NEVER FORGET

Christian and Jewish Perspectives
on
Edith Stein

D0870645

Edith Stein during her years in Speyer

NEVER FORGET

Christian and Jewish Perspectives
on
Edith Stein

Edited by Waltraud Herbstrith, OCD

Translated by Susanne Batzdorff

ICS Publications
Institute of Carmelite Studies
Washington, DC
1998

NEVER FORGET: CHRISTIAN AND JEWISH PERSPECTIVES ON EDITH STEIN is a translation of *Erinnere dich – vergiß es nicht: Edith Stein – christlich-jüdische Perspektiven,* edited by Waltraud Herbstrith (Essen: Verlag Plöger, 1990). It has been re-edited (with additions and deletions) for the English language edition by the translator, Susanne Batzdorff.

Cover design by Nancy Gurganus of Grey Coat Graphics

ICS Publications
2131 Lincoln Road, N.E.
Washington, D.C. 20002
202-832-8489

Library of Congress Cataloging-in-Publication Data

Erinnere dich, vergiss es nicht.   English.
    Never forget : Christian and Jewish perspectives on Edith Stein /
edited by Waltraud Herbstrith ; translated by Susanne Batzdorff.
        p.   cm. — (Carmelite Studies ; 7)
    Includes bibliographical references and index.
    ISBN 0-935216-62-6
    1. Stein, Edith, 1891-1942.   I. Herbstrith, Waltraud. II. Title.
III. Series.
BX4705.S814E7513   1998
248.2'46'092—DC21   97–39247
                                                        CIP

Our being and our life are forced upon us as a problem. We cannot avoid the question of who we are and what we want. And not just the reflecting mind confronts us with this question. Living itself has made our life into a problem.

Edith Stein, Zürich, 1932

In a sense Edith Stein is also an advocate for Judaism, because for Christians she will in the future be witness and symbol for Jewish martyrdom. And it is hoped that she will withstand efforts to play down or appropriate [her death] for triumphalist purposes.

Daniel Krochmalnik, Munich, 1987

Edith Stein, who entered the Carmelite convent in Cologne in 1933, was a daughter of the Jewish people; in solidarity with them and in Christian hope she shared their sufferings on the way to the "Shoah." "After all, salvation is from the Jews," said Jesus during his talk with the Samaritan woman at Jacob's Well (Jn 4:22). We Christians must never forget these roots of ours. The apostle of the nations reminds us that "You do not support the root; the root supports you" (Rom 11:18).

John Paul II, Cologne, 1987

Note to the ICS Edition

The present volume has a peculiar history. In the wake of Edith Stein's beatification in 1987, Sr. Waltraud Herbstrith, OCD, of the Edith-Stein-Karmel in Tübingen, Germany, collected varied reactions to this important event from a wide range of Jewish and Christian authors, as well as reminiscences from former friends and acquaintances of the new Blessed. These were published together in her anthology *Erinnere dich—vergiß es nicht* (Annweiler/Essen: Plöger Verlag, 1990), which was then promptly translated into English by Edith Stein's niece, Susanne Batzdorff, and offered to ICS Publications. Though we gladly accepted, circumstances prevented us from bringing out the book as quickly as we had hoped.

Delays, however, can prove providential. The announcement of Edith Stein's canonization has raised afresh all of the same questions originally addressed herein. We have condensed or eliminated only a few passages from the German edition that now seem dated or dispensable. But we have also added some articles that should be of special interest to English-speaking readers. In particular, John Sullivan, OCD, and Kieran Kavanaugh, OCD, here outline the actual steps involved in Edith Stein's beatification and canonization for those unfamiliar with the process.

As a collection of essays more informational than devotional, this work seems best suited to our *Carmelite Studies* series. Indeed, it can be read in conjunction with the beatification texts found in *Carmelite Studies IV*. This new volume is certainly not the last word on Edith Stein, but more like a series of excerpts from an ongoing conversation. The contributors often disagree with each other, and the opinions they express are, of course, their own. But we are confident that an open and honest exchange of views is an important step toward a better understanding of Edith Stein's significance, and a deeper friendship between Jews and Christians.

Steven Payne, OCD
Editor-in-Chief, ICS Publications

Table of Contents

III. ADDENDA

Foreword to the ICS Edition

by William Cardinal Keeler

Edith Stein, Sister Benedicta of the Cross, must be reckoned a giant of the twentieth century. Brilliant, analytical, mystical, she was a deeply religious woman with political sensibilities. This volume presents a variety of perspectives. Nonbelievers have contributed and so have believers, Jewish, Catholic, and Protestant. Viewpoints come from relatives, friends, and strangers, each a prism reflecting and refracting the light cast by an attractive yet enigmatic personality.

Here you will read of a beloved daughter who left her parents' faith decisively when she was fifteen years old and came to a new faith with an equally clear decision when she was thirty, five years after she had earned her doctorate in philosophy with highest honors. That Edith Stein did not intend by her conversion to reject either her parents or her admiration for the Jewish faith can be seen vividly in her loving depiction of both in her autobiographical book, *Life in a Jewish Family, 1891–1916,* which she began in 1933 in order to combat negative portrayals of Jews and Judaism then so tragically common in Germany. Throughout her life she continued along a path of study and teaching, writing and reflection that saw her address such issues as the role of women and the place of religious faith in this century.

In 1933, eleven years after her baptism, with the Nazis controlling Germany, Edith Stein entered the cloistered Carmel at Cologne. In November 1938 came *Kristallnacht* and an open, brutal demeaning of German Jewry. Sister Benedicta transferred to a Carmel in Holland but remained in solidarity with her Jewish family, still hoping against hope.

When the Netherlands fell to the German blitzkrieg, she explored the possibility of finding a refuge in a Swiss Carmel with

Rosa, her own sister who had joined her in the Dutch exile. This effort failed, and the protest of the Catholic bishops of Holland over earlier German action against Jews provoked the Nazis to round up Catholics of Jewish descent. And so Sister Benedicta and her sister were arrested. Their difficult trip to Auschwitz-Birkenau and the spoken and written messages of Sister Benedicta to strangers and to friends along the way tell an extraordinary story of martyrdom in the making.

As Pope John Paul II raises Blessed Benedicta of the Cross to sainthood at the completion of a long an careful process, new questions will be asked about this woman from Breslau (now known as Wroclaw) whose character and writings have touched profoundly so many people. In this volume are answers to those questions—and reason for further study of the life and work of this extraordinary woman of faith.

William Cardinal Keeler
Archbishop of Baltimore and Episcopal Moderator for Catholic-Jewish
Relations for the National Conference of Catholic Bishops (USA)
October 27, 1997

Foreword to the German Edition
by Bishop Anton Schlembach

As bishop of the church of Speyer I feel a special bond with Edith Stein and her fate. The parish church in Bad Bergzabern is her baptismal church. In the city of Speyer one encounters her traces in many locations. For eight years she was active as a teacher and lecturer at the Dominican School and Teacher Training Institute. Here she wrote many important letters to high-placed as well as ordinary people. Here she translated the *Disputed Questions on Truth* of Thomas Aquinas. The Dominican Sisters still own the manuscript, more than 2,000 pages long. Here she composed the first major lectures on the status of women. At the same time, she also quietly supported poor people and families in the parish.

It is impressive to go through the archives of the Dominican Sisters of St. Magdalena or to visit the permanent exhibit about Edith Stein that the sisters have lovingly and knowledgeably organized. Sisters Adele Herrmann, Theresia Mende, Agnella Stadtmüller, Reinhildis Ferber, and Dolorosa Leister deserve special mention for their efforts in compiling the voluminous exhibition catalog and publishing reports by many fellow-sisters who were friends of Edith Stein.

The modest room in which Edith Stein lived in the monastery has been made into a meditation room and invites contemplation. The *prie-dieu* in the convent church upon which she often knelt, steeped in meditation and veneration, is a particularly precious memento. In the chapel of the bishop's residence in Speyer she was confirmed on February 2, 1922. She often prayed and went to confession in the cathedral. More than thirty of Edith Stein's former students now live as retired teachers in the Palatinate and keep alive many personal memories of her. On the way to her death, while

Edith Stein passed through Schifferstadt in a sealed railroad car, she tossed out a message to the chaplain, Pastor Ferdinand Meckes, who stood on the platform, and asked him to remember her to Canon Lauer and the Sisters of St. Magdalena. And so we come to the subject that always shatters us anew and that permeates this entire book! How could it happen, how was it possible that such crimes against humanity could be committed in our country? How was it possible that German Jews and a large portion of European Jewry could simply be extinguished, without public protest? We won't be able to settle this question for a long time.

In her violent death she saw a real connection with the redemptive death of Jesus on the cross, but most certainly also as a member of the Jewish people. Edith Stein died in the Auschwitz extermination camp. With all Jews who were murdered, she was a blood witness of the chosen people of God, Israel. Neither Edith Stein nor her Jewish brothers and sisters sought this martyrdom. They were forced to die their horrible death because too few people resisted the beginnings of Hitler's barbarism.

We cannot think of Edith Stein, of her murder, and her beatification without considering her Jewish fate and that of her brothers and sisters. The Shoah, the destruction of millions of Jews in Europe by German henchmen, must remain a reminder for us and the world, so that similar things may never happen again.

May this book, created by Christians and Jews, by friends and relatives of Edith Stein, contribute to the reconciliation between Christians and Jews. May it also further the veneration of Blessed Edith Stein, which is a special gift for our diocese Speyer and a call not to be ignored.

Speyer, August 9, 1990
firty-eighth anniversary of the death of Blessed Edith Stein

Most Rev. Anton Schlembach
Bishop of Speyer

Translator's Preface

Biblical quotations in the material I have translated are taken from *The New Jerusalem Bible* (Garden City, NY: Doubleday, 1985). Translator's footnotes are followed by "—Trans." Occasional brief translator's remarks are given within the text and enclosed in square brackets [ ]. Wherever English translations of the sources cited exist, they are given here. Sources that are only available in the original German are cited as such.

The foreword by Cardinal Keeler and the articles by John Sullivan, OCD, Eugene J. Fisher, Daniel F. Polish, Victor J. Donovan, CP, and Kieran Kavanaugh, OCD, were written especially for the English language edition. The article by Nancy Fuchs-Kreimer is reprinted from the Winter 1991 issue of *Lilith*, and Leo Sudbrack's letter, recently retrieved from the archives of the Cologne Carmel, is published here for the first time. All other contributions are from the original 1990 German language edition of this book, and many were written a number of years earlier. Thus the opinions expressed represent the views of their authors at the time of writing.

The translator acknowledges with profound gratitude the assistance of Sr. Josephine Koeppel, OCD, of the Carmelite monastery in Elysburg, PA, who prevented me from committing major errors due to insufficient knowledge of Catholic usage and nomenclature and who offered expertise and cautionary advice; and of Fr. Boniface (Carl von Nell) of St. Anselm's Abbey, Washington, DC, who helped deepen my understanding of terms and concepts relating to the Roman Catholic Church. Thanks are also due to Volker Schachenmeyr for his editorial suggestions.

Susanne Batzdorff

Acknowledgments

Thanks to the following for their kind assistance with this book:

Sr. Marie Louise, OCD, for many years Superior of the Carmelite Monastery in Echt (now in Carmel Beek, Holland) for facilitating the translation of the articles of Herman Leo van Breda, Sr. Stephanie a Magna Domina, OCD, Hélène Vérène Borsinger, P. O. van Kempen, and Pierre Cuypers [into German];

Pater Angelus Scholz, OCD, from the monastery of Geleen, Holland, translator [into German];

Sr. Susanne Gerstmayr, OCD, Edith-Stein-Karmel Tübingen, translator of the article by Menahem Benhayim [into German];

Frau Carola Bloch, who, in the course of conversation, gave me hints about Edith Stein's friendship with the Hirshler family, Ludwigshafen, who were also friends of Ernst Bloch;

Eugen Fouquet, son of Stationmaster Valentin Fouquet, who gave me detailed information about Edith Stein's days in Speyer;

Susanne Kölbel, Cologne, for many comments about Christian-Jewish reconciliation;

Dr. Christine Lipp, née Lipps, daughter of Prof. Hans Lipps, who supplied background information through her stories about the Lipps family and her revered father;

Dr. Eberhard Avé-Lallemant for his tireless support;

Prof. Karl Schuhmann, University of Utrecht, for his help through his research on the philosophers Adolf Reinach, Alexandre Koyré, and Jean Hering, and the details he provided on matters of Husserl research;

Father Martin Cunz, Director of the Foundation for Christianity and Judaism.

Waltraud Herbstrith, OCD

Part I

Edith Stein: A Figure for Our Time

Chronology of Edith Stein's Life

1891	Born into a Jewish family in Breslau
1911–1913	University studies in Breslau (German, history, psychology, philosophy); loss of her faith
1913–1915	Philosophical studies in Göttingen under Husserl
1915	Work as Red Cross volunteer
1916	Receives her doctorate *summa cum laude*
1916–1918	Assistant to Husserl in Freiburg
1919–1923	Private philosophical work; unsuccessful attempts to gain university position
1922	Baptism, First Communion, Confirmation
1923–31	Instructor at Teachers College, Speyer
1928–1932	Public lectures, translations, and other work
1932–1933	Lecturer at German Institute for Scientific Pedagogy in Münster
1933–1938	Enters and joins Cologne Carmel (Sr. Teresia Benedicta a Cruce)
1938	Final profession of vows
1939–1942	Stay at Echt Carmel; resumes writing
1942	Arrest, deportation, and death at Auschwitz
May 1, 1987	Beatification in Cologne, Germany
Oct. 11, 1998	Canonization in St. Peter's Square, Rome

Introduction
by Waltraud Herbstrith, OCD

In 1991, Edith Stein—Jewish-Christian, philosopher, lecturer on current problems of woman—would have been 100 years old. She is one of the victims of the Shoah, the Holocaust, one of those millions of people who were murdered solely because they were Jews. The beatification of Edith Stein has met with both positive and critical responses. Her fate as a Jewish martyr of the Shoah and, through the witness of her life, as eminent Christian believer, is surely unique in this synthesis. Through Edith Stein we learn how careful we as Christians must be to avoid assumptions and triumphalist tendencies in our speech. True ecumenism, and Edith Stein's personality is ecumenical, means that we take the thought and belief of others seriously and allow them to stand in their individuality. The visit of the pope to the synagogue of Rome and the pope's prayer for peace in Assisi were such a beginning.

Our Jewish brothers and sisters, who have not forgotten the annihilation of their people by Germans, call our attention to the fact that we must not extol the horrible death of Edith Stein boastfully with such expressions as: "The resurrection of Christ triumphed over the flames of Auschwitz" or "Edith Stein sacrificed her life for her Jewish people, so that they might turn to Christ," etc. As Christians we must abandon such statements, if we seek out the reasons for the murder of this Christian Jew and her millions of fellow-victims. It is evident that for Edith Stein, her last, terrible road to death took place in surrender to the Crucified Christ, but that does not help the Jews of today to comprehend the horror of the Shoah. Auschwitz, Treblinka, Bergen-Belsen and all other places of remembering the horror should make us silent, because silence in the face of this atrocity is the most appropriate prayer.

3

In view of a fate such as Edith Stein's, Christians must ask themselves: What has the centuries-old theological anti-Semitism in the church contributed so that Hitler could carry out his mad anti-Semitic destruction almost unhindered? We cannot pass judgment on people of the past, but in view of such horrendous events as the Shoah, we can ponder and begin to take new paths religiously and politically: paths of reconciliation, of listening to one another, of nonviolence.

This book is a gleaning of thoughts that occurred to Jewish and Christian individuals in connection with the beatification of Edith Stein. In the first part of the book, under the title "Christian-Jewish Perspectives," there appear first of all Edith Stein's relatives, such as her nieces and great-nieces Susanne Batzdorff, Ilse Gordon, Waltraut Stein, and her nephew Gerhard Stein. Then there are colleagues and friends, such as Nikolaus Lauer and Jan H. Nota. It is surely most significant how the second and third generation after Edith Stein views the past, and does not repress it but confronts it in Edith Stein's example and poses questions for today and for the future. A troubled Jewish professor writes, "What has been disturbing me especially in recent days was the beatification of Edith Stein. People acted as if she had voluntarily gone to her death for the sake of Christ. In fact she was murdered because of her Jewish birth. Is not this a falsification of the Shoah, yes, a Christian triumphalism that is not justified by anything?" The thoughts of Ernst Ludwig Ehrlich, the director of B'nai B'rith, and of Daniel Krochmalnik, Doctor of Philosophy, deepen or supplement this query. Referring to the papal visit in the synagogue of Rome, Pastor Martin Cunz speaks about the importance of an unprejudiced encounter between Christians and Jews. The journalist Menahem Benhayim seeks to interpret the "between" of the fate of Edith Stein between Christianity and Judaism. Questions upon questions, but also good replies.

Surely it was not just a matter of course up to now that a Protestant scholar such as Leonore Siegele-Wenschkewitz should preach about the fate of Edith Stein in a Catholic church at the opening of a Protestant Church Congress, or that a senior teacher, Irmgard Rech, should give a morning address in the Southwest Radio Program about the dignity of woman in church and society, based on Edith Stein's guidelines for the integration of woman into the professional world.

Church historian Joachim Köhler looks at Edith Stein as the focus of controversy involving Christianity, Anti-Judaism, and National Socialism. He poses challenging questions toward mastering the past. Equally challenging are the queries of the Jewish philosopher F. G. Friedmann. He makes it clear that we can only remove prejudices by listening to each other.

In the second part of the book, students of Edith Stein, colleagues, friends, and acquaintances testify to her great and unusual personality, her devotion to people, her objectivity, and her loyalty. Let the words of the vicar at the Speyer cathedral, Canon Karl Hofen, represent all these authentic testimonies that have been preserved for us by retired bishop Markus Emanuel:

> Edith Stein was a highly intelligent, extremely modest, deeply religious, and self-sacrificial personality who enjoyed great respect from her students and the Sisters of St. Magdalena. She demonstrated her warm interest for needy persons in the parish by her participation in the so-called Vincentian Conferences, whose minutes she kept for a time.[1]

Concerning Edith Stein's escape from Cologne after the November pogroms of 1938 until her final road from Holland to her death, we have testimony of loyal helpers who dared, despite the murderous regime of the National Socialists, to put their lives on the line. Thus we have the Cologne physician Dr. Paul Strerath, the Dutch citizens P. O. van Kempen and Pierre Cuypers, the Swiss Doctor of Church Law Hélène Vérène Borsinger, who tried desperately to help Edith Stein escape to Switzerland.

Unknown until now were the efforts of the Breslau publisher Otto Borgmeyer who, after his fruitless efforts in Nazi Germany, tried to publish Edith Stein's main philosophical work, *Finite and Eternal Being*, in Holland. Until now it was not known that the wife of the Dutch journalist Anthony Mertens, a friend of Swiss President Etter's daughter, attempted to rescue Edith Stein.

Help came too late for six million Jews. It is important for us to let the memory of these innocently murdered people rise once more. Wherever we find traces and signposts of their lives, we ought to follow them. Their forcibly terminated lives should be an admonition for us to change our ways.

At the dedication of a chapel at the Benedictine priory in Nitschau/Bad Odeslohe, on May 1, 1987, the prior, Gaudentius Sauermann, said:

> What this inner space of silence and veneration means to us, we can best learn from a woman who has become profoundly close to us on our Christian path. First of all, I see in Edith Stein simply the human being of our time, placed willy-nilly amidst the difficult problems of life.[2]

After the beatification of Edith Stein, Pope John Paul II met with representatives of the Central Council of Jews in Cardinal Höffner's residence. In his address the pope said that God did not permit the powers of death to have the last word, but that, even in Germany, Jewish congregations again take up the old traditions and are allowed to develop and to live. He pointed out that in the fate of Edith Stein both her unconditional love for her Jewish people and her love for the Crucified Christ shine forth:

> Let us pause in reverent silence to reflect on the terrible consequences to our conscience which can arise from a denial of God and from collective racial hatred. In this connection we recall the suffering of many peoples in Europe in recent times, and we declare our commitment to a common effort on the part of all people of good will to establish a new "civilization of love" here in Europe, inspired by the highest Jewish and Christian ideals. At the same time, we must speak out when necessary, not lose sight of our examples, and remain alert for all new forms of anti-Semitism, racism, and neopagan religious persecution. Such a joint effort would be the most precious gift Europe could give the world in its arduous effort to develop and attain justice.[3]

I especially thank Auxiliary Bishop Rieger of Rottenburg for his support for this book, Mrs. Margarete Helferich of Schweinfurt for her tremendous help, and Mrs. Margarete Bossert-Kleiner of Pforzheim. Without their involvement this book could not have been published.

Edith-Stein-Karmel, Tübingen, April 21, 1990
fifty-second anniversary of the Solemn Profession of Edith Stein

The Path to Beatification

by John Sullivan, OCD

In the most general terms, according to Catholic belief, those persons the Catholic Church canonizes earn the distinction; they are not ultimately selected on tactical or strategic grounds. Rather, candidates for sainthood show that they heeded the call to "be holy as their God is holy" (cf. Lv 19:2 & 1 Pe 1:16). Afterwards the church intervenes to guide a process designed to acknowledge the holiness of God at work in them. This does not preclude long and sometimes tedious-sounding procedures for determining their worthiness. The complexity involved is designed to assure that care is exercised throughout the work of discernment; it obviously also depends on human factors derived from the structures in place.

The religion editor of *Newsweek*, Kenneth Woodward, has shown in his best-seller *Making Saints* (1990) just how intricate the exertions of those in charge of the canonization process can be.[1] He did the reading public a favor by illustrating their often seemingly byzantine dealings with case histories of some contemporary figures currently under examination. The centerpiece of the chapter on modern martyrs is Blessed, soon to be Saint, Edith Stein; and Woodward even weaves in eyewitness remarks about the beatification in Cologne (May 1, 1987) where he covered the ceremony for his magazine.

The following chronological outline traces the basic steps taken over almost forty years to bring Stein (Sr. Teresia Benedicta of the Cross) to the "honors of the altars" conferred on her that spring day in Germany. Four decades, more or less from 1948 to 1987, seems a short time span for reaching beatification, but in the contemporary high tide of blesseds and saints declared by Pope

John Sullivan, OCD, *is publisher of ICS Publications and has served on the General Definitory of the Discalced Carmelites in Rome, Italy.*

John Paul II, one may consider it a suitable period of gestation. The detailed rules and procedures governing the church's canonization process can be studied either in Woodward's book, or in the more technical treatment of the same process found in Michael Freze's *The Making of Saints* (1991) with its useful 21-page Glossary of Terms.[2]

The Forties and Fifties

In spite of the great difficulties rebuilding community life in the wake of World War II's devastation, the nuns who had lived with Stein in Cologne began to gather documentation about her once hostilities ended. Facing an initial dearth of information about her deportation and death in August 1942, they assembled as many data and autograph copies of her correspondence as they could. Inquiries arrived at the monastery about the fate of Stein, sometimes with requests for a memento of her. Her former novice mistress become prioress, Sr. Teresia Renata Possent OCD, organized the available information and published a biography entitled (in German) *Edith Stein, Life Portrait of a Philosopher and Carmelite* in 1948. It was enlarged and reprinted several times until it reached its seventh edition in 1954 (an English translation of the initial edition appeared in 1952).

Recognizing the inherent importance of Edith Stein's life for Catholics and their growing interest in her, Cardinal Frings, the Archbishop of Cologne, petitioned the Vatican for powers to begin initial steps toward opening an official cause by investigating her life, virtues and writings (a necessary step because normally the diocese in which a person dies is entrusted with conducting the cause). He received this permission on May 13, 1958. Father Edward Precht, OCD, the German general definitor of the Discalced Carmelites, sent word on August 20 asking Sr. Possent to draft a shorter biography of Sr. Teresia Benedicta Stein suitable for inclusion in the official documentation.

Publication of the first five volumes of the collected works of Stein by Nauwelaerts Publishers in Belgium took place between 1950 and 1958. Through both spontaneous and formal initiatives

Sr. Teresia Benedicta became better known, and interest in her life and thought continued to grow.

The Sixties

Almost twenty years after her death, Cardinal Frings opened the Ordinary Process on January 4, 1962 (to be followed afterward by the Apostolic Process conducted out of the Vatican). The Cologne beatification commission issued, on that same day, a 101-page booklet about the virtuous life and conduct of Stein, containing Sr. Posselt's biographical sketch and additional chapters completed by Sr. Teresia Margareta Drügemöller, who was a novice with Stein but at this period prioress after Posselt died in 1961. A canon of Cologne Cathedral, Monsignor Jakob Schlafke, began serving as vice-postulator of the cause for beatification.

Cologne enlisted the help of other dioceses around the world, to gather eyewitness testimony and petitions in support of canonization. For the former, sworn statements came from individuals in twenty-two locales: New York, Regensburg, Westminster, Southwark, Speyer, Bamberg, Trier, Roermond, Liège, Aachen, Berlin, Namur, Munich, Malines, Basel, Paderborn, Augsburg, Bruges, Münster, Limburg, Salzburg and Freiburg-im-Breisgau. Among the 109 persons interviewed (36 at Cologne and 73 in the other places) three Jewish women gave their replies to the prepared list of questions. Doctor Erna Biberstein, beloved sister of Sr. Teresia Benedicta, made her declarations on October 28 and November 6, 1963. The cumulative list of petitions asking for canonization of Stein (dated November 18, 1981) indicated 436 requests had been submitted to the officials of the cause.

Two theological evaluations of the thought of the "Servant of God" (title assigned to Stein once the diocesan process began) were drafted at this point: one by Cornelio Fabro, a noted Italian philosopher of religion, the other by Juan Lozano, a Spanish expert on the theology of religious life. The Discalced Carmelite Postulator General published these texts privately in the late seventies (1977). Ten volumes make up the "Copia Publica" of the Ordinary Process's acts.

The Seventies

Cardinal Joseph Höffner, successor to Cardinal Frings, sent the entire set of beatification process materials to Rome in 1972. The Congregation for the Doctrine of the Faith gave its "Nihil obstat" on September 19, 1972, thus opening the door to preparations for the Brief for the Introduction of the Cause. The latter document was some time in coming. In fact, after the steady flow of documentation up to 1972 progress slowed down until 1983. One commentator adduced as reason for the hiatus the sheer volume of the material submitted.

In the meantime the nuns of Cologne Carmel observed commemorations of Stein's death and received letters of gratitude for favors granted through her intercession. Most frequently the assistance obtained through prayer concerned finding either employment or residence—quite fitting, symbolically, from a person who out of prejudice was blocked from following her professional career and had to go into exile.

The Eighties

In 1980 the vice-postulator of the cause published a small work containing documents found in the Dutch Royal Institute for War Documentation in Amsterdam. Canon Schlafke proposed a new premise for future work, a premise he derived from these documents about the death of Stein: that she suffered martyrdom for the Catholic faith. This hypothesis had already been suggested by some of the texts in the Petitionary Processes but not studied in depth to this point by Rome, because from its inception the cause had been aiming to prove the heroic virtues of Sr. Teresia Benedicta. The Vice-Postulator's booklet produced no immediate reaction.

By 1983 the Brief for the Introduction of the Cause was ready: over 1,000 pages of text with thirty-five tables in an in-folio volume synthesized the documentation at Rome's disposal. On March 3 that same year Cardinal Höffner, as President of the German Episcopal Conference, wrote another formal petition to the Holy

Father (seconded soon after by the Polish Episcopal Conference). The letter embraced Schlafke's position in favor of martyrdom, but no immediate reply to this issue was forthcoming. Instead, on May 20, 1983 the Congregation acceded to a second part of the letter and dispensed from a rule requiring a fifty-year moratorium before discussion of the virtues of a Servant of God.

On January 25, 1983 the Vatican issued new regulations for the causes of saints and for the Congregation to which they are entrusted. These updated rules simplified the procedures and removed much duplication of effort by abolishing the Apostolic Process. In the case of causes begun under the former regulations one had to devise carry-over solutions. The change-over took time regarding examination of Stein's cause.

Nonetheless, by May 11, 1984, the Congregation appointed to the cause of Sr. Teresia Benedicta one of the new examining judges, i.e., an official called a "Relator." He was the Dominican Father Ambrosius Eszer, and his early efforts led him to familiarize himself with the work of Canon Schlafke.[3] When he weighed the arguments found in the 1983 letters of the German and Polish episcopal conferences, he started leaning toward the possibility of promoting acceptance of Sr. Teresia Benedicta as a martyr. In the meantime he ordered some new depositions and conducted further research designed to meet expected objections to the martyrdom thesis.

Fr. Eszer's intense work by early 1985 had produced a Report to the Congregation. Monsignor Luigi Porsi, Advocate of the Cause, assembled supplementary documentation joined to it. On the basis of their submissions the Congregation declared the validity of the Cause on November 15, 1985.

Two months later on January 10, 1986, the Father Postulator General of the Discalced Carmelite Order, alluding to the letters sent separately by the German and Polish Episcopal Conferences among other reasons, wrote a petition to Pope John Paul II. The letter requested that the pope allow the new Brief of the cause of Sr. Teresia Benedicta to go beyond the question of her heroic virtues, and specifically "investigate martyrdom."

The Congregation at its meeting of January 17, 1986, in the name of the pope, consented to this request and martyrdom was included with heroic virtues in the Supplementary Brief that appeared in March that year.[4] On October 28, the Theological Consultors of the Congregation met to consider the heroic virtues and martyrdom of Sr. Teresia Benedicta as expounded by the Brief and Supplementary Brief. Then, on January 13, 1987, the plenary convocation of the Cardinal and Archbishop/Bishop Members of the Congregation examined those materials along with the results of the theologians' discussions. Each meeting voted favorably to approve Stein for beatification on the basis of both her heroic virtues and martyrdom. This led to the final step of approval: in the presence of the Holy Father the Decree confirming the heroic degree of the virtues as well as the martyrdom of Sr. Teresia Benedicta was promulgated on January 26, 1987, an event without precedent in the centuries-old history of the Congregation.

The Vatican had accepted the martyrdom of Sr. Teresia Benedicta, thereby dispensing the cause from the need for a miracle to proceed to her beatification. The Relator, Fr. Eszer, offered a lengthy account of this question of Stein's martyrdom to *Carmelite Studies* soon after the beatification: the text of this key promoter of Stein's cause is available in Volume 4 of *Carmelite Studies*. Here only a brief summary is needed. In 1942 the Nazi leaders in the Netherlands had decided to wipe out Dutch Judaism. Dutch Christian religious leaders were especially worried about the Jews' fate; and all the Christian churches energetically protested the deportation underway in a telegram sent on July 11, 1942 to several ranking German occupation authorities in Holland. In that telegram the ecclesiastical authorities underscored their distress over the discrimination against the "Christian Jews." Despite warnings the Catholic bishops "went public" with their opposition to Nazi policies and had a pastoral letter read out at all Sunday Masses on July 26, 1942. The reaction was swift: hundreds of Jews who had embraced the Catholic faith were rounded up for deportation on August 2, among them Sr. Teresia Benedicta with her sister Rosa Stein (who was in residence as a lay Carmelite at the Echt monastery). The Nazis lost no time in attacking the church and its pastors by moving against these faithful. The Nazis acted with *odium fidei* (an ancient adage that means "hatred of the faith"), i.e., they struck at the church through its members, thus adding a special qualification to their sufferings, that of witness to their faith. The root meaning of the word "martyrdom" is witnessing. Stein in the eyes of the Vatican was properly a martyr and as a martyr she was then beatified on May 1, 1987, in Cologne where she had lived as an exemplary Carmelite nun for five years and two months.

A Concluding Glance Backwards

Most noteworthy in hindsight is the double qualification with which Stein's cause for beatification concluded, i.e., approval of her heroic virtues as well as approval of her martyrdom. During her life she earned her doctorate in 1916 with the distinction "summa cum laude"; thus posthumous "full marks" do not seem unwarranted for this great woman. All the same, one would have welcomed a decision by the Vatican authorities to include the other Catholics who met their deaths with her in the Nazi reprisal against their bishops' gesture of solidarity with Dutch Jews.

Church history has seen many individuals made saints along with their "companions," similarly holy persons whose separate names do not generally show up on lists or in worship books. If that approach had been taken in this case, her blood sister Rosa, who also became a Catholic, would be commemorated liturgically along with Sr. Teresia Benedicta, as well as many other people like the five Cistercians of the Loeb family, Lisamaria Meirowsky, Alice Reis and others we know from the correspondence of Stein herself. After all, Stein told Rosa on the day of their arrest "Come, we go for our people." A communal note to the church's commemoration of her is, in a way, missing, though Catholicism's faith vision does include them all in the "communion of saints." At this point no one can turn the clock back. But now that Stein's cause has been completed, why not consider the possibility of promoting the cause of these other Catholic Jews who were deported and killed in the summer of 1942? Official acknowledgment of their deaths would spread the honors wider and offer an attempt to heal at least some of the misunderstandings that have resulted from her beatification.

Of course, far in advance of controversies stirred up by the 1987 beatification, and before there was any hint tensions would surround it, signs of a definite "fama sanctitatis," or a renown for holiness, existed at grass roots level in many quarters. None other than the famed author of *Brideshead Revisited*, Evelyn Waugh, published a review of Sr. Posselt's biography of Stein the year it appeared in English (1952). One excerpt from that review (found in a 1977 collection of his journalism writings, *A Little Order*) suffices to show the attractiveness of the future Saint Teresia Benedicta for someone of his caliber:

> Her spirit shines out, very clear and lonely; a brilliant intelligence; a pure, disciplined will; a single motive power, the Grace of God. The circumstances of her death touch us for they lie at the heart of contemporary disaster. The aimless, impersonal wickedness which could drag a victim from the holy silence of Carmel and drive her, stripped and crowded, to the gas chambers and the furnace, still lurks in the darkness. But Edith's death is perhaps an irrelevant horror. Her life was completed in Carmel. She did not sit, waiting on God. She went out alone and by the God-given light of her intelligence and strength of purpose, she found Him.

Waugh could see how the liturgical dictum addressed to the Lord about the saints remains both inspiration and seal for canonizations: "In crowning their merits, you crown your own gifts." Saints are not proposed for veneration to promote agendas; they are recognized as intently faithful recipients of God's grace and generosity.[5]

Washington, DC, 1998
This article was written especially for the
English-language edition of Never Forget.

Edith Stein's Beatification: Annoyance or Sign of Reconciliation?

by Anna Maria Strehle, OCD

"One can be Jewish and yet be present in Cologne to honor Edith Stein," said Susanne Batzdorff, a niece of Edith Stein (daughter of her favorite sister Erna) and she added:

> It is surely bitter: Today millions looked on as the pope beatified our aunt. But in 1933 she received no reply from the pope, when she called his attention to the fate of the Jews. Still I see the beatification of my aunt as an attempt of the Catholic Church to improve its relations with the Jews, also as a sign of atonement for things which could perhaps have been done but were not done.

Mrs. Batzdorff's brother, Ernst Ludwig Biberstein, had not accepted the invitation to the beatification that Cardinal Höffner had sent to all of Edith Stein's relatives. Another guest, Prof. Waltraut Stein, a member of the Episcopal Church, remarked: "True, it is a joyous event, but it also reminds us of the Holocaust, the terrible time which our family had to experience." [Four of the Stein siblings—Paul, Frieda, Rosa, and Edith—died in concentration camps; three—Else, Arno, and Erna—were able to emigrate in time.] Waltraut's father, Prof. Gerhard Stein, who also traveled to Cologne, wrote to Cardinal Höffner:

> I consider the beatification of my dear aunt, who lost her life in a gas chamber of Auschwitz, a spiritual memorial which the Catholic Church is raising for all who perished because of Nazi

---

Anna Maria Strehle, OCD, *is a former prioress of the Edith-Stein-Karmel in Tübingen, Germany.*

15

persecutions. I lost my parents in the concentration camp of Theresienstadt. [His father was Edith Stein's brother Paul.] My prayer at the Holy Mass will be dedicated to all these victims.[1]

Critics within the Catholic Church formulated their concerns less cautiously than Edith Stein's relatives. At a meeting of the "Initiative Church from Below" concerning the papal visit and a radio program by SWF (Southwest Broadcasting)—to name just a few well-known examples—the reproach was forcefully raised that by beatifying Edith Stein and Rupert Mayer the Catholic Church wanted to "cover up" the "failure" of the Catholic bishops in the time of National Socialism.[2]

Let us then ask: Who was Edith Stein? Who was this woman who has become interesting in our day, not only because of her fate, but also because her thought and the way the church has recognized her life have drawn her into the interplay of reproaches, criticism, and defense? Edith Stein, in childhood fancies, dreamed of a "brilliant future," of "happiness and fame." In her autobiography she writes:

> In my dreams I always foresaw a brilliant future for myself. I dreamed about happiness and fame, for I was convinced that I was destined for something great and that I did not belong at all in the narrow bourgeois circumstances into which I had been born.[3]

Yet she imagined a different greatness than that for which we admire her today.

Edith Stein was a Jew, and consciously so. In the short *vita* that she added to her dissertation printed in 1917, we read: "I am a Prussian citizen and a Jew."[4] After Hitler's assumption of power in 1933, eleven years after her conversion, she began to record reminiscences of her mother and herself (*Life in a Jewish Family*). She wanted to report "what I, child of a Jewish family, had learned about the Jewish people, since such knowledge is so rarely found in outsiders." She felt a special responsibility toward young people, who at the time were being raised with racism from early childhood on: "To all who have been thus deprived, we who grew up in Judaism have an obligation to give our testimony."[5]

Edith Stein experienced anti-Jewish discrimination prior to National Socialism. That is evident, for instance, from her remark that in Prussia it was almost impossible for a Jewish woman to obtain employment in the school system.[6] For this reason, her older sister Else, who had passed the teacher's examination, applied for a job in Hamburg, and was lucky. Some passages in her dissertation *On the Problem of Empathy* hint at her own painful experiences:

> Suppose that I have taken over from my environment a hatred and contempt for the members of a particular race or party. For example, as the child of conservative parents I may hate Jews andSocial Democrats, or, raised with more liberal views, I may hate "Junkers" [aristocratic landowners]. Then this would be an entirely genuine and sincere hatred, save for the fact that it is based on an empathic valuing, rather than on a primordial one. This hatred may also be increased by contagion of feeling to such a degree that it is not legitimately related to the felt disvalue.[7]

Edith Stein is one of many who were victims of the racial hatred of the National Socialists. She represents many nameless ones. When we think of her and honor her (beatify her!), we also honor those victims whose names no one knows. However, we cannot honor Edith Stein today, cannot cite her, unless we ask ourselves: What is our attitude toward Jews and other minorities, guest workers and refugees, toward the ever-growing number of unemployed, drug addicts, homeless? Do we feel solidarity with them, do we take their part even when it leads to disadvantages for us? Are peace and reconciliation only catchwords for us, or do they demand of us a lifelong effort that challenges us anew every day?

In surveying the life of Edith Stein, we are struck by her inexorable search for truth, her unconditional honesty. She invested all her might in finding the truth and then in doing what appeared to her to be required. We cannot use her as an example and at the same time leave everything uncommitted, without deriving consequences for our actions.

At first neither books nor abstract information played a part in Edith Stein's road to faith, but real people did: her mother, the Reinachs, Max Scheler, and finally the life of Teresa of Avila. Are we aware that this is also the way for many people in our own time? Do we take our responsibility seriously? Are we prepared to render an account of our faith if someone asks? Has our daily life any connection with our faith? Today, too, witnesses of faith are indispensable (cf. Diocesan Synod Rottenburg-Stuttgart 1985/86 on the theme "Passing the Faith on to the Coming Generation"). It is important that we dare to speak of our faith with others, that we account for the basis of our life as Christians. Edith Stein, whose life witness the church has acknowledged as authentically Christian by means of her beatification, can give us courage to meet this challenge.

In 1962, Cardinal Frings of Cologne opened the process for Edith Stein's canonization. In January 1987, Pope John Paul II decided that Edith Stein should be beatified as a martyr. This decision met with criticism.

Was Edith Stein gassed because she was a Catholic nun and thus because of her witness of faith for Christ (the traditional meaning of martyrdom)? Or did she, together with her sister Rosa and many others, suffer this fate because of her Jewish origins? If Edith Stein is considered a martyr, what about the millions of murdered Jews?

The destruction of the Jews was carried out in Christian countries. Anti-Semitism has a long Christian Catholic history (charges of "deicide," the "Reproaches" of Good Friday). But the Second Vatican Council's Declaration *Nostra Aetate* (1965) brought a change in Catholic thinking. In Article 4, dealing with the relationship between Christians and Jews, it states that "the Church reproves every form of persecution.... [She] deplores all hatreds, persecutions, displays of anti-Semitism leveled at any time or from any source against the Jews."[8] During his visit to the synagogue of Rome on April 13, 1986—an historic event—Pope John Paul II reiterated this passage and added, "I repeat: by anyone."[9] At the service on May 1, 1987, Cardinal Höffner picked up this phrase once more in his request to the pope to beatify Edith Stein. Why wasn't it possible at the Second Vatican Council, in the synagogue of Rome, or in Cologne, to be concrete and say, "even by the Catholic Church, even by Catholics"? Where is the admission of complicit guilt on the part of the official church, where is the plea for forgiveness? In his homily at the beatification the pope stressed Edith

Stein's identification with the Jewish people. Repeatedly he spoke of her as a "daughter of Israel." Her baptism, he said, did not signify a break with her Jewish people. And he quoted Edith Stein's comment that it was important for her "that she was related to Christ 'not only in a spiritual sense, but also in blood terms.'"[10]

The efforts of the pope not to make light of the uniqueness of the Shoah, the cruel annihilation of the Jews, nor to coopt their sacrifice by Christianity with the beatification of Edith Stein, were appreciated. Mrs. Batzdorff stated in a telephone conversation with one of my fellow-sisters, "I have the impression that the pope did what he could not to reopen old wounds."

During the meeting with the Central Council of Jews in Germany the pope apparently succeeded in allaying fears. He called the existence of Jewish congregations in Germany "a sign that God does not allow the forces of death to have the last word." He called Edith Stein a "daughter of Israel, who during the Nazi persecutions is bound in loyalty and love to the crucified Lord Jesus Christ as a Catholic and to her people as a Jew. Together with millions of brothers and sisters she suffered humiliation and pain to the end, unto inhumane destruction, the Shoah." He called for vigilance and courage in the face of "all new forms of anti-Semitism, racism and neopagan religious persecution" and stressed the common responsibility for peace.[11]

The religious philosopher and Europe's Director of B'nai B'rith, the largest Jewish lay organization in the world, Dr. Ernst Ludwig Ehrlich, who lives in Basel, was impressed by "how tactfully and carefully" the pope "phrased what had to be said." Ehrlich states that he did not engage in apologetics nor emphasize the resistance of the church.[12] Ehrlich was very critical of the beatification and had declined the place of honor offered him in the stadium in Cologne. In the summer of 1986 he had written in an article that for Catholics "Edith Stein remained one of the great human symbols of how this Church largely abandoned Jews, persons of Jewish origin, whatever faith they may have had." He felt that "the Catholic Church would do well not to claim Edith Stein as their martyr but to reflect on how this martyrdom could occur. Edith Stein is not suitable as a showpiece nor for historical apologia. She should rather be an incentive for reflection."[13]

Edith Stein and Father Rupert Mayer, SJ, the second blessed on this papal trip, are not figures for an alibi. They are, as a reporter expressed it, "thorns in the flesh of the Catholic Church."[14] They prevent us from forgetting and displacing our past, our most recent history ("The mystery of redemption is remembrance!") and challenge us to vigilance, courage, and responsibility.

Beyond that, the beatification of Edith Stein is, in the view of Willehad Paul Eckert, a Dominican friar engaged in Jewish-Christian dialogue, "a challenge for a new encounter between Jews and Christians." At least it should lead to a more intensified acquaintance with Judaism, for this is an "indispensable prerequisite for a true dialogue between Jews and Christians."[15]

The literary critic Paul Konrad Kurz views Edith Stein in a more general framework. For him she is:

> a great woman and an exemplary German Jew. She belongs— even after her beatification—not just to the inner realm of the church. Edith Stein is not a sacred decorative figure. She does not stand in an imaginary museum but with a questioning eye looks at us as her contemporaries. Involuntarily she became a provocation for Jews, for Catholics, for Germans, and for intellectuals. It is fortunate that Edith Stein, the woman, finally becomes a public figure in her own right.[16]

From a lecture held on May 16, 1987, at the Academy of the Diocese Rottenburg-Stuttgart in Stuttgart-Hohenheim

What Significance Does Edith Stein's Beatification Have for Her Family?

by Susanne Batzdorff

The last chords of the hymns sung at the beatification of Edith Stein had hardly faded away when the press asked me about the views of Edith Stein's family concerning the beatification. These questions were also repeated after our return to America. It is not so easy to give an answer, because we relatives are such a diverse lot with such varied ideological and religious beliefs that we don't all think alike by any means. In fact our origins are probably the only factor that unites us. That does not mean that this connection is insignificant. Our meeting in Cologne, at which we met some relatives for the first time and met others again for the first time after several decades, meant a great deal to us. We remain in contact with one another, probably a more intensive contact than before, and exchange information about the family, pictures, and family trees.

And so, in order to gather material for the theme "What has the beatification of Edith Stein accomplished?" I sent out questionnaires that dealt extensively with this subject to eleven relatives in the United States, Switzerland, and Germany. On the basis of the replies I received, I shall try to render the spectrum of diverse points of view. My report is based on seven carefully filled-out questionnaires and on the reactions of my husband and myself. Of these nine people five are Jewish, three Protestant, and one Catholic. Besides myself and Waltraut Stein, a great-niece of Edith Stein who has herself studied philosophy and who translated her great-aunt's

Susanne Batzdorff *is an author, translator, and former head of the Humanities Department, Northeast Regional Library, Free Library of Philadelphia. She is Edith Stein's niece and lives in Santa Rosa, CA.*

doctoral dissertation into English years ago, most of the other relatives had heretofore hardly occupied themselves with the work or
the personality of their famous relative. Despite that fact they had
traveled to Cologne to attend the beatification, partly out of curi-
osity, partly because of a desire to learn, to gain information, or to
establish contacts. That they have since then read much about
Edith Stein and also about Catholic-Jewish relations is attested by
the various articles which they sent me on this subject. Thus one
can say that Edith Stein's relatives pay much more attention to
this subject since May 1, 1987, than they did before. Now to the
replies:

Although only one of the relatives admitted to having made
changes in her life since her trip to Cologne, changes for the express purpose of reading more of the works of Edith Stein in order
to understand her spirituality better, most of the respondents
stated that they now had a better understanding of Edith Stein
and better knowledge of her importance for the church. Their participation in this ceremony has also deepened their perception of
the Catholic Church. And through insight into the life of the
Carmelites they have gained access to the life of Edith Stein. All
were glad to have been present at this celebration.

It may be of interest for outsiders that some of the participants admit to a feeling of trepidation prior to this event. A great-
niece felt obliged to send the pope a long letter in which she set
forth her differences with the position of the church on homosexu-
als and AIDS.

My own apprehension was based on many thoughts. First I
constantly kept thinking that thousands came together in Cologne
to rejoice over the new Blessed. But when she was sent to her death
in a cattle car, precious few gave any thought to this and no one
came to her aid. Secondly, it seemed to me as if, instead of attending a joyous festival, I was at a memorial service for my murdered
aunts. For, because of the way they died and the fact that we only
found out at war's end, there was no funeral and no real time of
mourning, as is otherwise customary. And so I was overcome by a
deep melancholy when I saw this ocean of faces, most of whom were
much too young to have known this woman who was being honored
here, too young to carry any guilt for the murder of six million Jews.
And third, when the pope came down after the service and greeted

us, the family of Edith Stein, I thought that the reigning pope of her time gave my aunt Edith Stein scant hearing. Why was he silent then in the face of the wicked regime of the National Socialists? Why could people like my aunt not be saved? And why did Pope Pius XI, whom she asked in the spring of 1933 for a declaration against the persecution of the Jews, answer only with a perfunctory blessing for her and her family instead of publicly taking a position? His defenders cite his encyclical *Mit brennender Sorge,* but that document was not published until four years later and, by the way, said not one word about the persecution of the Jews. Instead of giving moral guidelines to German Catholics and warning them of the godless doctrines of National Socialism, he concluded a concordat with the new Hitler regime of Germany. Therefore my apprehension never left me, even during the celebration.

It is perhaps worth mentioning that, in the destruction of the Jews during the Third Reich, Edith Stein's family lost not only Edith, but three of her siblings, a niece, and a large number of other relatives. It is only the Catholic Church that has elevated Edith from the larger group and chosen her for special honor and veneration.

To my question concerning the pope's sermon I received mostly very positive answers. My relatives were greatly impressed with the conciliatory, tolerant tone and found the description of Edith Stein as "a great daughter of Israel" a welcome sign that her Jewish origins were not overlooked. It is interesting that the rabbi of the Cologne Synagogue took exception to this term and expressed his view on Saturday, May 2, after the service: "When someone leaves the Jewish community and embraces a different faith, we may regret it, but we cannot view such a person as a great son or a great daughter of Israel." That the pope meant well by this terminology is certain. But it is also certain that in using this phrase he hurt some of us Jews. It is probably inevitable that such misunderstandings occur, for we still have a long way to go in mutual understanding of both religions.

Harvey Sachs, a great-nephew of Edith Stein, remarked after first experiencing the beatification ceremony and attending the Jewish Shabbat services on the following morning, that through these two experiences he had first become aware of the huge differences between the two religions: the mystical, mysterious aspects of

Communion, with its transubstantiation, which constitute the focus of the Catholic Mass, and in contrast to it, the intensive immersion in the study of Torah which is at the center of the Shabbat.
There are hardly any points of contact between the two. Those who
believe that the only difference between Judaism and Christianity
is the belief in Jesus of Nazareth as God's Son and Redeemer do
not understand the basic tenets of these two faiths. Only by truly
knowing them and from this basis, respecting the differences, ap-
proaching one another without intent to convert and without con-
descension toward the other, can one attain true understanding.

What some of us missed in the pope's homily was any mention of regret whatsoever over the failure of the church during the
persecution of the Jews in the Third Reich as well as the persecution of Jews by the official church in former centuries. It can hardly
have been coincidence that this subject was not even mentioned.
Although the pope strongly condemned the atrocities of the Nazis,
there was no idea of a confession of guilt in the name of the Catholic Church.

As Mary Gordon, a Catholic author, wrote: "The Church has
committed serious transgressions against the Jews. There is no reason for Jews to trust or forgive the Church before it has confessed
the depths of its transgressions" (*Tikkun* [September–October,
1987]: 53).

Several of my relatives expressed their displeasure over the
pope's omission of the subject of women, even though Edith Stein
stood in the vanguard of the women's movement and in her writings discussed some matters that today are still among the unsolved
problems of the church. She could well be a signpost on this subject, but the pope preferred to avoid this theme. It is not surprising
that the Synod of Bishops that adjourned on October 30, 1987,
totally dropped the many proposals for expanding the role of
women in the life of the church (*Neue Zürcher Zeitung*, October
31, 1987).

To my question regarding the ways in which the pope's actions in subsequent weeks and months harmonized with his
homily, I was surprised that my non-Jewish relatives had paid
little attention to certain events during that time. They made no
mention of the controversial reception of Kurt Waldheim, which

had created a sensation in the Jewish press. I myself wrote to the pope in July 1987 and asked for an explanation of his stand. The pope's reception of this man, who had been declared *persona non grata* by the governments of the major powers on the basis of his only recently discovered questionable past, gave Waldheim a welcome boost in prestige without which he probably would have been humiliated before the world. The answer that I received two months later from the papal nuncio in Washington was quite unsatisfactory.

One of my Jewish cousins gave the pope poor marks for continuing to withhold diplomatic recognition to the State of Israel. Such a step would go far in diminishing Jewish distrust.[1]

It is clear to me that the positive impression we got from the pope's homily on May 1, 1987, can have lasting meaning only if it is confirmed on an ongoing basis by consistent deeds. Without such confirmation these mellifluous words remain just words.

My eldest son Ronald was present at the beatification. He understood little of the German-language celebration. But he was greatly impressed. After the pope had passed along the row of relatives and had greeted them all, Ronald said to me: "The pope has promised much, and he gave me his hand on it." Let's wait and see whether the promises we heard on May 1, 1987, will be fulfilled.

This thought leads me directly to my next point. Will the pope's noble sermon have a lasting effect on the attitude of the church? My relatives are not in agreement on that question. Two say no. They base their opinion on the ponderousness of the church "apparatus," the reluctance to change long-established customs and thought patterns or to give up prejudices. Two believe that it might perhaps lead to improved conditions, one did not even answer this question and the last said simply: "We must wait and see what happens."

To the question of improved Catholic-Jewish relations, I received greatly varying replies. Only a single one was affirmative. Another one hopes for it. Two said it might perhaps be possible, and one answered in the negative. He believes that Catholics in leading positions do not understand Judaism and vice versa; and that this is even more true of the public at large. But because the thoughtful segment of the public knows what can happen when we fail to work for better relations, they will continue their efforts and once in a while achieve small successes. In summary we can only say: If one does not expect too much, one can perhaps live to see some pleasant surprises.

I asked whether they believed that the beatification of Edith Stein has deepened the understanding of the so-called Holocaust. Three of my relatives believe that a knowledge about Edith Stein's fate brings the events of that time closer to people than statistics are able to do. Her example may alert and sensitize some people to the gruesome deeds of the Nazis. No, says another one. She is being honored as a Christian martyr, not as a persecuted Jew. Thereby the church shows that it has not comprehended the plan of the National Socialists for the so-called "final solution" that found expression in the Holocaust. Also by the establishment of the monastery on the site of the crematorium in Auschwitz, the church shows little empathy with the suffering of the Jews who see this site as a Jewish mass grave. And to build a church in such a place is viewed as an act of desecration. Such a step is often seen by Jews as an attempt to "Christianize" the Holocaust and to turn Auschwitz, the place where people acted on their meanest, most cruel impulses, into a place of triumph of Christian faith. That is untenable for Jews, for we believe that spiritual triumph is to be found in life, not in the death of millions.[2]

What the Stein family found very impressive was the opportunity to meet leading personalities of the church and the Carmelite Order. People like Fr. Ulrich Dobhan, Sr. Maria Amata Neyer, Cardinal Lustiger (himself a convert from Judaism) and Cardinal Macharski sat at our tables and held conversations with us that made us forget the differences in our origins and history and allowed us to meet face to face as individuals. Other relatives sat with Cardinal Mayer and Cardinal Ratzinger. In such a situation we are not Jews or Christians, Catholics or Protestants, Americans or Germans, but simply human beings who must somehow cope with this life, on this earth, with its manifold problems, who need each other and want to get along with one another. That was a positive experience that we shall not soon forget.

But that was not all. The beatification brought us something else, something that no one else could experience there and that meant a lot to us: The chance to be together as a family. It was really moving how in that little hotel we met with people whom we had not seen for a long time; with others whom we knew only through the stories of our parents or grandmother. Harvey, for instance, writes:

> Meeting new family members was an incredible, spine-tingling experience. Having cousin Angela walk up after the ceremony and join us, in that crowd, is just unforgettable and deep in symbolism. Some memories will fade: Language and cultural problems limit the gap that genes can span. Others, like Angela's happiness at finding us, will stay for a long, long time.... The Holocaust is decimation, so that discovering others who survived must be one of the greatest pleasures and affirmations of life.

Angela Javitz is a young woman who survived the war in Berlin. She had found her way to her American relatives years ago, when she came over to America for a visit and was a guest in my mother's house. She is the great-granddaughter of my grandmother's brother.

A daughter of Edith's cousin Richard Courant was also in Cologne. She stressed repeatedly how glad she was to meet these relatives. Her father had no special inclination to cultivate such relationships, and therefore his children had no contact with the extended family.

I believe it was a fitting tribute honoring Edith Stein that family connections could be restored through her. After all, she had labored for years on the book *Life in a Jewish Family*. She was deeply rooted in this family, and it is a tragic irony that, while she joined a new family as a religious, she continued to live on in her former family and simultaneously became estranged from it. Her life distanced itself from that of her loved ones, and yet her cruel death reunited her with the fate of her relatives in a horrible manner that she perhaps foresaw.

My mother, who often said, "A living sister would have been worth a thousand times more to me than a dead saint," did not understand Edith's road to Carmel, but she knew that Edith was following her conscience, even though thereby she caused deep pain to her family, and especially to her mother. I thought a lot about my mother as I sat in the stadium and experienced this impressive celebration. How would she have felt about this event? We are religious Jews, and the beatification is something foreign to us. In Jewish teaching, there are no intermediaries between God and human beings. Everyone can and must find his or her direct way to God. To pray to a human being is not permitted, be he or she ever so virtuous and exemplary. But if the beatification of my aunt can help to bring people closer to each other and lead to a better understanding among them, so that a horror such as we experienced can never occur again, then that would be a wonderful thing indeed.

I conclude my remarks with warmest thanks to Alfred Batzdorff, Gerhard Holti, Gertrude Moser, Harvey Sachs, Lotte Sachs, Ronald Stein, Waltraud Stein, and Wolf Stein. Without their valuable contributions this essay could not have come about.

l.r.: Susanne Batzdorff and Sr. Josephine Koeppel, OCD

Life in a Jewish Family:
Aunt Edith's Legacy to Her Descendants
by Susanne Batzdorff

I. A Memento From Days Gone By

On my desk lies a yellowed prayer book in German and Hebrew, a Golden Wedding Anniversary present to my great-great-grandmother. It must have been beautiful then and probably expensive, too; it is covered in violet velvet, although a bit worn by now, gilt-edged and bearing her name in gold Gothic letters, "Ernestine Burchardt, December 5, 1866." Inside is a dedication, likewise in gold lettering:

> For the Golden Wedding Celebration
> in Love and Recognition of her special merit
> by the Women's Club of Lublinitz.

With its petit-point embroidered bookmark that bears the initials EB in tiny gold beads, this book looks as if the old lady had just placed it on my desk. Holding this book in her hand, my ancestor may have prayed for the return of the Jewish people to Zion, or perhaps quite simply for the recovery of her husband, who at that time suffered from paranoia and no longer trusted her. In this book Ernestine lives for me just as in the early pages of the autobiography of my aunt Edith Stein. Ernestine was the grandmother of my grandmother Auguste Stein.

Susanne Batzdorff *is an author, translator, and former head librarian of the Humanities Department, Northeast Regional Library, Free Library of Philadelphia. She is Edith Stein's niece and lives in Santa Rosa, CA.*

29

II. The Opinions Vary

A folder in my file cabinet contains the voluminous correspondence concerning the publication of Edith Stein's family history. These numerous old letters flew back and forth between Brussels, Cologne, and New York from early 1963 until the summer of 1964, in order to resolve a conflict concerning a sometimes violently disputed publication. The Archivum Carmelitanum in Brussels, where Edith Stein's manuscripts were kept and organized, was then planning to publish her book *Life in a Jewish Family*.

My mother knew only its first part, which Edith had written while yet in Breslau and in which she describes the early history of the Courants (Edith's mother's maiden name was Courant) and the Steins, going back about three generations, according to descriptions and stories of her mother. The Cologne Carmel, however, had a last will and testament of Edith Stein which stated:

> As for the family history, I ask that it not be published as long as my siblings are alive, and that it not be handed over to them. Only Rosa might have a look at it, and after the death of the others, their children. Even then the Order should decide about the question of publication.

When, on the basis of this provision, the Carmelite Sisters of Cologne refused to give their consent to the publication of the book, my parents were drawn into the debate. The archive in Brussels, having prepared the text for publication, wrote to my mother (who at that time did not yet know about Edith's will) and asked for her consent. This letter says:

> The legally valid testament of Edith Stein was destroyed by the Sisters in Cologne prior to Edith's flight to Holland in order to avoid possible danger for the Cologne Carmel. The contents of this testament are not known. For years we have been pressured to publish the manuscript and been subject to spirited criticism of our discreet reluctance; and now, despite complete awareness for months that we were preparing this work for publication, the clerical court of Cologne is being presented with a letter which Edith Stein composed for the Sisters after her flight to Holland. This hitherto unknown text has no

legal validity whatsoever. It contains a postscript in which Edith expresses her wish that the manuscript be published only after the death of her siblings. You, dear Professor and Mrs. Biberstein, are the only surviving "siblings." For us there is no doubt that at this time, Edith would not add this codicil any more or would cross it out without hesitation....

The letter is not dated but must have been written in early May 1963.

It is amazing how nonchalantly the author's handwritten request not to present her text to the public until after the death of her siblings was simply shoved aside and how, on top of that, the archivists claim to know that Edith would surely have changed her mind if she were living today. My mother answered, still rather innocently, and asked for an explanation of what might stand in the way of publishing the book during her lifetime:

> Of course I have no objection against the publication *per se*, on the contrary, I eagerly await its appearance... I have full confidence that you will not do anything against Edith's wishes. Of course I am curious to hear about the further development of this matter and hope that you will let me know. (Letter of May 19, 1963)

My mother, however, received no reply. In spring 1964 a letter arrived from Sr. Teresia Margareta, who at that time was the custodian and arranger of the documents by and about Edith Stein [in the Cologne Carmel]. Written on March 20, the letter announced that "the large, voluminous manuscript" was en route to my mother, so that she might decide "whether it was really her wish to let this book appear already at this time."

Immediately, my parents began to read this book that, of course, had to be fascinating for them, because, after all, it portrayed not only Edith's but also their youth in all its delight and beauty, but also with unvarnished honesty. I have galleys that my parents pored over and in many cases provided with the marginal comment "omit." Everything that might hurt or injure a family member was to be omitted. And although at first they felt that the book should not be published at all, as long as any relatives of

Edith's generation were still alive, and that it was both morally and legally correct to respect her last will and testament, finally an amicable agreement was reached among the Archivum Carmelitanum, the Carmel of Cologne, and my parents (representing the family). Following my parents' annotations, an abridged text was to be published with the offensive passages removed. This was done, and in 1965 the book was published. Only in 1985, seven years after the death of my mother, the last "obstacle," did the complete text appear.

III. Plans and Intentions

On September 21, 1933, four days before my twelfth birthday, Aunt Edith sat at her desk in Breslau and appended the date to the introduction of her family history. She planned to record the chronicle of her Jewish family according to the stories of her mother and her own observations. The main purpose was to allow thereby an insight into the nature of a possibly typical Jewish bourgeois family, as counterweight to the distorted picture given by Nazi propaganda. My aunt had as yet hardly any idea how far this anti-Semitic rabble-rousing would lead within a few years. She worked diligently on the first part of this book and within one and a half years had made quite a lot of progress. The attentive reader will notice that she appears to have forgotten her original intent. The book became instead the story of her own youth. And the urgency of her plan to offer the German reader an accurate picture of Jewish family life must have receded in her consciousness, for she required a lot of time to ready this work for publication. For it happened that in May 1935, one and a half years after her entrance into Carmel, other tasks interfered, so that she had to pause for almost four years. She could not resume this work until the beginning of January 1939. Add to this that Edith Stein made the above-mentioned disposition in her last will and testament, which would postpone a publication of her book far into the future.

At that time her six brothers and sisters were still all living. Thus, her family history would not be reaching its readers very soon, and her intent to help inform the German people and serve as an antidote against malicious and mendacious Nazi propaganda would not be fulfilled.

All who know her life story will realize that she was under much greater pressure in January 1939 than at the time when the main portion of this work originated, from September 1933 to May 1935. In between lie the death of her beloved mother in September 1936 and the ever-worsening political conditions in Germany with ever more radical intrusions into the existence of the Jews and descendants of Jews that culminated in the pogroms of November 9 and 10, 1938. Following these, Edith Stein had left Germany on the last day of the year and had been transferred to a Dutch monastery. On January 7, the day on which she resumed this work, she had been in Echt barely one week. The foreign surroundings, her shock at what she had experienced in Germany, the necessity of adjusting to new fellow-sisters whose political views she could not yet know, and above all, the knowledge that a second world war was probably imminent and that a horrible future loomed ahead, can surely have contributed to a feeling of great insecurity and exhaustion.

The book breaks off quite suddenly. What else did Edith have in mind concerning her autobiographical notes? We find several references to later passages that she intended to write. But that never came about. It was not granted to her to complete her autobiography. The question arises: Would not Edith have made some revisions before publishing her book? We have no way of knowing. But it is tempting at times to speculate a bit.

I believe, for example, that Edith added the above-mentioned instructions concerning the disposition of her book to her testamentary letter because she was not sure whether she would yet be able to finish the planned revision of her manuscript or whether her life might end prematurely. We know she was prepared for that. She did not wish to hurt any of her relatives by her all too truthful presentations. Hence the caution not to show this text to any of her siblings but Rosa, who had very likely already seen this work in part during a visit to Cologne.

It is quite imaginable that Edith thought: *If I get around to revising this book, I can change this proviso later, since in that case there would be no reason not to publish the entire text. But if I die beforehand, I must protect my siblings from the uncensored text.*

IV. Unvarnished Truths

It was her concern to report truthfully what had occurred between 1891 and 1916, the favorable and the less flattering, and in this reportage she did not spare any of her fellow-humans. She promised also to describe and criticize herself just as relentlessly as the others (p. 18), but those who read it later felt differently about it. Of course, Edith could not know that these reminiscences would be available in bookstores after only thirty years and that therefore some relatives, a real sister and her husband among them, would get to read them. She also could not know that of her six siblings, three besides herself would fall victim to the systematic German persecutions of the Jews.

If Aunt Edith, like Cassandra, could have looked into the future, she might have pictured her relatives with more restraint, because we all know that one ought not to speak ill of the dead. This way, however, she wrote the truth as she saw it and felt it. Especially in the beginning chapters, Edith criticizes relatives and acquaintances quite sharply. Her self-criticism, written with disarming pleasantness, appears gentler and pleads for extenuating circumstances. Besides, one always gets the impression that these faults have since been corrected. She is speaking of weaknesses from earlier times.

> We never again had a falling-out such as we sometimes had during our student years. This was because I had completely changed my attitude towards others as well as toward myself. Being right and getting the better of my opponent under any circumstances were no longer essential for me. Also, though I still had as keen an eye for the human weaknesses of others, I no longer made that an instrument for striking them at their most vulnerable point, but, rather, for protecting them.[1]

When writing about her relatives, however, things are portrayed just as they were in Edith's recollection, and even if, in the meantime, the person concerned had long changed his view or acted differently, the story remains and characterizes him forever.

For these reasons, some of her relatives felt impelled to take a stand on Edith Stein's portrayals. My father, for instance, wrote a twenty-three-page letter to his son Ernst Ludwig and to me, his daughter, in which he set down his comments on the facts as Edith had described them. It was very important to him that we should know his views as well. He suffered at that time from severe heart disease and definitely wanted to have his say before it might be too late. His comments refer mainly to what had been written about his relationship with his wife Erna and about him and his mother. What Edith reported about her eldest sister Else and her family probably even now makes painful reading for her children. Else's youngest daughter Anni Meyer, née Gordon, wrote to me on this subject, in a letter of March 5, 1988.

> It contains too many things that do not concern the public and can be seen one-sidedly. In my English translation (i.e. *Life in a Jewish Family,* trans. by Josephine Koeppel, OCD [Washington, DC: ICS Publications, 1986]) I have inserted slips with data that I myself remember, and with corrections.

The question also arises whether such a detailed discussion of a problematic marriage serves to give non-Jews a positive impression of a Jewish family. By the time the first edition of this book appeared, Else and her husband had died. Paul and Trude, whose sloppy housekeeping had here been sharply criticized, were also dead, victims of the Nazis. Their son, Gerhard, however, had survived to cope with this unsympathetic description of his mother. Only years later did Gerhard write a defense of his mother that showed why these two very different women, his grandmother and his mother, could not understand one another.

V. Self-Portrait?

Edith saw herself in the role of a peacemaker. At times she was successful. She portrays herself as a wise, calm, serene soul, unprejudiced and therefore often consulted for advice.

Her friends and relatives loved her as a merry, loyal companion. She wrote humorous occasional verse, took part in all jests and sociability and contributed her share in entertaining the others.

In her book, one scarcely notices these traits. Here Edith portrays herself largely as a serious, well-behaved person, even a bit of a bluestocking who wants to waste no time on frivolities. That her aunt Cilla called her a "go-getter" did not please her. But it must have contained a grain of truth. According to the remarks of her teacher Hermsen and her fellow-students at *Viktoriaschule,* her somewhat condescending attitude towards others had attracted attention as well. Unfortunately it is these traits that often stand out in this autobiography. She describes herself as modest and shy.

> For me it was always most embarrassing to have to thread my way through the tightly packed rows of girls all the way up to the podium where the entire faculty was seated; one was the center of attention for all those present in the hall while the principal spoke a few friendly words.[2]

> I did not like to have so much fuss made about them [my good marks] nor to have all the relatives and acquaintances told of them.[3]

And yet one notices in her self-portrayal a strong need for admiration. ("I was apt to skip right to the front of the teacher's desk with index finger raised in order to 'get my turn.'")[4] and the characteristics of an ambitious achiever ("I cared less about the award than about the actual rank in class").[5] And much later, at the university, "whenever possible, I sat in the first row in class so I could follow the lecturers without distraction."[6]

Aware of her own talent and intelligence, she looks down upon the mass of her fellow-students: "But the mass of students I considered a negligible quantity."[7] That also fits in with her characterization of the students in her adult education class on German composition and spelling as "a herd,"[8] as well as her estimation of the philosophy students whom she was to introduce to the ideas of Husserl as her "philosophical kindergarten."[9] She found it embarrassing to have her fellow students meet her mother, to whom she was devoted with tender love, because of her "work clothes and her rough, toil-worn hands."[10] Edith admits this frankly and with remorse.

Some readers who did not know Edith Stein personally and who form an opinion based on reading her autobiography may have an unfavorable impression. A great-grandniece, for example, remarked, "I hope you won't be offended, but I don't think I would have *liked* her very much if I had ever met her. She seems to me, from her writings and from what other people have said, to have been a very self-centered, judgmental, and intolerant individual."[11]

One gains the same impression from the description of her service with the Red Cross.[12] Her manners appear prudish and puritanical. One is tempted to think that Edith is here making an effort to portray herself as overly virtuous.

She was, after all, a nun in the Carmel of Cologne and her writings doubtless had to be submitted to the prioress for her attention and possible censorship. And not only that: The new postulant may have been eager to make a good impression through piety and virtue, in order to find among her fellow-sisters and superiors the recognition that in former times had been hers in abundance from colleagues, friends, relatives, and lecture audiences. Already as a child, Edith knew that it was much more important "to be good than to be clever."[13] And as an adult and a nun it was at least as important to keep this goal in view.

My father had the impression that Edith Stein had written her family history "not only as a tribute, but actually a glorification of her mother."[14] He meant it most likely as criticism, but for me it was something very positive. In this book Auguste Stein came alive as the "Woman of Valor" in the Book of Proverbs, a matriarch who knew life very well, from its sunny as well as its bleak side, and always grasped it with both hands and wrested her reward from it in daily hard work. For us children she was, without a doubt, the head of the family and when we moved away from her large home in 1933, it seemed to us as if suddenly a much harsher wind was blowing. Even today I am still glad that Aunt Edith depicted our grandmother so vividly and lovingly. Also, the milieu of the Courant family gives a good picture of the lifestyle and the way of thinking that characterized these people. This world no longer exists. All the better that it is portrayed so vividly here. How typical the Stein family was for German-Jewish society in the first half of the twentieth century is debatable. Perhaps it was more characteristic of the

German middle class in general. The manner in which family crises were dealt with, the attitudes toward morality, divorce, women's rights and much more are clearly shown here.

VI. Idyllic Times

Particularly vivid are Edith's descriptions of student life. On April 1, 1964, Erna Biberstein, Edith's sister (and my mother) wrote: "We, that is my husband and myself, have read this book with feverish eagerness [and] enjoyed parts of it very much... During this reading, our entire youth came alive for us once again."[15] This picturesque, nostalgic view of student days in prewar Germany could rekindle the enthusiasm of those readers who had once been university students. It was so totally different than in America, for example, and probably also in Germany today. The relationship of students and professor, here called "master," can hardly be imagined in an American environment. The personalities of professors and instructors, Husserl, Scheler, and Reinach, live in this description, and one can well imagine what a charismatic influence they had on this young, impressionable student. The hikes in the scenic surroundings, the comic newspapers and humorous verses, the self-organized seminars and introductory courses, the student lunches and finally the "little refreshments" consisting of delicious cakes available in the pastry shop, all appear here in living color as if seen on stage in a comedy. The nostalgia with which Edith dreams of her time in Göttingen contrasts so dreadfully with the termination of her life that one reads these passages with an aching heart.

> Dear Göttingen! I do believe only someone who studied there between 1905 and 1914, the short flowering of the Göttingen School of Phenomenology, can appreciate all that the name evokes in us.
>
> I was twenty-one years old and looked forward full of expectation to all that lay ahead.[16]

She loved the German landscape and made frequent excursions into the most scenic parts of the country, mostly on foot, only occasionally by train. She was always accompanied by fellow-students, both male and female, happily and in a spirit of adventure. For us Aunt Edith always held some mystery, because she came on vacation from the Rhineland, which one knew only from epic poems, ballads, and student songs, an unknown, romantic land for which one always longed a bit. And this aunt, who came to us from this fairyland, somehow brought some of that magic with her. The same feeling I also get when I read these lyrical passages. *My* Germany, of course, looked quite different, for by the time we had reached the age of reason, National Socialism was already in power, and for us Jews in Germany that meant a very restricted life. One began to think of emigration. Every day brought new restrictions and harrassments to which one tried to adapt as best one could. The fairytale dreams of the Rhineland had to remain dreams, for as a Jew one no longer traveled within Germany but spent one's vacations beyond the German border in order to recuperate a bit.

When we were in Cologne in May 1987 for the beatification of my aunt, we subsequently drove down along the Rhine River by car. Our son Ronald was with us. Suddenly he asked: "Why have you never told me how beautiful it is here?" He was right. Due to our grief over past experiences, we had forgotten or overlooked the charms of this country that had once been our homeland. The beauty of the landscape has remained, but we have become strangers here. For Edith it was a treasure that, feeling herself to be German, she enjoyed fully.

When she talks so brightly and freely of those happy days, the reader rejoices with her.

VII. Edith Stein and Judaism

It is important to examine Edith Stein's Jewish connection of which, even in later years, she was so proud that she "felt part of it" even after her conversion. In her description of her family she states: Mika (a younger sister of her mother) was "the only one in the house who had preserved the faith of her parents and who saw to it that the traditions were carried out while the Jewish identity of the others had lost its religious foundation."[17] In her mother's house she observed a similar trend. The younger generation no longer greatly valued the tradition that gave their mother support and direction. The daughters of the family received no religious instruction and did not learn Hebrew. The sons were prepared for their Bar Mitzvah, learned a little Hebrew and probably also a bit of Jewish history. At that time there was no equivalent (Bat Mitzvah) for girls, so one saw no particular reason to give them religious instruction.

Numerous passages of her book show that Edith's familiarity with Judaism had many gaps. For example, she does not know that the commandment against eating leavened bread throughout the week of Passover stems directly from the Bible (Nm 28:17). That these laws were "expanded with the stubborn consistency characteristic of the Jewish mind"[18] is simply not true and shows that Edith's judgment is based on prejudices here, not facts. A similarly critical remark, concerning the Sabbath prohibitions against carrying loads, offends the observant Jew:

> One day when out walking with [Metis] I had an errand in one of the houses we passed. In the doorway I suddenly handed him my briefcase to hold while I went in. Too late, it occurred to me that it was Saturday and one ought not to carry anything on the Sabbath. I found him dutifully awaiting me in the doorway. I apologized for thoughtlessly causing him to do something forbidden. "I haven't done anything forbidden," he replied quietly. "Only on the street is one not to carry anything; in the house it's allowed."
>
> For that reason he had remained in the entrance-hall, taking care not to put even one foot into the street. This was an example of the talmudic sophistry which I found so repugnant. But I made no comment.[19]

Edith's comment shows her unfamiliarity with the practice of observant Jews. In her assimilated milieu orthodox Jews were an exception.

Her views concerning the Jewish attitude toward death can likewise be attributed to misunderstandings and lack of knowledge. Her comparison of a Jewish funeral with a Catholic one contains the following description:

The rabbi began the eulogy. I have heard many such talks. They gave a résumé of the life of the deceased, recalling all the good things he had done, thereby rousing the sorrow of the bereaved all the more; there was nothing consoling about them. To be sure there was a prayer pronounced in solemn tones: "And when the body returns to dust, the spirit returns to God who gave it."

However, nothing of faith in a personal life after death, nor any belief in a future reunion with those who had died, lay behind these words. Many years later, when for the first time I attended a Catholic funeral, the contrast made a deep impression upon me. The one then being buried was a very well-known scholar. But no longer was mention made of his achievements or of the reputation he had won in the world. Called by his baptismal name alone, the humble soul, in all its poverty, was commended to divine mercy. But how consoling and calming were the words of the liturgy which accompanied the deceased into eternity! [20]

Admittedly these two ceremonies differ. But Edith Stein mentions nothing of the prayers and psalms that are always recited at Jewish funerals. Because she did not know Hebrew, she probably did not understand them. Speaking of the deceased is designed to help the mourners express their feelings instead of keeping them bottled up inside. The Jewish funeral instructions are considered reasonable from a psychological point of view. The seven days of *Shiva*, the thirty days and the eleven months are designated periods of mourning of different degrees, enabling the mourner to find his way from deep mourning back to a daily routine and to work by means of carefully graduated stages. Edith Stein probably knew nothing of the wisdom of these regulations, because she was unfamiliar with these customs.

Finally we read here that suicide is more frequent among Jews than among the rest of the population. That does not correspond to the facts, at least not in normal times. However, during the years of Jewish persecution, when this text was written, there were very logical reasons why more Jews than others put an end to their lives. These reasons are to be found not in the Jewish religion but in the diabolical Nazi politics.

Other examples could be cited, but these may suffice. We often asked ourselves why our aunt, so intelligent and always eager to learn, could not have devoted to the study of Judaism a fraction of the time she gave to studying philosophy and later, Christianity. She dismissed the Jewish religion without having given it a real chance. The comparison with Franz Rosenzweig comes to mind. He, too, considered conversion to Christianity for a while, but, prior to doing that, he made a serious attempt to recapture a relationshipwith the faith of his ancestors. He returned to Judaism and became a renowned Jewish scholar.

When considering Edith Stein's attitude to Judaism, an understanding of the society in which she lived and in which anti-Semitism was widespread is essential. Her youth was spent in imperial and later in democratic Germany. Hitler's thousand year, anti-Semitic Reich did not yet exist. Nevertheless anti-Semitism was alive and well in Germany. Among the many academics who converted to Christianity at that time, only a few did so out of religious conviction. For many it was the springboard to a professorship. As Jews they were condemned to a strictly limited academic career that terminated at the level of "ausserordentlicher Professor" (assistant professor). Edith mentions that she owed her employment as a teacher at the municipal *Viktoriaschule* to the First World War, because most of the men were away on active duty.

> Because of our Jewish descent and because the *Viktoriaschule*, as Professor Lengert once mentioned at one of the conferences, "had always been considered as Protestant," neither of us would have had any prospects of employment in the institution in former years.[21]

Her older sister Else had been unable to obtain a teaching job in the Prussian school system in peacetime and finally had to take a position at a private school in Hamburg.[22]

Edith's frequent references to the non-Jewish appearance of various persons shows that that was a definite advantage and something thoroughly desirable. Aside from that, it unfortunately also shows that, while herself a Jew, she had taken on the prejudices of the population at large to a certain degree. She herself emphasized proudly: "By the way, this [the fact that I was Jewish] used to astound people since no one took me to be Jewish."[23]

She once made a condescending comment about Eastern Jews:

> Nor had he even the slightest trace of that unpleasant intonation common to the uneducated Eastern Jews which irritated the German "assimilated Jews" even more than it did the "Aryans."[24]

She had thoroughly accepted a prejudiced way of thinking. By the way, the adjective "uneducated" as applied here to Eastern Jews was often inappropriate. Many of these immigrants or students from Eastern Europe spoke a broken German with a Polish or Russian accent, but there were renowned and high-ranking academics and Talmud scholars among them.

As a last example for the prejudices of pre-Hitler times let me cite the case of Suse Mugdan. Suse was a good friend of Edith's during her service with the Red Cross. Stein described her as follows:

> By descent, the Mugdans were Jewish; but Frau Mugdan had had all her children baptized as Protestants after her husband died...to insure for them a more prosperous future.... Her mother's preventive measure was never a source of gratitude for Suse.... In the lazaretto, of course, anti-Semitic remarks were to be heard at times. On such occasions Suse forthrightly envied me the ability to come forward with a simple acknowledgment that I was Jewish... Yet if she wanted to say anything, she would have had to give such a complicated explanation that it would have appeared odd and would not have been understood.[25]

On careful reading of the above paragraph it is striking that Edith considers it a matter of course that she and her colleague sometimes heard anti-Semitic remarks in the hospital. It is characteristic of these pre-Hitler times that as a Jew one accepted such remarks as almost routine. There was even a term for it: The good old-fashioned *Risches* (anti-Semitism). It differed from the later,

state-sponsored official anti-Semitism that resulted in legislated in-
justice, deprivation of rights, and finally destruction of the Jews.

VIII. Status of Women in Edith Stein's World

Just as Edith Stein's reminiscences characterize the existence
of the Jews in Germany at that time extremely well, we can also
derive quite a bit from her descriptions concerning the position of
women in society during the same period.

Female university students were then, about 1910, a rarity.
[Prussia first admitted women students in 1908.—Trans.] My
mother (Edith's sister Erna), Edith, and their friends considered
themselves privileged women, and as members of the Prussian Organization for Women's Suffrage they fought for complete equal-
ity, especially the right to vote. Eagerly they debated the problem
of couples with two incomes: "I was alone in maintaining, always,
that I would not sacrifice my profession on any account," Edith
wrote.[26] Out of a deep sense of obligation these young women entered the women's movement in order to achieve full political
rights for women.

In the life of the university campus, women were still an exception. One did not quite know how to deal with them. And the
women students themselves had a hard time with it. For the cen-
tennial celebration of the university in the summer of 1911, for
example, the women did not want to absent themselves. On the
other hand, they worried that the fraternity party could end in a
brawl. It was only after an urgent invitation by the rector of the
university that the women students decided to attend. For their
protection, it was suggested to place several professors' wives at
their table, but now such "mothering" seemed ludicrous to the
young students.[27] Even so, the table with the young girls dressed in
white caused a sensation and drew the attention of the alumni.

In the workers' courses where Edith taught for a while, the relations between women students and male teachers were not yet clarified. First, it had to be decided whether the ladies would prefer to
study in mixed or segregated classes. Most were greatly relieved and
grateful for not having to attend the general course: "They would
have felt so awkward in the presence of the young men."[28]

In the small university town of Göttingen, too, the population did not view women students without prejudice. Some landladies did not like to rent rooms to female students. Edith's pleasant young landlady had confessed that:

> She had never had any woman students in her home before and thought they would all be old and ugly.... Many landladies refused women boarders. Some had moral prejudices. Others feared their kitchens would be in demand too frequently for washing, ironing, or cooking.[29]

And finally she tells of a female student whose mother accompanied her to Göttingen to take care of her daughter and provide for her. The father had to be left alone all year long.[30]

We find it strange that these young women could not fix their own meals but had to take their meals at student lunch tables. At most, they prepared their own breakfast. While Edith lived for a time in the apartment of her cousin Richard Courant, a cleaning woman came every day to service the coal furnace and cook breakfast for the young student.[31]

IX. Love of Germany in Edith Stein's Family

Not without bitterness do we read today in Edith Stein's reminiscences about her great love of her country and her family's patriotism. The description of the plebiscite after the First World War shows this clearly.

> Lublinitz is not far from the Polish border. During the entire war, troop transports passed through it, and my aunts were very active in caring for the soldiers.... The German authorities entrusted my uncle with the distribution of food.
> The entire family antagonized the Poles by their decisive pro-German partisanship.... More than fifty descendants of the Courant family who had been born in Lublinitz returned for the voting.... The sad event after so much strain and effort was the more painful: Lublinitz became Polish....My relatives could not and would not think of remaining there; they sold the family seat and left their homeland.[32]

As a student, Edith felt:

...a deep gratitude to the state which had granted me academic citizenship with its free access to the wisdom of mankind.

I regarded all the small benefits to which our student's pass entitled us, such as reduced prices for theater and concert tickets and the like, as the loving providence of the state for its favored children. This stirred in me a desire to discharge my debt of gratitude to the people and the state, later, by making a professional contribution of my own.[33]

And when in 1914 war broke out, the student body was seized with a passionate patriotism. The war fever of the young lecturer Reinach found a distinct echo in Edith's heart:

Only the coming events [the war] were talked of.
"Must you go, also, Doctor?" Kaufmann asked.
"It's not that I *must;* rather, I'm permitted to go," Reinach replied.
His statement pleased me very much. It expressed so well my own feelings.[34]

She traveled to Breslau as soon as she could:

Though feverishly tense, I faced the future with great clarity and determination.
"I have no private life anymore," I told myself, "All my energy must be devoted to this great happening. Only when the war is over, if I'm alive then, will I be permitted to think of my private affairs once more."
... Meanwhile, with jubilant cries of victory, we followed the progress of our army into France: we used colored pins to mark the route on our big maps and awaited the day when "we" would march into Paris.[35]

Her mother's objections could not prevent her from going into a hospital for infectious diseases in Moravia as a volunteer nurse's aide. How bitter all the more was the fate that this woman later experienced because she came from a Jewish family. Hitler would later deny every patriotic impulse, every noble deed, every bravery that was performed by Jews in times of war and peace. Jews were maligned as cowardly shirkers and opportunistic war profiteers and a few years later they were exterminated like vermin. The thought that, prior to her death, Edith was shipped once more into the area where her beloved home had once been, and that the hospital where she had nursed sick soldiers was situated not far from Auschwitz, increases the irony even more. When she, herded together with hundreds, was transported through the country, she must have remembered all this with an aching heart.

What had begun as a young woman student's gratitude and willingness to sacrifice herself, ended in Auschwitz/Birkenau on August 9, 1942.

The pre-war student idyll, the adventures and conflicts within the family, the hopes and ambition of an unusually gifted student, the disappointments and triumphs of her career, and the ever more intensive search for truth form a vivid, connected narrative that ends abruptly. We who are tied to our aunt by bonds of family cannot read this book without pain, because we cannot get over the tragic outcome of this promising and hopeful human life.

The pope greeting members of Edith Stein's family after the beatification in Cologne, May 1, 1987
l.r.: Alfred Batzdorff, Susanne Batzdorff, Bernhard Rosenmöller, Jr., Pope John Paul II,
Cardinal Joseph Höffner (photo by Ronald Batzdorff)

The Family Awakens to Edith Stein's Destiny

by Waltraut Stein

Everything depends on love, because in the end we are judged according to love.

Edith Stein

On May 1, 1987, Edith Stein was beatified in Cologne, Germany by Pope John Paul II in a soccer stadium, with 75,000 people in attendance. As Edith Stein's grandniece, I had the privilege of participating in this event in a very special way.

On the eve of the beatification we family members, twenty-five strong, from the United States, from Colombia, South America, and from Switzerland, gathered together for a reunion at the invitation of the Archbishop of Cologne. My father from Pennsylvania, my brother from Seattle, and two of my sister's children from Idaho were there. There were also relatives I had never met before. We were most graciously received and treated with great respect and warmth as guests of the archbishop. The church had planned a formal dinner for us at a fine restaurant and a number of church dignitaries, who had come to Cologne for the ceremonies, were also present.

After the beatification, the pope himself came over to us and greeted each one of us personally.

That evening we family members again assembled, this time with four cardinals, and had a chance to meet at length over dinner. The cardinals were Joseph Ratzinger of Rome, Franciszek

---

Waltraut Stein *is Edith Stein's great-niece and has translated several of her works into English. A philosopher, she now lives in Atlanta, Georgia.*

49

Macharski of Cracow, Jean-Marie Lustiger of France, and Augustin Mayer of Rome. My cousin Susanne Batzdorff, who is Jewish and deeply spiritual, told me that Cardinal Macharski told her and her husband about things that happened to him during the Nazi time that he had never told his Christian friends. A number of the rest of us, too, had the chance to talk about things very close to our hearts but seldom discussed. All during those few days I heard my family speaking and listening on a level I had never heard before. We stopped arguing and really tried to understand each other. Somehow, it seemed to me, the love and joy of this grand occasion and the good will and sensitivity to differences among us had broken down the personal and religious barriers we had raised against each other.

In the early 1930s, when Edith Stein left her family to become a Carmelite nun in Cologne, many of the staunch Jewish members of the family who were being harrassed by the Nazis thought that she was deserting her people. But my cousin Sue now says, "Maybe she did the right thing [as she saw it]." [1] Because she allowed God's plan to be worked out in her to its final, tragic conclusion, bearing the cross of Christ and also continuing to identify herself as part of the Jewish people, she can now be an instrument of reconciliation between Christians and Jews.

My hope is that the reconciliation that I saw beginning in my family in response to this beatification will be the beginning of a wider reconciliation among all of us.

After the beatification, Jan Robitscher, who is also from Atlanta, and I joined forty-eight other people for a week-long pilgrimage sponsored by the Edith Stein Guild of New York City and led by Father John Sullivan, OCD, of the Institute of Carmelite Studies in Washington, DC. We visited a number of places important in Edith Stein's spiritual life: the church of her baptism in Bergzabern, the Dominican school in Speyer where she taught for nine years, and the Benedictine monastery in Beuron where she used to spend Holy Week and Christmas. The climax of the pilgrimage was a visit to the first Edith Stein Carmel, founded ten years earlier in Tübingen.

We were enthusiastically received everywhere we went, and it was evident that Edith Stein was held in great esteem. We began to get a sense of how much this woman has already influenced the spirituality of German Catholics, and we were ourselves deeply moved by the evidence of her faith and steadfastness. These experiences led us to desire to find ways to make her better known in America.

From the Church Bulletin of the Archdiocese of Atlanta, Georgia, 1987

l.r.: Wolfgang Stein, Anni Meyer-Gordon, Gerhard Stein

Edith Stein holding young Courant relative (1921)

My Experiences with My Aunt Edith
by Gerhard Stein

I Gerhard Stein, am the son of Paul Stein. He was the eldest child of Auguste Stein, née Courant. Edith Stein, my aunt, was the youngest of seven siblings. Even though she was my aunt, Edith Stein was only ten years older than I. When I attended elementary school, Edith was in the upper classes of Victoria School, a girls' high school. Her scholastic achievements were so excellent that she was awarded the Schiller Prize, a recognition of outstanding achievement in honor of Friedrich Schiller's 150th birthday. Frau Stein, my grandmother, told me at the time that one day Edith had come home laden with books, the complete works of Schiller. About that time my parents' apartment was being renovated and I was sent to stay with Grandmother. Edith took over the supervision of my homework. Given my poor talents, that was no easy task for Edith, so she had to take great pains.

After many vain efforts to get a teaching position as a woman at a university, Edith held private courses in phenomenology from 1920 on in her mother's house in Breslau at Michaelisstrasse 38. I was one of her students. We sat with Edith at a long table in the large so-called "Saal" with four windows, located on the second floor.

At the same time, 1920, Edith wrote a short dramatic piece for the wedding of her sister Erna and Dr. Hans Biberstein. In this play I appeared as a stork and my cousins Wolfgang and Erika prophetically appeared as babies of the bridal couple: The Bibersteins later had a boy and a girl. As stork I said to the babies:

Gerhard Stein, *nephew of Edith Stein and father of Waltraut Stein, worked as a professor of electrical engineering in Pittsburgh, PA.*

...Here you simply cannot stay.
This camp ain't forever, no, it's not,
From here you must go to another spot...
Look through my spyglass, and don't tarry.
You'll see a couple who just did marry....

One of the babies replied:

You just pick us up, it doesn't make sense,
And never ask us *our* preference.
I belong to the Babes' Commissariat,
And I know my rights, you can bet on that...
All your promises could be a hoax,
No, no, we'd rather choose our own folks.

These verses reveal Edith's interest in trade unions!

In 1931, Edith's first volume of the translation of St. Thomas Aquinas's *Quaestiones disputatae de veritate* (Disputed Questions Concerning Truth) was published. Edith asked my father Paul, her brother, to type the text. My father had taken early retirement from his bank at the age of fifty-five. With this typing job Edith gave my father something to do as well as some small earnings.

My mother Gertrude, née Werther, was a distinguished woman. She studied music theory at the University of Breslau and taught at Humboldt Society. She composed music for violin, viola, and piano. She lectured on important composers.

On the day following her forty-second birthday, October 13, 1933, Aunt Edith said goodbye to her family in Breslau, espcially her mother. She took the train to Cologne to enter the Carmelite monastery as a postulant. As she changed trains at the *Schlesischen Bahnhof* (Silesian Station) in Berlin, my wife Hertha and I met Edith and spoke to her for the last time in our lives.

In 1936, while working in the United States, I accepted an appointment to the Chair for Electrical Engineering at Peyang University in Tientsin, China. On that occasion, Aunt Edith wrote to me:

Recently I saw a letter from the Bishop of Tsingtao to our Reverend Mother. Since you will probably have few social contacts when you arrive in China, it occurred to me that you could pay him a call. When you do, you might explain to him that you are not thinking of converting.

That was the last communication I received from Edith. Since I never got to Tsingtao, I could not make use of Edith's suggestion. Concerning Edith's personality, I remember her as always serious and reserved. But whatever she said was clear and to the point. She never particularly stressed her religious convictions toward persons of another faith. She was no missionary, as her letter to me concerning a social contact with the Bishop of Tsingtao proves.

People claim that Edith's mother, my grandmother Gustel, was greatly upset over Edith's conversion to Catholicism. I believe that one has to look at two changes in Edith's life: her baptism in 1922, and her entry into Carmel in 1933, eleven years later. Grandmother was actually a fairly liberal-thinking woman. After my wedding in 1930, which was prior to Edith's entering Carmel, she welcomed my gentile wife Hertha very cordially. Both went for a walk together arm in arm. Edith's entry into a convent would not have been so painful for Frau Stein, if it had not been for the strict monastic rules. Frau Stein knew that she would never see her daughter again.[1] In contrast, nuns in our day are permitted to leave their cloistered residence to visit their parents in fulfillment of the commandment, "Honor your father and your mother."

The question arises whether the Catholic Church did everything it could to prevent Edith's deportation into an extermination camp. To achieve success, Pope Pius XII would have had to appeal personally to the *Führer,* referring to Edith's significant achievements in Catholic cultural life. As Eugenio Pacelli, former papal nuncio to Germany, and through his negotiations concerning a concordat with the Nazi government as papal secretary, the pope not only had a great deal of diplomatic experience but certainly knew some German members of the government. The bishop of Utrecht, Holland, too, should have turned directly to the *Reichs–kommissar* of Holland, Seyss-Inquart, with the same concerns for Edith. However, several problems stood in the way of such an action by the pope or the bishop:

1) There was little time. Just one week lay between the arrest of Edith on August 2, 1942 and her execution in Auschwitz on August 9.[2]

2) At that time it was not yet known that those who were deported to the East were murdered immediately upon arrival. Quick action on the part of the church therefore appeared unnecessary. The gas chambers of Auschwitz-Birkenau in which Edith lost her life had only recently been put to use. Only two years later, Auschwitz became known to the world as an extermination camp when a few young Jewish workers were able to escape. Edith's fate in Auschwitz became officially known only in 1950, when the death dates of the deported Jews were published in the *Niederländischen Staatsanzeiger.*

3) At the time of Edith's arrest and execution in August 1942, the German government was at the height of its military might. That same month its troops reached Stalingrad on the Volga.

4) Edith herself had refused to be exempted from the deportation without her companions. It was not to be expected that the government in Berlin would revoke the destruction of all Catholic Jews, as ordered by the *Reichskommissar* of Holland, because of an appeal. This destruction was, after all, a response to the bishop of Utrecht's pastoral letter, read in all Catholic churches in Holland. The Nazis would have preferred to keep this letter secret.

5) Despite all that, Pius XII was criticized after the war for not having taken a public stand against the persecution of the Jews. On the contrary, Pius XII had, according to a report, prepared a pastoral letter against the persecution. However, he did not make it public because the Catholic Jews of Holland had already been deported because of a pastoral letter. The pope therefore limited himself to protecting Jews and other victims against the Nazi persecutions by private means without public statements. He took care that churches and monasteries, including the Vatican, gave refuge to victims of persecution and that Jews were marked as Catholics with the help of forged baptismal certificates. He used gold from the Vatican as ransom against the deportation of Jews. Of the two million Jews who escaped from Nazi persecution, it is said that 860,000 owe their life to the influence of Pius XII.[3]

Among those who were saved in this way was the present Pope John Paul II. As a young student for the priesthood he got on the hit list of the Gestapo because he had helped Polish Jews to escape. He found refuge with the archbishop of Cracow, Stefan Cardinal Sapieha.

Among the victims of the Nazis were my parents (Paul and Gertrude Stein), three aunts (Rosa, Frieda and Edith) as well as my cousin Eva.

Edith Stein's journey from Holland to Auschwitz was, in her view, a way of the cross like that of Jesus to Golgotha. This way of the cross meant being imprisoned in a cattle car under dreadful sanitary conditions. To perish in a gas chamber was Aunt Edith's cross. As by heavenly providence, the deportation train stopped in her hometown Breslau, so that one day before her death she was able to see the towers of the city one more time.

According to reports, Edith went to her death by gas in full awareness as a sacrifice for her beloved Jewish people. She did so in the faith of Jesus who gave his life for the sins of all humanity.

There are portents for the destiny of Edith. She was born on the Day of Atonement, on the Jewish day of reconciliation with God for all transgressions. Her death on August 9 is, for the Jews, the day of mourning for the destruction of the Temple in Jerusalem, *Tisha b'Av*, the ninth day of the month of Av, the fifth in the Jewish calendar.[4]

With Edith Stein's beatification, a spiritual monument is now being erected for all those who lost their lives through the Nazi persecutions. All these are also being blessed by her beatification. This public monument is witness that a mass destruction of Jewish people really happened, a fact that some people deny.

Edith Stein holding Ilse Gordon (Hamburg, 1906)

A Great, Exceptional Human Being
by Ilse Gordon

Dear Sister Waltraud,

Your kind message and the beautiful picture postcard of the monastery deserve a reply, although writing is becoming a chore for me because of many other matters that I have to take care of daily, despite my age and my limited vision, due to cataracts that even multiple eyeglasses cannot correct.

First I want to tell you what my mother often told me: How that very young aunt took care of my brother, then only a few months old, as well as myself, aged about two, and how she was pretty reliable and skillful one time when my mother had to be away from the house for several hours (I cannot recall for what reason). From that time stems the attached photo (cut out from a larger photo) that appears in the book *Life in a Jewish Family*.[1] In this family history she herself reports on this stay in Hamburg that lasted about eight months.

I still remember another event, which I have never seen mentioned, probably because nobody considered it as important as it was to me at the time: When I was about fifteen and had outgrown my children's clothes and it was very difficult to buy new clothes, I received a navy blue wool skirt from Aunt Edith, used, but still in good condition. Aunt Edith at that time evidently could afford, perhaps was even expected to buy, new clothes for herself. A few years later, when I was a university student and had very little

---

Edith Stein's niece Ilse Gordon *has a diploma and doctorate in law and political science, and has worked with Hans Meyer, the director of the International Assistance Organization for Jews, in Bogota, Colombia.*

money, she helped me again with a sum of money that today appears very small, but at the time sufficed to finance a two-week stay in a resort in the Lüneburger Heide. Otherwise I remember her mainly seated at her desk in Breslau and working on the big translation of St. Thomas Aquinas, a job at which she was not to be disturbed. And above all, I recall her last visit with us in Hamburg, when, beaming with happiness, she told us of her impending entry into the Cologne Carmel. Even though we could not understand her conversion to Catholicism, we, my mother and I in particular, honestly rejoiced that this fervent wish was to be fulfilled. At that time we also assumed, of course, that she would be safer and better off in the convent than we, for whom the early measures of the Nazi regime had already made life much more difficult. I also want to mention here that only a few years later Aunt Rosa, just as happily, took leave of us when she, too, came to Hamburg after her baptism and prior to her emigration (which was unsuccessful at first).

I believe that she [Edith] herself gave the best testimony to her development and her life in her memoirs, written from 1933 and almost up to her last days in Echt. By and large most of it is in agreement with what I myself experienced and found out during my vacations spent in my grandmother's home. But the book contains a few errors or perhaps misprints, for instance the family tree on which both the birth and death date of my mother are wrong. The correct dates are 1876 and 1956. How correct the other dates are, I cannot say. And concerning what Aunt Edith says about her stay in my parental home 1906–1907, I would like to add that it sounds too curt and even judgmental to me when she writes "there was no religion there." It is true that my parents did not attend synagogue and did not observe the traditional forms of the Jewish religion at home, nor educate us children in accordance with them. Yet I myself have a different concept of religion, which goes far beyond these forms and which, I suppose, I got from my parents. It is likely that Aunt Edith might have found another expression or might have supplemented her account if she had had time and leisure to review her manuscript carefully once more before it went to print. I also believe that my mother did not—as is stated somewhere else—"consider herself superior to her environment and look down upon others," even though she, like anyone, had some faults and imperfections. But her sister, who was so much younger than she, must have gotten this impression and never rid herself of it in the course of the years. After all, Else, my mother, had to take a mother's role for several years; she loved Edith very much until the end, just as she always spoke of "the two little ones." My mother never spoke a harsh (let alone an angry) word about these youngest sisters and would surely have been surprised and disappointed to find this opinion expressed in Aunt Edith's memoirs. This book lacks several pages, not only where the editors expressly mention the omission, e.g. the passage that deals with the engagement of my parents in Hamburg in 1903, but then a lot is missing and the second paragraph tells about events in Breslau that took place in the years 1910–1911.[2] Therefore I also believe Aunt Rosa is unjustly suspected of having removed a few missing pages from the manuscript that portrayed her in a bad light. I believe in that case she would have had to remove a few prior pages, and, after all, she had become truly pious and had long been devoted to Aunt Edith and recognized her superior intellectual abilities and saw in her a role model, so that she would not have done such things. On the other hand, I also believe that our Aunt Frieda was always underrated, not just in these memoirs. Her harsh fate always pains me. She was deserted by all and had to send her only daughter to Palestine into an uncertain future. Likewise I cannot get over the thought and I believe that Aunt Edith would agree; that people talk and write so much about her—understandably so, since she was a great human being, helpful and self-sacrificing and exceptional—but that they already appear to have forgotten the other six million Jewish victims, to say nothing of the many other millions.

No one speaks of the Gordon family, for example. And as for Ruth Kantorowicz [also deported from the Netherlands to Auschwitz at the same time], a dear friend of my childhood and youth, she is only mentioned in connection with Aunt Edith. And how many Jewish young people whom I met in the early years of my professional life over there and of whom I never heard again, do I think of again and again! I know times were hard then for other Germans as well, who did not want either the Hitler regime or the war, but that is, after all, a different matter. And I see from the picture postcards of Cologne as well as Tübingen, that the rebuilt convents are better than the Carmelite convents as Aunt Edith knew them then. I also believe I can infer from the pictures and descriptions that the nuns no longer live in such strictly cloistered conditions as she sought. And this greater closeness to life is probably good, suited to the times in which we live. With my very best wishes for you and the other Sisters of the Edith Stein Carmel.

I remain yours,
Ilse Gordon

Edith Stein with friends and relatives in Breslau

women in back row, l.r.: Frau Platau, Frau Dorothea Biberstein,
Frau Auguste Stein
women in middle row, l.r.: Rose Guttmann, Erna Stein,
Hede Guttmann, Elfriede Stein Tworoger
women in front row, l.r.: Edith Stein, Lilli Platau
(holding Erika Tworoger, Frieda's daughter), Rosa Stein

Edith Stein: A Jew's Path to Catholicism

by Daniel Krochmalnik

I as a Jew want to speak of the convert Edith Stein. Hence I have to state right at the start that I intend neither a sermon nor an indignant reckoning (although there is material enough for both, God knows.) The vocation, sanctity, and suffering of the faithful, just like the thinking of a philosopher, must have a significance that bridges religions. To be sure, a Jew would hardly succumb to the temptation to portray an Edith Stein who—already during her life-time—was affected by saintly pallor. A Jew will distinguish as a matter of course between the merits of the individual and the merits of the institution that uses her as decoration. And finally, a Jew won't be able to comprehend all expressions of her religious convictions and will even be repelled by some manifestations of her new faith, particularly when they are directed against her former faith. Yet if a Jew has retained a sense for a religious dimension of the Holocaust, he won't be able to deny his respect to this exceptional woman that was Edith Stein.

I. Baptism, Teresa of Avila, and the Jews

Edith Stein was baptized on New Year's morning 1922. She chose the baptismal name of Theresia Hedwig. This is an indication of the specific circumstances of her conversion. Her later mistress of novices and prioress of the Cologne Carmel, Teresia Renata

---

Daniel Krochmalnik, Ph.D., *is active in adult education in Munich, Germany.*

de Spiritu Sancto [Posselt][1] has published Edith Stein's report on her conversion. In the summer of 1921, Edith Stein had been a guest in the home of her friend Hedwig Conrad-Martius on an orchard in Bergzabern. One evening, while Edith was alone in the house, she happened upon the autobiographical *Life* of St. Teresa of Avila on the bookshelf. "I began to read," she states, "was immediately caught up and did not stop until the end. When I closed the book, I said to myself: *This is the truth.*" Just as the *Confessions* of St. Augustine had been for Teresa of Avila, Teresa's autobiographical confessions turned out to be decisive for Edith Stein's faith. Her conversion was the fruit of her reading.

The report of the Jesuit Erich Przywara sounds a bit different: Edith Stein allegedly told him during a walk along the banks of the Rhine in Speyer that she had found a copy of the *Spiritual Exercises* at her bookdealer's while yet an atheist.... With that little book as a guide, the atheist Edith Stein went on a 30-day "Spiritual Exercises" retreat and emerged with the decision to convert.

These reports, made in private, need to be supplemented by the impressions that the young philosopher received from her teachers at the University of Göttingen. The leading minds of the phenomenological movement to which she belonged—Edmund Husserl, Max Scheler, and Adolf Reinach—were all converts from Judaism. Her first contact with Catholicism, which in her Silesian hometown was the primitive faith of Polish foreign workers, goes back to the summer of 1913. During that time the eager convert Max Scheler gave impassioned lectures to the inner circle of Husserl disciples, of whom Edith Stein was one. She reports:

> He was quite full of Catholic ideas at the time and employed all the brilliance of his spirit and his eloquence to plead them. This was my first encounter with this hitherto totally unknown world. It did not lead me as yet to the Faith. But it did open for me a region of "phenomena" which I could then no longer bypass blindly. (*Life in a Jewish Family*, p. 260)

Whoever may have inspired Edith Stein to change her religion, in the end it was the testimony of Teresa of Avila, this impressive and charming woman known simply as "madre," which was to become decisive for her declaring herself a Catholic. On New

Year's Day 1922 Edith Stein was baptized in the Catholic church of Bergzabern with the names—Teresa and Hedwig—of her spiritual godmother and her real one (who incidentally was a Protestant of Jewish descent, according to her nephew, the sculptor Roland Friedrichsen). A parenthetical comment: For another philosopher of Jewish descent, the encounter with the Spanish mystic was also religiously decisive: Henri Bergson. In 1932, in his last great work about the two sources of religion and morality, he wrote that Christian mysticism surpassed the mysticism of the Jewish prophets and was the purest embodiment of the divine *élan vital* and that, as the highest form of mysticism, selflessly loving and acting, it relates to all of creation. However, Henri Bergson wrote on February 8, 1937:

> My reflections led me ever closer to Catholicism, which I consider to be the ultimate achievement of Judaism. I would have converted if I had not, for some years, witnessed the rise of a formidable wave of anti-Semitism that began to break over the world. I wished to remain among those who, tomorrow, will be the persecuted.

In a conversation with her former fellow-student Alexandre Koyré in Paris, long after her conversion, Edith Stein once said of Henri Bergson, "He, too, is one of ours." She could not then fathom what Alonso Cortés would discover in 1946, in the Archives of the Inquisition; that St. Teresa, too, was "one of ours." Teresa probably knew that on her father's side she was descended from *conversos* or, as they were also called, *marranos,* and that according to the *limpieza de sangre* (purity of blood) statutes valid for all religious orders, she was no *limpia* (pure one). The saint who embodied political skill, educational ability, and the most exalted mystical consecration, had to be fascinating to people like Henri Bergson and Edith Stein for whom mystical experience and worldly involvement were connected.

All these are, to be sure, only outward clues to an inner struggle, that Edith Stein kept secret even from her closest confidants. Once during the time of her decision in Bergzabern she put off her friend Hedwig Conrad-Martius with the words *Secretum meum mihi* (My secret belongs to me). Thus the process of her conversion, as long as it cannot be observed, can only be understood empathically on the basis of the known testimony, somewhat the way young Edith Stein proposes in her dissertation *On the Problem of Empathy:*

> I can be skeptical myself and still understand that another sacrifices all his earthly goods to his faith. I see him behave in this way and empathize a value experiencing as the motive for his conduct. The correlate of this is not accessible to me, causing me to ascribe to him a personal level I do not myself possess. In this way I empathically gain the type of *homo religiosus* by nature foreign to me, and I understand it even though what newly confronts me here will always remain unfulfilled. (p. 115)

However, comprehending her conversion, which involved all levels of her personality, depends upon how the life of Edith Stein is told. The arrangement of the stages of her life establishes the intent.

For hagiography this sequence is most appropriate: Jew, Christian, Martyr. In this way the old theological theme of supersession is repeated. This scheme Edith Stein also used in her self-portrait, and—in the words of the Benedictine Paulus Gordan—she is not free of "pre-coined...formulae." In contrast to that, Ludwig Ehrlich has obviously based his biographical considerations on a different sequence: Assimilated Jew, anti-Jewish Catholic, non-Aryan Christian abandoned by the church. At the beatification the pope skillfully avoided both these tendencies, in that he mentioned Edith Stein's atheistic phase between the Jewish and Christian stages of her life, and rightly so, and thus avoided both Christian triumphalism and Jewish embitterment. And yet one could select very different focal points. Thus the Polish philosopher Roman Ingarden, a former fellow-student and friend of Edith Stein, rightly placed the totally neglected philosophical aspect of her life in the foreground and showed the changes from the Jewish liberal psychologist, to the liberal arts phenomenologist, to the Christian personalist.

A more socio-psychological view—such as the Munich biographer Elisabeth Endres recently constructed it—must deal with the stages in Edith Stein's political development, which can be enumerated as follows: While growing up, Edith Stein took radical democratic positions. Before and during the First World War she changed into an involved, yes, even chauvinistic nationalist, like many assimilated Jews of her generation. She was convinced of Prussia's invincibility, meaning "the inner Prussia, whose thinking is apparent only to the inner human being," and which has "its ancestral homeland in the realm of thought." After the *a priori* impossible defeat she, like many other establishment Jews, e.g. Walter Rathenau, joined the National Liberal Party. At the same time she shared in her sociopolitical writings—like Rathenau—the social criticism of the youth movement: She contrasted the organic community that is in solidarity and embodied in a leader, with the opposing soulless, splintered bourgeois society. This romantic social criticism made an impact not only on the Catholic, but also on the nationalist youth movement.

Finally we must characterize not only the breaks but also the transitions and phases in terms of religious considerations. Erich Przywara has shown in his albeit somewhat tiring typology how Edith Stein gradually experienced the various forms of monastic culture of Catholic Christianity with typically Jewish approaches. With his help she moved from the (in his estimation) religiously decisive Jesuit environment into the Dominican circle and there learned, while teaching at the Dominican college in Speyer, to combine scientific phenomenology and Christian faith in the cosmological philosophy of St. Thomas. Besides, she had led a liturgical life among Benedictines that E. Przywara calls an "immanent Christianization of Jewish tradition." But in these positive statements of Christian faith a dramatic trait of her religiosity breaks through that finds fulfillment only in the rigorous and total mysticism of the Carmelite sphere. In her essay on the history and spirit of Carmel, dated 1935, she does not trace her order back first to the Spanish reformers Teresa of Avila and John of the Cross, but rather to the legendary founder, Elijah (for Jews probably the most popular prophet), and his hermits upon Mount Carmel. To the sequences enumerated here, certainly tied to particular positions, I do not want to add, nor will I tell a new version of the life of Edith Stein. I merely want to show by means of two central concepts how in Edith Stein's view the continuity of her life's path from Judaism to Catholicism can be portrayed. These two concepts are the Jewish Day of Atonement, Yom Kippur, and the Biblical figure of Queen Esther.

II. A Life Under the Sign of Yom Kippur

Edith Stein was born on October 12, 1891, on Yom Kippur, the highest holy day of the Jewish calendar. On this fast day, the conclusion of a stringent time of repentance, even the so-called Yom Kippur Jews who are not otherwise seen in synagogue wrap themselves in their white shrouds and, in continuous prayer for "the livelong day," as Christians call it, remorsefully confess their sins and plead for God's mercy. In order to counteract an often-denounced mechanical atonement routine, on that day Isaiah's rebuke against hypocritical fasting and his appeal to be builders of the city of justice is read. Further, the reading of the Book of Jonah is intended to recall Israel's mission for humanity. One can hardly think of a more appropriate portent for the life of Edith Stein, which was, above all, a liturgical life.

In the Stein family there was a liturgical tradition. The great-great-grandfather on her mother's side was a cantor in the Upper Silesian town of Lublinitz. After the onset of the Industrial Revolution, he became a manufacturer of surgical cotton in Silesia and established a house of prayer of his own for his extended family. Edith Stein's grandfather, the soap boiler and candlemaker Salomon Courant, was able to set himself up as a grocer with the help of his well-to-do father-in-law, and founded for his fifteen children a Jewish private school where they could learn the rudiments of Hebrew, translate Holy Scripture, practice ritual law, and learn the psalms by heart, in German.

On the Sabbath, they were introduced to liturgy under the choleric supervision of their grandfather in his private synagogue. True, their knowledge of Hebrew was too poor even to understand the liturgy fully. Auguste Stein followed the liturgical rules, but not with her grandmother Ernestine's fervor. The "Hanna," as the Prussian prayerbook for mothers was called, was a sacred object in the secular and somber household of this single mother with her seven children, who, since the death of her husband, managed a prosperous lumber business and was known as "the only real man" in Breslau's lumber circles.

Among the industrious and socially established Jewish bourgeoisie the liturgy had become a rigid ceremonial routine that was designed to document a sense of duty and order. However, a rapid decline of tradition had accompanied their accelerated social advancement and entry into German culture. The greater religious context of Jewish liturgy, rabbinic study, and customs were lost; prayer had deteriorated to a formality devoid of meaning.

Edith Stein, born under the sign of liturgy, did not know the rich life of prayer of the mystical and Hasidic-styled Polish Judaism. Although in Breslau and in Lublinitz one was very close to Eastern Judaism, there was all the more desire to distance oneself from it. The culturally assimilated and legally emancipated Prussian Jews did not want to be confused with the backward immigrants from the East, and at best felt pity for them. How might the strongly *mystical* talent of Edith Stein have been touched by Hasidic piety? One can hardly imagine this woman, *Prussian* in the best sense, with a strongly developed sense of order, at a Hasidic "Farbrengen" as these Hasidic "happenings" are called in Yiddish, or busy with a labyrinthine Talmudic or Hasidic discussion. And yet her emotion-based liturgical piety might have been better able to express itself in this milieu than in the official religious service of a Prussian district rabbi.

After her conversion to Catholicism, Edith Stein occasionally accompanied her pious mother to synagogue and joined her in reading the psalms. Even though she persisted in imploring her daughter to reverse her decision, the mother confided in a friend "I have never seen prayer so devout as Edith's." Edith Stein was also strongly attracted to the prayer-oriented Benedictine piety, the "immanent Christianization of the Jewish tradition." She found her spiritual home in the monasteries of Beuron and Maria Laach, the centers of the liturgical movement that in the twenties stood at its zenith. "Ecclesia orans" found strong response in academic circles as well. This liturgic-monastic spirituality shaped Catholicism in the second decade just as modernism shaped it in the first and personalism did in the third decade of the century. The spirit of this movement finds expression in the decorative frescoes of the crypt of Monte Cassino—the cradle of occidental monasticism which was formed at the beginning of the century in the manner of Beuron. Statuary hieratics, measured gestures, and inward emotional expression characterize this movement. Edith Stein called herself Benedicta after entering the cloister, and she felt secure in this liturgical Christianity.

After the death of Auguste Stein on September 14, 1936, she received the "Hanna" [her mother's prayer book] from the estate. In her letter of thanks to her sister she writes: "Now I immediately opened it to the prayer for the dead and found in it the same faith that to us is so matter-of-fact and on which I now rely. It is not foreign to Judaism, only unfortunately not alive in most [Jews]...". At the same time she writes an essay about the "Prayer of the Church" and in it refers expressly to the "developed liturgy" of Judaism from which Christian liturgy derives. But she also says, as in Pauline shadow theology, that the old liturgy was revived only through the life, death, and resurrection of Jesus. For Edith Stein, who only got to know Jewish prayer and especially the psalms via the Catholic liturgical movement, this may well be true.

The other typically feminine and eucharistic traits of her mystical piety could also have found very different nourishment in a religiously intact Judaism.

Of particular significance for the emotional charge and affective shading of Eastern Jewish piety is the motif of exile and of the suffering of *Shekhinah* in the world; a motif that was first developed in the Talmudic midrash and in Kabbalah and that penetrated into the folk piety of the Eastern European Jew. *Shekhinah* is the feminine personification of the indwelling of God in the world. As the *Ecclesia Israelis*, the *Shekhinah* is, so to speak, the divine mother of the people Israel, and she shares the suffering of her children in exile. And conversely, Israel also mourns the exile of *Shekhinah* in the world, separated from her husband, the Father in Heaven. It was a widespread custom among the Hasidic masters to lament the lot of *Shekhinah*. Rabbi Zaharia Mendel of Jaroslaw reports about this: "As soon as the clock strikes midnight, the masters wake up from their sleep, trembling in every limb, strew ashes upon their heads, squat on the floor and lament brokenheartedly about the exile of *Shekhinah....*" Here we find the beginnings of a sentimental religion of lamentation, a self-pity encoded in the image of a suffering divine mother that in many respects resembles the veneration of Mary, the suffering mother of God, the *Pietà* of Catholicism.

A strongly developed sense of mission corresponds to this, as in all matriarchal religions of lament. All religious performances are understood, in Hasidic piety, as the support of the children for their forsaken mother. Every religious act is understood as a work of redemption of Shekhinah and her union (*yihud*) with her divine husband and is introduced by the ritual formula, "for the unification of the Holy One, blessed be He, and His Shekhinah, I do this or that."

By the way, we are dealing here with a peculiar confusion of Biblical theology. It is not God who redeems his people from exile and gathers them in, but it is the community that, as it were, redeems God, gathers him in and restores him in his unity. This idea is expressed by yet another kabbalistic motif. In the theosophic events preceding the creation, there was an explosion in the divine realm of light (*shevirat ha-kelim*) and, to use a concept of Meister Eckhart, the sparks of the divine *pleroma* were scattered in the realm of creation and are imprisoned in the *qelipot*, the "shells" of material things that, as it were, encapsulate the divine sparks. The religious mission of the Jews consists in redeeming from imprisonment the divine sparks scattered all over and to restore (*tikkun*) the divine realm of light. This patient work of the redemption of God is not only a coded self-redemption; in the end it concerns all people and the act of bringing nature back home to God. This religious intent especially concerns all objects in the profane sphere. Rabbi Jacob Israel of Polonoye, a direct disciple of the Baal Shem Tov, the founder of Hasidism, writes: "There is nothing large or small in the world that can be isolated from God, for he is present in all things. Therefore the perfect human being can perform deep meditations and contemplative acts of unification even in his worldly deeds, as for example in eating, drinking, and cohabitation, yes, even in business transactions." The ideal of a totally sacramental course of living would surely have accommodated Edith Stein's requirements, who, as a Catholic, stressed eucharistic piety so firmly.

In the festival cycle of traditional Jews in Breslau there were surely rudiments of sacramental actions, as in the *Pesach* (Passover) festival. On this occasion the memory of the exodus from the Egyptian house of slavery and the migration to the Promised Land is celebrated with symbolic actions, stories and prayers. At that time the duty is expressed that "in every age the Jew is to look upon himself as if he himself had gone out of Egypt," so that the remembered past together with the suffered present and the hopeful future may be tied together eschatologically. Because the whole ritual is conceived as an answer to the four questions by the youngest child (for the Steins this was Edith), the celebration must be considered the sacramental visualization of God's salvation and practice for the interpretation of Jewish destiny for the coming generation. In Prussia, of course, one sat around the fleshpots, and no one thought of exodus. In addition, there was no guardian of tradition in the Stein family. The older siblings, who had to take the place of the deceased father and did not understand the customs, "talked my mother out of some of it," according to Edith Stein's memoirs. "The brothers whose task it was, as substitute for their deceased father, to recite the prayers, did so with little respect. [One of them] made clear his opinion that it was not to be taken seriously" (*Life in a Jewish Family,* pp. 69-70).

In the second part of the second chapter of her autobiography, Edith Stein describes the Jewish customs in her family. She, who had been born on Yom Kippur, was especially attracted by this holiday. Shortly after entering Carmel, she recalled that she "loved" the fast day, which her mother also considered her birthday, more than all others. Strangely, however, she opens her autobiographical report with a description of the Levitic customs of the Day of Atonement from chapter 16 of the Book of Leviticus:

> The highest of all the Jewish festivals is the Day of Atonement, the day on which the High Priest used to enter the Holy of Holies to offer the sacrifice of atonement for himself and for the people; afterward, the "scapegoat" upon whose head, symbolically, the sins of all the people had been laid was driven out into the desert. (*Life in a Jewish Family,* p. 71)

This has obviously no connection with the piety she experienced in her youth. But as a Christian she interprets Yom Kippur in the sense of the Letter to the Hebrews (9:3-14, 25ff., 13:11ff.): as a model and foreshadowing of Good Friday. In her essay *The Prayer of the Church*, Edith Stein has reduced the ritual of the Day of Atonement, which, after all, she knew, to the sacrifices of the Levites. The expiatory sacrifice of Jesus becomes the true fulfillment and abolition of these Levitic rites point by point. She says nothing about Isaiah's rebuke against useless sacrifices and Jonah's example of a universalist message, let alone the mystical meaning of prayer. She had to set Judaism's place in salvation history at a lower rank in order to surpass it with Christian theology.

From now on Teresia Benedicta a Cruce places her life, under the sign of the exalted Yom Kippur, under the sign of the cross. To the Ursuline Agnes [Petra] Brüning she writes:

> I must tell you that I already brought my religious name with me into the house as a postulant. I received it exactly as I requested it. By the cross I understood the destiny of God's people which, even at that time, began to announce itself. I thought that those who recognized it as the cross of Christ had to take it upon themselves in the name of all. (December 9, 1938, #287 in *Self-Portrait in Letters*)

Thus the cross is, for Edith Stein, originally a symbol of her community of fate with Judaism, but with a Christian interpretation. In her report about her road to Carmel she recalls an evening in the spring of 1933: "It became clear to me all at once that God had put a heavy hand upon His people, which was also my people."[2] In dialogue with Jesus, Edith Stein realizes "that it is His cross which was being laid upon the Jewish people." With her testimony—thus can her remark of 1933 be understood—she wants to point out the religious dimension of the persecution of the Jews. For this purpose, she wishes to offer herself as a sacrifice of atonement or—as she once wrote to Sr. Adelgundis Jaegerschmid in connection with the difficulties of converting Edmund Husserl—as a *holocaustum*.

Jews cannot comprehend this interpretation of their persecution as a religious message, not even religiously speaking. Jews obviously see Yom Kippur not as the final reconciliation of humanity, but as the annual reconciliation of ever-relapsing individuals with their fellow-humans and with God. *Pesach* they understand not as the resurrection from the dead, but as liberation and coming home. For Jews several religious interpretations of the persecution of the Jews exist, but as far as I can see, the symbol of the Holocaust is inappropriate. Elie Wiesel introduced the term in connection with the Biblical terminology of sacrifice. These crematories are no altars, the victims did not serve as restitution, and above all the perpetrators did not act for the "joy of the Lord" (Lv 1:9) as it says in connection with the corresponding writings about sacrifice. No matter how foreign Edith Stein's interpretation of suffering may be, from the Christian viewpoint it is understandable. From the Jewish viewpoint it is an anachronistic and alienating interpretation of Yom Kippur.

There is the danger, however, of another stereotyped Christian interpretation of the idea of expiation. Such an interpretation is highly regrettable for a Christian who is so sympathetic to Judaism, and it is hurtful to Jews. After the November 1938 pogrom, Edith Stein states her interpretation of suffering with new undertones that are actually age-old: "That is the shadow of the cross which falls upon my people. Oh, if only they could see the light! That is the fulfillment of the curse which my people have called down upon themselves! Cain must be persecuted, but woe to him who touches Cain!" [The authenticity of this remark, allegedly overheard by one of the Carmelite nuns, has never been confirmed.—Ed.] The suffering of the German Jews is presented here as the punishment for a branded, fratricidal people who perpetuate the deicide by their unbelief, and a call to conversion. The true murderers fulfill here the role of God's scourges who exceed their assigned task. We shall refrain from attempting to unravel the psychological skein that may lie at the basis of this convert's utterances. Let us put John XXIII's prayer opposite Stein's accusatory intercession:

> We understand that a mark of Cain is inscribed on our foreheads. In the course of centuries our brother Abel lay in the blood that we have shed or he wept tears that we have caused because we forgot Your love. Forgive us the curse that we wrongfully attached to the name "Jew." Forgive us that we crucified you, in their flesh, for the second time.

(Admittedly, the Curia feels it must question the authenticity of this prayer.)

No matter how Edith Stein understood her fate in the end—as a sacrifice of reconciliation in the sense of a testimonial for the "humanity of Christ" which is being persecuted in the persons of the Jews, or as atonement for alleged Jewish guilt, or finally, unconsciously, as a desperate religious interpretation of a genocide against a people whom she loved by a people whom she loved—she thus realized her Yom Kippur.

III. Queen Esther

Another symbol for Edith Stein's life and fate is closer to us Jews: the figure of Queen Esther. The Book of Esther tells the story of a beautiful Jewish orphan who was married to King Ahasuerus (Artaxerxes) and of a plotting minister, Haman, who persuades the king to issue an order to exterminate the Jewish people "which separates itself from all other peoples" (Est 3:8). Esther appears unbidden before the king, a violation of court etiquette that could cost her her life. The king, however, receives her graciously, and she is able to uncover Haman's intrigue. The king cancels his extermination order and has Haman hanged on the gallows intended for the Jews. "The festival of Purim," as we read in the Greek version of the Book of Esther, "is to be celebrated for all time and all generations under the eye of God among God's people" (10:3). In the Jewish tradition Haman is seen as the archetype of the destroyer of Jews and Esther as the vigorous woman who averts the disaster. In Christian folk piety, in the *Bibles of the Poor* ("Armenbibeln") and concordances of the late Middle Ages, Esther is an Old Testament figure in scenes of intercession.

When the Haman of her generation was entrusted with sovereignty in Germany, Edith saw herself in the role of Esther. In October 1938 she writes to Agnes [Petra] Brüning, "Again and again I have to keep thinking of Queen Esther, who was taken from her people precisely that she might represent them before the king. I am a very poor and powerless little Esther, but the King who chose me is infinitely great and merciful" (#281 in *Self-Portrait in Letters*).

Edith Stein undertook her first initiative deserving the name of a Jewish Esther, even before entering the convent. At Easter 1933, she decided to travel to Rome to ask the Holy Father in a private audience for an encyclical denouncing anti-Semitism. The pope, however, could not receive her, "due to the great crowds," evidently greater than at the Persian court. She writes: "I abandoned my travel plans and instead presented my request in writing. I know that my letter was delivered to the Holy Father unopened; some time thereafter I received his blessing for myself and for my relatives. Nothing else happened."[3]

This initiative of our Esther presumably helped Pope Pius XI conceive the suggestion of an encyclical against racism and anti-Semitism in the summer of 1938. True, Edith Stein could not have known about such plans, since the drafts by the Jesuits John LaFarge, Gustav Gundlach, and Desbuqois were first made known thirty years later, in 1968, through an indiscretion in the *National Catholic Reporter*. Why was this encyclical never published? Upon reading the results of Jesuit Father J. H. Nota's research, the following course of events appears, purged of all euphemisms: Count von Ledóchowski, Superior General of the Jesuits who was equally anti-Soviet, anti-Semitic, and anti-German, received the completed drafts in October 1938, one month before the November pogroms in Germany and Austria, and put them aside for some obscure reason. Then Pius XI received the drafts, but had more important things to do. In February he died. His successor Pius XII, in contrast to his predecessor Achille Ratti, "this obstinate old man" as Mussolini called him, wanted to maintain a pact of expediency with the Axis powers. After the start of the war, Pius XII obviously represented Christian viewpoints, but, despite being well informed, avoided taking a stand on the Jewish question, with the exception of a few hints in his Christmas speeches....[4]

After the empowerment of Hitler and the National Socialists, measures were promptly taken to exclude Jews, even converts, from public life. Edith Stein understood that she had become untenable as a lecturer at the German Institute for Scientific Pedagogy. She announced her resignation on April 20. In accordance with the true situation, she wrote in theological code: "I had become a stranger in the world" and sought admittance to the monastery.

Her Jewish relatives had also become "strangers in the world," but they could not flee into a cloister. For Edith Stein, unlike the usual situation for converts, her entry into a religious order did not mean a break with her earlier life. As a diplomatically failed Esther, so to speak, she now wants to give public testimony for Judaism. In the convent she records her mother's and her family's memoirs, in order to confront Hitler's mad portrayal of the Jew. She counters with the reality of a normal middle-class and patriotic Jewish family, as she states in her September 1933 preface. Yet she prohibited the book's publication during her lifetime. Aside from that, this elucidation about loyal German Jewry was hardly suitable for stopping the anti-Semitic madness. In no way did her portrayal resemble the monstrous stereotypes in Julius Streicher's *Stürmer*. Actually, Edith Stein does not deny the possible reality of the hostile image, the Jew as exploitative capitalist, the revolutionary Communist, and the educated anarchist. Yet, however unavailing her initiative may have been at the time, for us it testifies to a lost and destroyed world. Edith Stein appears to have intended as much. In her preface she writes that "we who grew up in Judaism have an obligation to give our testimony" for the sake of "the young who, these days, are being reared in racial hatred from earliest childhood" (*Life in a Jewish Family*, p. 24). As Esther, Edith Stein later turned above all to the King of Heaven in prayer. In a dialogue that she wrote two months before her deportation on August 2, 1942, she characterized herself in the end as Esther, the stranger, who knocks on the doors of the convent and is admitted by the mother, the prioress.

Stranger: I have traveled far,
　　　　　From land to land and from door to door.
　　　　　I am seeking lodgings.

Then she reveals herself as Esther and tells her story.

Esther:　This is how the highest Lord freed his people
　　　　　Through Esther, his maidservant, from the hands of Haman.

Mother:　And today another Haman
　　　　　Has sworn to annihilate them in bitter hate.
　　　　　Is this in fact why Esther has returned?

Esther: You're the one who says so—
          Yes, I am traveling through the world,
          To plead for lodgings for the homeless,
          The people so scattered and trampled
          That still cannot die.

Then Esther explains to the Mother why she has left the realm of heaven.

The church had blossomed, but the masses
Of the people remained distant, far from the Lord
And his mother, enemies of the cross.
The people are in confusion and cannot find rest,
An object of disdain and scorn....

Finally Esther shows the prioress how she must understand her mission.

Mother: Her people, which are yours; your Israel,
          I'll take it up into the lodgings of my heart.
          Praying secretly and sacrificing secretly,
          I'll take it home to my Savior's heart.

Esther: You have understood, and so I can depart.
          ("Conversation at Night" in *Hidden Life,* pp. 128-133)

A bit more openness would surely have been helpful. Many monasteries, however, opened not only their hearts but also their doors to the hunted *Ahasuer.*[5]

When Julius Streicher, the former district leader of Franconia, walked his last walk to his place of execution, he said, "This is my Purim Festival, 1956."[6]

The murder of Edith Stein was prosecuted in criminal court, a rare exception. On February 24, 1967, Robert M. W. Kempner represented the Stein family as joint plaintiff in a suit against the former commander of the security service in Holland, Dr. Wilhelm Harster, before the district court Munich. His intention was to personalize the mass murder trials by means of an individual suit. It was due to Harster that the deportation of the Jews from Holland to Auschwitz ran its course with fewer hitches than elsewhere. Adolf

Eichmann once remarked: "It was magnificent how the Jewish program functioned in Holland." Dr. Harster also directly participated in the deportation of the so-called "Catholic Jews" in the summer of 1942. In contrast to other lawsuits against leading former SS members, Dr. Harster admitted his guilt and showed remorse. After the joint plaintiff reminded the court that at the beginning of the year a Dutch worker had been sentenced to twelve years in the penitentiary for two cases of attempted murder, he concluded his summation with the remark: "These crimes here are so horrendous that, despite my experience, I am unable to recommend any appropriate length of punishment." The court sentenced Dr. Harster to fifteen years in the penitentiary for joint assistance in 82,854 cases of murder. After a short time, Dr. Harster was paroled. The philosopher Emmanuel Levinas, who in a talmudic exegesis reflects upon the inclusion of the Book of Esther in the biblical canon, characterizes the ethical and religious value of the book as follows:

> Think of Mordecai's warning to Esther: "If at that time you keep silent, salvation and liberation will come to the Jews from another place. You and the house of your father, however, will perish" (4:14). Rather than accept the death of the others, leaving the others to die, ...Esther prefers her own death. Esther replies: "Well, I shall go to the king, contrary to the law! If I perish, I perish" (4:16). The death of another individual troubles her more than her own.... It is the holiness of a book that gives (it) admittance to the Holy Scriptures.

The courageous sacrifice, if that is what it was, in the sense of the Book of Esther, makes Edith Stein, like Janusz Korczak and others, holy in the eyes of the Jews. In a way Edith Stein is also an advocate for Judaism, because in the future she will be a witness and symbol for Jewish martyrdom in the eyes of the Christians. And it is to be hoped that her example will not be used to play down [the Shoah] or to seek glory.

Lecture held before the Friends of Hebrew University, Jerusalem.
Stuttgart, December 7, 1987

Joseph Schwind, Vicar General of Speyer

Edith Stein and Christian–Jewish Dialogue
by Waltraud Herbstrith, OCD

During the years 1925–1933, the religious philosopher and theologian Erich Przywara collaborated with Edith Stein in an active exchange of ideas. He supported her return to scholarly work after her conversion and stimulated her to lecture tours on women's issues. Edith Stein devoted herself to the professional, political, and religious integration of women in society. Przywara remembers that Edith Stein took a fervent interest in the Zionist efforts in Palestine and would have liked to transfer to a Carmel there during the Nazi period.

In 1919 Edith Stein wrote to her friend Roman Ingarden, the Polish phenomenologist, that Germany was beset by an incredible anti-Semitism, and she strongly criticized the murder of Jews in Lemberg. Edith Stein never abandoned the political concerns that she had displayed early on. In contrast to the political apathy common at that time, even in church circles, which would thrust Germany into disaster, she remained true to her political belief that everyone and every people needs a place to realize their human and cultural values. Her treatise on the state appeared in 1925. But in his memoirs, Przywara also wrote about something else. Of his encounter with Edith Stein and the Vicar General of Speyer we read: "Dr. Schwind told me in advance that Edith Stein would be a surprise: He had never seen anyone who showed so little of her racial characteristics as Edith Stein."[1]

Waltraud Herbstrith, OCD, *of the Edith-Stein-Karmel in Tübingen, Germany, is the author of numerous works on Edith Stein and Carmelite spirituality.*

"Not a Jewish type," was in the German usage of those days the highest praise, even among upright, benevolent Christians. Edith Stein, the Jew searching for truth, the intellectual who had lost her childlike faith early, had become alerted to Christianity through her intellectual environment. Here she found fulfillment for her deepest religious longing. Simultaneously, however, she found a Christianity in which theological anti-Judaism and subliminal anti-Semitism were bound to hurt her.

Father Felix M. Schandl, a Carmelite in Bamberg, pursued the following theme in his doctoral dissertation: "I Saw the Church Growing Out of My People: Jewish References and Structures in the Life and Work of Edith Stein." Here we find the first copy of the complete text of a note from Edith Stein to the Apostolic Administrator of Innsbruck-Feldkirch, Bishop Sigismund Waitz, dated March 6, 1932. She writes:

> For a long time I have owed you thanks for your last kind note, and longer yet the requested comments on the second volume on St. Paul: I have the impression that here—in the treatment of apostolic activity—the pastoral applications can be tied in much more organically than in the depiction of his life. I was somewhat painfully struck by occasional remarks, here as in volume 1 before, concerning Judaism. Those who were born and raised in Judaism know its high human and moral heritage, which is largely hidden from the outsider. And such a person finds those judgments which pertain only to the manifestations of decay, which are very conspicuous to the outsider, harsh and unjust.[2]

One year later, in her reminiscences about her own family she opposes the slander by the National Socialists in these words:

> Recent months have catapulted the German Jews out of the peaceful existence they had come to take for granted. They have been forced to reflect upon themselves, upon their being, and their destiny. But today's events have also impelled many others, hitherto non-partisan, to take up the Jewish question. Catholic Youth Groups, for instance, have been dealing with it in all seriousness and with a deep sense of responsibility. Repeatedly, in these past months, I have had to recall a discussion I had several years ago with a priest belonging to a

religious order. In that discussion I was urged to write down what I, child of a Jewish family, had learned about the Jewish people, since such knowledge is so rarely found among outsiders. A variety of other duties prevented me from taking up this suggestion in earnest at the time. Last March, when our national revolution opened the battle on Judaism in Germany, I was again reminded of it. In one of those conversations by which one seeks to arrive at an understanding of a sudden catastrophe that has befallen one, a Jewish friend of mine expressed her anguish: "If only I knew how Hitler came by his terrible hatred of the Jews." She had her answer in the programmed writings and speeches of the new dictators. From these sources, as though from a concave mirror, a horrendous caricature looked out at us.[3]

Here Edith Stein begins a dialogue between Jews and Christians. Because Jewish people knew their high moral and religious values, Edith Stein's jottings were aimed in the first place at Christians. For centuries, a theology of condemnation had been built up against Jews. For centuries the Jewish ethos was barely noticed. Neither Protestant nor Catholic Christians allowed symptoms of decay in their own religion to mar the beauty and depth of their faith or culture. Edith Stein especially opposed the mad Nazi idea of "Jewish blood," which was made accountable for all the problems and faults of the Weimar Republic.

Is Judaism represented only by, or even, only genuinely by, powerful capitalists, insolent literati, or those restless heads who have led the revolutionary movements of the past decades? Persons whose reply to that question will be in the negative can be found in every stratum of the German nation. These persons, having associated with Jewish families as employees, neigbors, or fellow students, have found in them such goodness of heart, understanding, warm empathy and so consistently helpful an attitude that, now, their sense is outraged by the condemnation of this people to a pariah's existence. But many others lack this kind of experience. The opportunity to attain it has been denied primarily to the young, who, these days, are being reared in racial hatred from earliest childhood. To all who have been thus deprived, we who grew up in Judaism have an obligation to give our testimony.[4]

In nearly 400 pages, Edith Stein bore witness to a Jewish family life that had a high human and ethical standard and was totally integrated with German identity. She sought to pursue the theological and spiritual relationship between Judaism and the church in her article "The Prayer of the Church" (1937). Without having the knowledge of today's exegesis at her disposal, Edith Stein, the Jew, emphasized the Jewishness of Jesus. Israel is the root of Christianity. In Edith Stein's interpretation, the Old Testament does not harden into a mere prefiguration of the New Testament. As a Jew, Edith Stein is a daughter of Israel and as such she has a love for and prior understanding of Jesus's origins and for the roots of the church. Thus she writes:

> The Gospels tell us that Christ prayed the way a devout Jew faithful to the law prayed. Just as he made pilgrimages to Jerusalem at the prescribed times with his parents as a child, so he later journeyed to the temple to celebrate the high feasts there with his disciples. Surely he sang with holy enthusiasm along with his people the exultant hymns in which the pilgrims' joyous anticipation streamed forth: "I rejoiced when I heard them say: Let us go to God's house" (Ps 122:1). From his last supper with his disciples, we know that Jesus said the old blessings over bread, wine, and the fruits of the earth, as they are prayed to this day. So he fulfilled one of the most sacred religious duties: the ceremonial Passover seder to commemorate the deliverance from slavery in Egypt. And perhaps this very gathering gives us the most profound glimpse into Christ's prayer and the key to understanding the prayer of the church.[5]

Edith Stein explains to Christians how very much the New Testament is enlivened by the images and ideas of the Old Covenant. In Jesus the joy of biblical creation theology comes alive, which was often portrayed in abridged form through St. Paul's theology of the cross. Edith Stein saw the surrender of Jesus Christ on the cross as a single great thanksgiving, both in the celebration of the mass and in eternity. In this thanksgiving Jesus is wholly formed by biblical faith.

But we also know that Christ used to give thanks when, prior to a miracle, he raised his eyes to his Father in heaven. He gives thanks because he knows in advance that he will be heard. He gives thanks for the divine power that he carries in himself and by means of which he will demonstrate the omnipotence of the Creator to human eyes.[6]

Only someone who grew up in Judaism can interpret with such joy the biblical images that Jesus absorbed quite naturally.

Some understanding of this eucharistic character of prayer had already been revealed under the Old Covenant. The wondrous form of the tent of meeting and, later, of Solomon's temple, erected as it was according to divine specifications, was considered an image of the entire creation assembled in worship and service around its Lord. The tent around which the people Israel camped during their wanderings in the wilderness was called the "home of God among us" (Ex 38:21). It was thought of as a "home below" in contrast to a "higher home." "O Lord, I love the house where you dwell, the place where your glory abides," sings the Psalmist (Ps 26:8), because the tent of meeting is "valued as much as the creation of the world." As the heavens, in the creation story, were stretched out like a carpet, so carpets were prescribed as walls for the tent. As the waters of the earth were separated from the waters of the heavens, so the curtain separated the Holy of Holies from the outer rooms. The "bronze" sea is modeled after the sea that is contained by its shores. The seven-branched light [candelabrum] in the tent stands for the heavenly lights. Lambs and birds stand for the swarms of life teeming in the water, on the earth, and in the air. And as the earth is handed over to people, so in the sanctuary there stands the high priest "who is purified [anointed] to act and to serve before God." Moses blessed, anointed and sanctified the completed house as the Lord blessed and sanctified the work of his hands on the seventh day. The Lord's house was to be a witness of God on earth just as heaven and earth are witnesses to Him (Dt 30:19).[7]

Christians who venerate Edith Stein as an exemplary human being should not forget her Jewish origins and development, but should let themselves be introduced into her "joy over Israel" as she formulated it in a poem based on Psalm 47:

To us He gave His legacy,
Delight in Israel has He....
God rules over all the world,
High o'er the earth His tent's unfurled.
Princes of nations, they stream to His throne,
Acclaiming our God their very own.[8]

Edith Stein can help us find the basic change in Christian attitude toward their Jewish brothers and sisters which Ernst Ludwig Ehrlich hopes for. Such a change, however, presupposes knowledge and acknowledgment. Ehrlich stresses the need for individual Christians to accept the change made by the Second Vatican Council regarding the "Jewish Question"; that way, Christians can free themselves from pseudo-theological views concerning the Jews. Let us take Edith Stein's suffering seriously. One of her fellow-Sisters in the Carmel of Echt/Holland remembers: Edith Stein "took it hard whenever she heard anyone making unfavorable remarks about the Jews; she would say that they were all calumnies."[9] We often think of ourselves as tolerant. "Tolerance, however, is not yet love," says the Swiss Bishop Streng. "Love is honest, heartfelt, mutual goodwill." Streng admonishes Christians to avoid polemics in speech or writing. "Sermon and religious instruction, parish newsletters and brochures must be kept free of any untruth and lovelessness toward those of different faiths, while at the same time stating differences clearly and openly."[10]

Herman Leo van Breda, the long-time head of the Husserl Archives in Löwen[11] met Edith Stein in Echt five months prior to her cruel death. In 1967 he gave a memorial address in her honor for the 25th anniversary of her death. In it he describes his first visit to the former concentration camp, Auschwitz.

To honor Edith Stein's memory, I went on a pilgrimage to Auschwitz in the autumn of 1957. I want to say just this about my visit of several hours' duration to this unholy place:

No human eye has ever seen, no ear has ever heard, and it has never penetrated a human mind what was perpetrated there, in Auschwitz, by human hands.

After I had turned my back to this place of misfortune again, I needed many hours before I could bear to hear the sound of a human voice again or simply to talk to anyone.[12]

The President of Israel, Chaim Herzog, said on the occasion of a visit to the former concentration camp Bergen-Belsen on April 6, 1987:

> At this horrible place, the valley of murder, and at the start of my road on this soil, I place before you, my brothers, victims of the Holocaust, a rock, hewn from the rocks of Jerusalem, in which are engraved, as a testimony to the destruction of my people, the words of the psalmist: "And my grief is ever with me." I have brought with me no forgiveness—and no forgetting. Only the dead have the right to forgive, and the living are not allowed to forget. For [it says]: "You will surely think of it, and my soul tells me so..." The grief over your death we will keep in our hearts in eternal remembrance. Not for the sake of eternal hostility, not for the sake of fruitless, paralyzing hatred, but to gain strength and steadfastness; to recognize the abysses of the human soul and to rise above them; to bring forth the opposite to evil, to Godlessness with all our being. "Desist from evil and do good, seek peace and pursue it."[13]

Originally published in
Christ in der Gegenwart *40 (1988): 373-74*

Edith Stein in 1926
(Instructor at Teachers College, Speyer)

Edith Stein's Timely Message
by Irmgard Rech

During his last trip to Germany the pope beatified a woman who had been a thinker and writer. Edith Stein was a philosopher, educator, and theologian.

Three qualifications make her thought interesting and unusual: She was a modern woman of independent thought, a Jew coming out of a living tradition, and a convert who was able to see many aspects of Christianity from a fresh perspective. As a modern young woman who gained great respect at a university shaped by men, she thought about the role and task of woman.

Edith Stein found it logical that women's activities in the congregation were described in the documents of the early church. Even St. Paul "emphasizes the praiseworthy achievement of women in the service of the first pastoral communities."[1] She notes with joy that there was even a consecrated position for women, namely as deaconesses. She deeply regrets that "in later historical developments, women were displaced from these posts... [and] there was a gradual decline in their canonical status."[2] She ascribes the causes for this to "the influence of the Hebraic and Roman judicial concepts."[3] She definitely considered it possible that in her time the church would meet the demands of many women by reintroducing the diaconate for women. She saw this as an act of fairness, to give back the character of ecclesiastically acknowledged service to the work of so many women who devoted their efforts to church charity and the care of souls. Of course she also asked herself whether women might be admitted to the priesthood. Her reply was: "It seems to me that such an implementation by the Church, until now

Irmgard Rech *is a high school teacher in Lebach-Talexweiler, Germany.*

89

unheard of, cannot be forbidden by *dogma.*"[4] Despite this frank attitude she herself still thinks in biological terms and has not surmounted her feeling that in Jesus, the male is especially distinguished and that therefore only men are destined to be his official representatives. Edith Stein had faith that the church of her time would introduce the diaconate for women. In this she was mistaken. As a convert she neither could nor wanted to criticize the church harshly. Should not the present-day church, which beatified her, see it as its charge to take up her ideas and give them the necessary emphasis in order to launch changes?

Edith Stein accorded to woman, just as to man, a vocation of her own on the basis of her special gifts. While she was not a feminist [in the current sense], she saw men and women together and thought of how to put an end to the "battle of the sexes."[5] The two versions of the creation story in the Old Testament were decisive for her understanding of man and woman. As a Jew, she was, of course, able to read these stories in the original Hebrew, and thus had a much more profound access to the images of these texts than we do. She loved these image-filled texts and saw in them texts for healing the dismal relation between man and woman. Here we are told what this relationship could be in its best sense. Edith Stein writes: "The first passage of the *Bible* which concerns humanity assigns a common vocation to both man and woman.... But mutually they are given the threefold vocation: They are to be the image of God, bring forth posterity, and be masters over the earth."[6] Not man alone is here addressed, but both, and therefore she concludes: "It seems to me that a common creativity in all areas was assigned in the original order, even if this was with a differing allocation of roles."[7] Edith Stein derives an important insight from this for woman: If woman, together with man, receives the charge of shaping the earth, then that obviously means that "*all* powers which the husband possesses are present in a feminine nature as well."[8] And that again is tantamount to a divine "instruction" that woman, too, should utilize all her powers "in corresponding activity."[9] If not, "wherever the circle of domestic duties is too narrow for the wife to attain the full formation of her powers, both nature and reason concur that she reach out beyond this circle."[10] What was obvious for Edith Stein was at that time not yet obvious by a long shot: that, in principle, woman should have access to all occupations, so as to enable her to find, by free vocational choice according to her ability, an occupation best suited to her. Even at the universities one had not come far enough to accord her a chair, though she was a gifted woman philosopher.

In what manner then should man and woman work together, and how is their mutual relationship ordered? Edith Stein found an answer to this in the second creation story: Adam received in the woman "a helpmate corresponding to him" (Gn 2:18). Edith Stein finds it difficult to translate into German the Hebrew term used here. "One can think here of a mirror in which man is able to look upon his own nature.... One can also think of a counterpart...so that, indeed, they do resemble each other, yet not entirely, but rather, that they complement each other as one hand does the other."[11] Edith Stein does not tire of stressing that there is no idea here of a sovereignty of man over woman: "She is named as *companion* and *helpmate,* and it is said of man that he will cling to her and that both are to become *one* flesh. This signifies that we are to consider the life of the initial human pair as the most intimate community of love."[12]

I once saw an old glass painting in which both Eve and Adam are portrayed as saints. Unfortunately the male theologians have wrested this halo from Eve forever. They have accorded greater weight to the story of the fall of man and subjugated woman for all time to the rule of man. And yet Jesus never mentioned one word of the story of the fall of man. On the contrary, he refers unambiguously to the passage of the creation story, "They will be two in one flesh,"[13] and posits as commandment of the new covenant, "What God has united, let man not put asunder."[14]

Is it not long overdue that the church, as Edith Stein suggests, put the emphasis on the right texts? Not the fall but the texts dealing with the creation of man and woman. They are texts of healing for us.

It might be interesting for men to learn what a woman who was recently beatified thought of them. Edith Stein's point of departure was that the world can't improve if only the women are forever being taken to task. In church sermons and instructions it has been a favorite practice to reproach females for their depravity, since woman was considered the gateway for evil in the world. The "fellows and menfolk" fared better for the most part.

Edith Stein, who observed the patriotism common during the time of the monarchy as well as the rise of National Socialism around her, appears to be strongly repelled by the conduct of the men of her time. It is striking how frequently she speaks of the "brutal lordliness"[15] which she must have perceived in her environment. She even goes so far as to seize upon a politically pejorative term from the Nazi ideology and sets it as a mirror image for male conduct. She calls their attitude a "denatured lordliness."[16] That the man is to be master, and that he is thus entitled to a certain position of priority, still was a matter of course for Edith Stein. However, she wants the term "Lord" to be understood quite differently. She starts out with the Lordship of God and replaces the word "Lord" with "King." In Jewish-biblical usage this does not accord to man a willful launching into power; rather, according to this image of royalty, man has the task of protecting all creatures in his realm, of preserving them and of promoting their development. Yet according to the first creation story this task is given jointly to man and woman. In the second creation story the woman is given to man by God as an indispensable companion. Edith Stein is appalled to note that this companion relationship has become a "brutal relationship of master and slave."[17] Here that word "brutal" appears again; she does not hesitate to repeat it often. Not only the suppression of woman by man is brutal in her view, but also the man's suppression of the children in the family. Just as the man tends to hinder the woman in developing her own natural gifts, so he also shows a tendency to avoid the duties of fatherhood. The lowest form of this denial she finds in the abuse of "sexual intercourse simply for the sheer satisfaction of sexual desires without any concern for offspring. On a higher level, he may assume his material obligations well, but perhaps he will disregard completely his duty to share in the child's formation."[18] Hence husband as well as wife must renounce the expansion of his professional work, if it causes him to neglect his family....

For centuries it was customary that the man's opinion decided everything. In the church one cited the word of Paul, "I give no permission for a woman to teach" (1 Tim 2:12). Edith Stein did not hold with that view. For her, who had become a Christian, these words did not express the spirit of Jesus. In Jesus's teachings, Edith Stein does not find any statements limiting women. For her he embodies the "ideal of human perfection: in Him...the masculine and feminine virtues are united."[19] "Manly boldness, proficiency, and determination" are here supplemented by "womanly tenderness and truly maternal solicitude."[20] Are not men and women brought to reconciliation in this way?

Süd-West Funk Baden-Baden, Kirchenfunk
Timely Message, August 10, 1987

Eugen Breitling, priest of Bergzabern
who baptized Edith Stein in 1922

Edith Stein: Remembering a Colleague
by Nikolas Lauer

It's a long, long way from Breslau to Bergzabern in the Palatinate,[1] a charming small town and health resort among vineyards and wooded hills, only seven kilometers from the French border. Edith Stein, "clever Edith," as she was already called as a child, had passed her *Abitur* exams in Breslau with distinction in 1911 and had registered at the university there. German and history were to be her major subjects, to prepare her for high school teaching. At age fifteen she had renounced her belief in God, to the sorrow of her devout Jewish mother: "Deliberately and consciously, I gave up praying" (*Life in a Jewish Family*, p. 148). She embarked on an intensive search for truth. The study of psychology in Breslau left her without an answer. In a journal she discovered the photo of a student, Hedwig Martius, who had brilliantly won a prize competition in Göttingen. A minor sensation at that time, since academic education was mostly closed to women! In Husserl's *Logical Investigations* a path opened up for her to genuine research in the humanities. Husserl proposed to trace the true essence of things from external appearances (phenomena). From autumn 1913 on, Edith Stein became his enthusiastic disciple. However, when she moved to Göttingen, she no longer found Hedwig Martius there. Shortly before, she had married her fellow-student Theodor Conrad and had followed her husband to Bergzabern. The couple lived in a beautiful house "near the Eisbrünnel," with a large orchard that contained delicious yellow plums. In popular parlance the owner was therefore called the "plum doctor." The house became a meeting

---

Nikolas Lauer, *a parish priest, was a colleague of Edith Stein as a high school teacher at St. Magdalena in Speyer, Germany.*

place for the Göttingen circle. During the very hot summer of 1921, Edith Stein was a house guest there for several weeks. She had passed her state board examination for higher education in 1915 and had earned her doctorate in 1916, both with highest honors.

She later described her state of mind as follows: "State of my soul prior to conversion: Sin of radical unbelief. Salvation purely through God's mercy without any merit of my own." In the house "Am Eisbrünnel" she experienced her hour of grace. When the couple went away on a trip for several days, Edith Stein was asked to look after the house; the large library was at her disposal. That first night she took from this library an inconspicuous book: *The Book of her Life, written by St. Teresa of Jesus, on the order of her father confessors.* This was the autobiography of a great woman of church history and a master of the mystical life. The young philosopher read and read. When morning dawned, she said, "This is the truth."

She bought a Catholic catechism and a missal, attended Mass in the nearby parish church, and afterward asked the priest of Bergzabern, Eugen Breitling, for baptism. Breitling was an outstanding, highly educated priest. Upon examination he found to his surprise that the petite young Jewish lady doctor had completely mastered the subject matter of Catholic faith. And so he scheduled her baptism for January 1, 1922. He wrote to his friend, Canon Josef Schwind in Speyer, "Josef, I have here a convert who is far superior to me and puts me to shame with her theological knowledge. You have to help me. I commend her to you." This letter decided the next ten years in Edith Stein's life. Canon Schwind found her a position as teacher in the convent teacher-training school of St. Magdalena in Speyer.

Edith Stein spent New Year's Eve (1921–1922) in prayer. On New Year's Day 1922, at age 30, she received holy baptism in the parish church of Bergzabern and her first holy communion. She wore her friend Hedwig Conrad-Martius's wedding cloak, and her friend also served as her godmother. Father Breitling invited everyone to an *agape*. For all participants the day remained unforgettable. Only the day of her clothing ceremony in the Cologne Carmel equaled the day of her baptism in splendor and happiness. Hedwig Martius who on that day, too, stood by her godchild, writes:

"Edith had always had something childlike in her nature, but the childlike joy, and sense of security she had now achieved, were, if I may say so, enchanting."

In 1922 Edith Stein faced a radical turn in her life. Her hope for a professorship at a university, which she might have expected as Husserl's assistant, did not materialize. The thought of an ideal marriage and a family of her own vanished forever. In her overflowing happiness she wished—radically, as was in keeping with her nature—to belong completely to God as a religious. But Canon Schwind, who became her confessor, imposed upon her a long waiting and probationary period. "What did not lie in my plan, lay in God's plan."

In the Gardens of St. Magdalena

Until the outbreak of the Third Reich, the Catholic women teachers of Bavaria were educated in convent-sponsored schools. For the Palatinate this task was the responsibility of the Dominican nuns of St. Magdalena in Speyer. In 1928, the women's monastery in the shadow of the imperial cathedral celebrated its 700th anniversary with Nuncio Pacelli [the future Pius XII]. King Ludwig I of Bavaria, on the occasion of the readmittance of monastic life in 1826, had obligated the nuns to administer public schools and high schools for the city of Speyer. Thus numerous school and dormitory buildings arose in the nineteenth century around the stylish convent church consecrated in 1718. An extensive garden with clumps of trees and a vineyard surrounded the convent. Edith's domicile was a large room in the oldest section, the gatehouse at the church gallery. When she wanted to go to town, she had to pass through the inner and outer gate, cross the schoolyard, and exit through the large outer gate into Hasenpfuhl Strasse. Thus she was largely shielded from the outside world. She kept the daily schedule of the Sisters. Her meals came from the convent kitchen. Two regular portresses took care of her. They saw to it that her room was always well heated. When Edith entered Carmel in 1933, these good souls had only one worry: The cells in the Carmel were not heated. Would Fräulein Doctor be able to stand the cold?

The teacher-training institute was housed in a wing of the convent barely one hundred meters from the gate house. The future women teachers of the Palatinate were educated along with the postulant nuns. Because of the small demand, the number of students fluctuated around one hundred and were divided into six sections. Almost all the girls lived in the convent dormitory. Everyone studied diligently. Discipline was exemplary, the separation from the outside world probably a bit too severe. At age twenty the young teachers left the house after two difficult examinations. It could not have been easy for either teacher or students to bridge the intellectual gap. Yet it worked. Harmony prevailed among the faculty, consisting almost totally of Dominican nuns.

The years 1923 and 1924 brought disputes with France over the Ruhr area. These led to the closing of bridges over the Rhine; deportations and inflation followed.

In the years up to 1927, Edith Stein was a frequent guest in the home of Canon Schwind and also met his relatives in the neighboring Schifferstadt. But occasionally Schwind, after a coffee hour with Edith Stein, would sit down on a chair, exhausted, and sigh: "My, how many questions that Fräulein Doctor asks! I simply can't keep up with her!"

With the improvement of the political and economic conditions in 1925, this "hidden life in God" underwent a return to other activities. Discovered and counseled by the well-known religious philosopher Father Erich Przywara, SJ, Edith Stein translated the *Letters and Diaries of J. H. Newman Before His Entry into the Church, 1801–1845* for the Theatiner Verlag. This project required her to familiarize herself with the English language but also demanded a thorough knowledge of contemporary theology and history. Again with Father Przywara's counsel, there followed the huge job of translating *Disputed Questions of St. Thomas Aquinas* in two volumes. The manuscript of more than one thousand handwritten pages is preserved in the convent archives at St. Magdalena. Teaching in a teacher-training institute also led to an intense involvement with the so-called "women's question." Edith Stein treated this multifaceted material in many publications and especially in her lectures which, since the Salzburg Academic Weeks of 1930, made her known all over Germany and led to her 1931 appointment as a docent in Münster, Westphalia. Beuron, however, had become her spiritual home.

In the Palatinate Once More

"She was always happy and very friendly, but reserved. No one could penetrate into her secret." Such was the judgment of the Schwind family. I can only confirm that. Even though we worked in the same school for three years, I only remember a single evening on which we were together with Father Przywara for an extended conversation. The first volume of the Aquinas translation was finished and vacations were imminent. Edith Stein was supremely happy, merry, and relaxed as we disputed and joked on an evening filled with sunshine, spirit, and promise.

Final Journey

In 1970 I visited the Carmel in Echt, Sr. Teresa Benedicta of the Cross's last refuge. In the visitors' lounge there was a library with works by and about Edith Stein; the grille had been removed. An urn with ashes from the death camp of Auschwitz was in the rear section. Her last journey in the prisoners' transport on August 7, 1942 passed through the Palatinate once more. The train stopped at the Schifferstadt station. At a window with bars the pale face of a nun appeared. The station master was standing immediately below the window. "Please," said the prisoner, "give my greetings to the Schwind family. They know me. I am Edith Stein, now traveling to the East." The railroad employee transmitted the message to the Schwind family and to the convent of St. Magdalena, where the devout believer has not been forgotten.

The urn with the ashes in Echt is not the end. Edith Stein combined rare intelligence with childlike faith, critical thinking, and mystical immersion, the science of the cross to its completion. I await the hour of her beatification. And out of conviction I shall call upon the name of the new Blessed, the saint of our century.

From Die Mitarbeiterin *30 (November/December, 1979): 170-171*

Edith-Stein-Karmel in Tübingen, Germany

Sermon for the Twenty-Second German Protestant Church Congress

by Leonore Siegele-Wenschkewitz

D ear Congregation:

First I wish to thank you most cordially for inviting me, as a Protestant minister, to celebrate with you a service in St. Mauritius Catholic Church on the occasion of the opening of the German Protestant Church Congress.

This congress and this service stand under the motto "Behold the Man!" This motto points to Jesus Christ, the basis of our Christian faith. Pilate characterized him during the trial, in view of the inevitable road of suffering that awaited him, as quite simply human. In his own path of life and suffering, Jesus demonstrated in all its depth what it means to be human. By his humanity he vouched for God's closeness to suffering, weakness, and powerlessness in the world.

As a sign of our ecumenical unity I would like to make this worship service a memorial to Edith Stein who was beatified in early May. She made the motto "Behold the Man!" her own, signifying the decisive turn to Jesus Christ. Having been captivated by faith in Jesus, she made her own humanity a path of exemplary emulation.

I would like to tell you how I became interested in Edith Stein. Nearly ten years ago a Carmel was founded in Tübingen. They named their monastery after a fellow-nun, Edith Stein, who was

Leonore Siegele-Wenschkewitz *is a professor of church history. A Protestant minister, she serves as Head of Education for the Protestant Academy in Arnoldshain.*

gassed in Auschwitz in 1942. I was living in Tübingen at that time and, as a Protestant church historian, was lecturing at the university on the history of the church during the Third Reich. Until then I had not occupied myself with Carmelites nor with Edith Stein. This monastic foundation awakened my interest and my sympathy. What kind of women were these who were founding a monastery in the midst of predominantly Protestant Tübingen? Who was this woman for whom they had named their monastery? After my first contact, my connection with the Tübingen Carmel and my involvement with Edith Stein have deepened and solidified. The sisters accompanied me with prayer and encouragement during a period of severe illness in my life. This was a great comfort for me. At the same time, Edith Stein's life and work, her philosophical and theological work, her spirituality—also her spiritual life with God and her fellow-humans have come to be increasingly important for me. I owe my knowledge of Edith Stein above all to the splendid writings of the Tübingen Carmelite Sr. Teresia a Matre Dei, who has been researching and explicating Edith Stein's works for decades under her civilian name Waltraud Herbstrith.

Who was Edith Stein, and why do we remember her today? Her life lasted just a little more than 50 years and ended violently, yet it has many facets. It merits consideration from many diverse angles. I would like to address the most important events in her life and after that, elucidate her path with respect to two themes:

How did Edith Stein live her Judaism?

How does she explain the meaning, for herself, of the cross of Christ?

Edith Stein was born in 1891 in Breslau as the youngest of eleven children in a Jewish family. Since her father died when she was not quite two years old, she was brought up solely by her energetic, religious mother, who took over management of the lumber business as an independent entrepreneur. When Edith was fifteen, during her adolescence, a crisis began for her. For almost a year she dropped out of school. During that time she gave up prayer and considered herself an atheist. After her *Abitur* she studied psychology and philosophy to find answers to life's problems. What meaning is there in my life? How can human beings contribute to a good meaningful world?

Under the influence of several fellow-students as well as her university professors, she found a way to Christian faith. In 1922 she was baptized a Catholic. Although she had at first been drawn to Protestantism, the inspiration for her conversion to the Catholic Church came through reading the life of St. Teresa of Avila. Teresa of Avila was a Carmelite; in the sixteenth century, together with her spiritual friend John of the Cross, she had reformed the Order. Edith Stein's encounter with the great Spanish mystic was the decisive moment of her conversion.

She concluded her studies with the doctoral examination, which she passed with honors as an assistant to the phenomenologist Edmund Husserl. She would have liked to teach philosophy at the university, but this path was barred to her, as a woman and as a Jew. The social barriers were too high, even for Husserl, her teacher, to take her seriously as a partner. And so she became a teacher and lecturer to Catholic women. In her lectures and discussions, she opposed discrimination and typecasting of women. She stressed "the idea that the low esteem of woman in the Church is based on socio-cultural reasons, but can hardly claim to be founded on the intention of Scripture."[1]

In 1932 she was appointed lecturer at the German Institute for Scientific Pedagogy in Münster. The first measures of the National Socialist persecution of the Jews deprived Edith Stein of continuing her professional work. The so-called "Aryan paragraph," issued in April 1933, expelled men and women from their jobs and positions if they were of Jewish descent. Now she decided to fulfill her longstanding wish to become a Carmelite. In the fall of 1933 she entered the Cologne Carmel, a convent that lived according to Teresa of Avila's reform. But even in Carmel she was not safe, not only because of the increasing pressure from the National Socialist regime but also because of the situation within the monastery, where she met fearful fellow-Sisters and heard disparaging remarks about her Jewishness. Thus, in spring 1938, Edith Stein tried in vain to convince her fellow-sisters not to take part in the plebiscite on the so-called "Anschluss" of Austria, which at the same time was a plebiscite about the politics of Adolf Hitler. Edith Stein consented to flee to Holland after the November pogroms of 1938, the so-called *Kristallnacht,* when synagogues in Germany were aflame and Jewish people were driven from their homes with rubber truncheons and shipped to concentration camps by the tens of thousands. In 1939 she witnessed the outbreak of the Second World War from a Carmel in Echt. In 1940 the National Socialists occupied Holland. Thus Edith Stein was again threatened. On August 2, 1942, following a protest by the Dutch bishops against the persecution of Jews, Edith, her sister Rosa, and other Catholic Jews living in Holland were deported into death camps by the Nazis. On August 9 she was murdered in Auschwitz-Birkenau because she was a Jew.

Edith Stein's fate, which I have described to you in broad strokes, has essentially been defined by recent German history. The assumption of power by National Socialism and its racist ideology confronted her with the decisive problems of her life and she would have to deal with them. Thus she had to work out for herself what her Jewishness meant to her; and furthermore, as a convert to Catholicism, she had to examine what the cross of Christ meant to her in this situation in life, at this historical moment.

First I want to describe the tension raised by these two themes in Stein's life.

As I mentioned before, Edith Stein came from a Jewish family in which, in contrast to many largely assimilated Jewish families, the Jewish religion and culture were a firm part of daily life. Her mother embodied Jewish faith and Jewish tradition. She expressed her conviction that one should remain in the faith to which one was born. Therefore, Edith's conversion to Christianity was shocking to her.

Since Edith, as the youngest child, had a very intimate and loving relationship with her mother, she was fully aware of how much her decision hurt her mother. Although she would have liked to enter a convent soon after her conversion, she did not do so because she did not wish to burden her mother, who had a negative attitude toward her path. To understand Frau Stein's position today, we must remember centuries-old Christian hostility against Jews, the innumerable attempts to convert Jews to Christianity forcibly, the persecutions and pogroms on Good Friday, and the longstanding doctrine that Christianity was superior to Judaism and that the Jewish faith should no longer exist after Jesus Christ.

When Edith Stein finally entered the Cologne Carmel in 1933, her family saw this step as "disloyalty in the face of extreme peril." Her being a Christian was seen as a distancing from the family, as an abrupt opposition to Judaism. How did Edith Stein deal with the feelings and the judgment of her relatives?

Certainly she did not take them lightly; she understood them and did not dismiss them. It was therefore a task for her to convince her family that her decision was not a step of distancing or disloyalty, but an act of connection with them.

She was not looking for separation but for reconciliation.

How did she attempt to realize this?

Shortly after the National Socialist takeover she wrote the following on Jewish persecution in Germany: "True, I had heard of rigorous measures against the Jews before. But now a light dawned in my brain that once again God had put a heavy hand upon His people and that the fate of this people would also be mine."[2]

"The fate of this people would also be mine."

Edith Stein never changed her mind about remaining in solidarity with her family and the persecuted Jews in general. In fact she proved it most strongly by setting out, together with her sister Rosa, on her deportation that led to the gas chambers of Auschwitz.

And yet Edith Stein could have acted differently. In 1933 she received a job offer from South America that, however, she did not follow, especially because of her aged mother. In 1941–1942 the possibility arose for her to find safety in a Swiss Carmel, but not for her sister Rosa. Again, Edith Stein could not accept.

Her indissoluble connection with the fate of her family and the Jewish people arose above all from the way in which she interpreted the Cross of Christ: "By the Cross I understood the fate of God's people which, even at that time, began to announce itself. I thought that those who recognized it as the cross of Christ had to take it upon themselves in the name of all."[3]

Since she herself understood it, she was prepared to go this way of the cross as an expression of her Christian being. In this insight and in this unshakeable determination lies Edith Stein's independence. Here is the special message which she brings to the church as a Jewish Christian. Since she herself and her family were directly affected by the National Socialists' anti-Jewish politics, she perceived, even before 1933, much more clearly and distinctly what the Nazi ideology was all about. She spoke about the fact that the hostility toward the Jews would not remain limited to the Jewish people but would also turn against the churches and against Christianity. For in her estimation the Nazi ideology was directed equally against the living God and against true humanity. Therefore Christians and churches ought to resist the Nazis together with the Jews.

With these appeals she wanted to cause awareness that anti-Judaism affects not only Jews but also the churches themselves.

Edith Stein followed her path in total isolation. Already in 1933 she tried to move the pope to issue an encyclical against racism and anti-Semitism and to offer the Jews the protection of the church. But Edith Stein's appeals were unsuccessful. Other problems, seen to be of higher priority, took precedence in Catholic and Protestant churches alike: they desired to avoid conflicts with the state in order to prevent church persecution. Thus they largely abandoned the persecuted Jews.

The legacy that Edith Stein left, with her message of the commonality between Christians and Jews, has gradually begun to enter our consciousness in the last few decades. Anti-Semitism of any kind is contrary to God's commandment. Whoever touches the apple of God's eye, the Jewish people, transgresses against God himself. The suffering of one's neighbor is the cross of Christ. Following after him means taking up the cross of Christ and showing solidarity with one's fellow men and women in distress.

Whence did Edith Stein derive the strength to walk this lonesome road of solidarity between Christians and Jews? She herself always pointed out in letters, notes, and articles whence it came: It was the power of the cross.

To be a Christian and to be ready to take up the cross was for her one and the same. Thus she writes: "A *scientia crucis* <knowledge of the Cross> can be gained only when one comes to feel the Cross radically. I have been convinced of that from the first moment and have said, from my heart: *Ave, Crux, spes unica!* <Hail, Cross, our only hope!>" [4]

She sees the hope of the cross in this:

Christ's suffering and death are continued in His mystical body and in each of His limbs. Every man must suffer and die. But if he is a living member of the body of Christ, his suffering and dying assumes redeeming power through Jesus Christ. That is the reason that all saints have wished for suffering. That is not a sick enjoyment of suffering. To the eye of reason it seems a perversion. In the light of the mystery of redemption it proves, however, to be the highest reason."[5]

Just as St. Paul said that the cross appears to human eyes to be a stumbling block and foolishness, Edith Stein saw that it was necessary to penetrate again and again to a deeper meaning and to understand the meaning of the cross of Christ anew. She no longer wanted to see it as the symbol of a triumphant national church and a powerful, missionary church. For her the cross is an expression of compassion, of God's solidarity with the powerless and the weak, the darkness and forlornness of the world. And by her own compassion and decision to follow after Christ, she wished to take part in the redemption of the world which Jesus Christ began.

For her this participation did not lead to practical charitable work such as was done by other Christian men and women who helped persecuted Jews during the Nazi period. Edith Stein's road led to the convent. Is this path understandable to us today and acceptable as a way of following Christ?

Once more I would like to recall that Edith Stein entered the convent only when her public activities were no longer possible. And she did not see her entry into the convent as flight from the world. "Gradually I realized," she writes, "that, even in the contemplative life, one may not sever the connection with the world. I even believe that the deeper one is drawn into God, the more one must 'go out of oneself'; that is, one must go to the world in order to carry the divine life into it."[6]

The divine life must be carried into the world. It is an ecumenical sign that Dietrich Bonhoeffer came to the same recognition during those years. His totally different path led, for similar reasons, to his resistance against National Socialism. And yet his path is in many respects comparable to that of Edith Stein. The opposition to National Socialism led both Christians in a similar direction.

Edith Stein tried in her own way to carry the divine life into the world: in prayer of praise and intercession, with comfort and consolation through letters and conversations, and in the community of Carmel. In the final analysis "to carry divine life into the world" meant not separating from her sister Rosa. For her Christian being, the cross was no reason to separate herself from the Jews but a means for reconciliation. She bore witness to the cross of Christ as a sign of hope for a life of reconciliation.

Frankfurt-Schwanheim, June 17, 1987
Sermon for the 22nd German Protestant Church Congress,
Delivered in St. Mauritius Catholic Church

Members of the Edith Stein Guild
visiting Edith-Stein-Karmel in Tübingen

nuns, l.r.: Anna Maria Strehle, OCD,
Waltraud Herbstrith, OCD

Not Like That!
On the Beatification of Edith Stein
by Friedrich Georg Friedmann

The question you will ask right away, no doubt, is: How is it that a mature person troubles his mind with the beatification of a Catholic woman of Jewish birth—in a world filled with war and civil war, a world that totters between technological power and moral powerlessness, and is barely able to come up with strategies for its own survival?

The answer depends in part on the background of the person who engages in these thoughts. I was born in Augsburg in 1912, and grew up in a German-Jewish family where the relationship between German culture and Jewish tradition was not an issue. For my Bar Mitzvah I received several hundred books from members of the Jewish community; they were India paper editions of German classics. It was a matter of course that the principal and vice principal of the Benedictine Gymnasium that I attended for nine years came to the synagogue on the High Holy Days as guests of honor.

When I was a student at the University of Rome in 1933, I regularly visited Benno Gut, a Benedictine priest at Sant' Anselmo who later became a cardinal and who gave me private lessons in philosophy. From 1934 to 1939 I went to the home of the editor of the *Osservatore Romano* in Vatican City twice weekly to practice German conversation with his son. The discussions within the Vatican concerning an appropriate political stance toward Nazi Germany were thus not hidden from me.

Friedrich Georg Friedman *is a professor of philosophy and former director of America House in Munich, Germany.*

I was expelled from Italy when the Nuremberg Laws were instituted there. I spent a year in England, including internment as a German-born person. In the fall of 1940, I arrived in the United States of America where I worked, with several interruptions, until 1960. In the southern state where I taught for a while at the state university, there was much prejudice against the Catholic minority. Due to the lack of qualified clergy, I came to lead the Newman Club there.

Shortly after my call to Munich I was received into a small circle of Catholic professors of which Cardinal Ratzinger was also a member for a short time. During the Second Vatican Council I started a correspondence with my colleague and later friend Karl Rahner about the awkwardness between Jews and Christians and what might be done to eliminate it. It was my first involvement with a Jewish or Jewish-Christian topic. It turned into my first contribution to the journal *Stimmen der Zeit*, to be followed by about a dozen more.

After my retirement on October 1979 I began to research certain well-known personalities of the pre-Nazi German-Jewish culture that no longer exists. In doing this, I dealt with the relations between Judaism and "Germanness," and between Judaism and Christianity. Hans Urs von Balthasar published a little essay that I wrote about Hermann Cohen, Franz Rosenzweig, Franz Kafka and Walter Benjamin. Piper published my book *Hannah Arendt: The Life and Work of a German Jew in the Age of Totalitarianism. Stimmen der Zeit* published a lengthy essay titled "Erich Fromm and the Search for God."

One day I visited the Husserl Archive in Louvain, where an assistant gave me a copy of an unpublished essay written in 1938 by Sr. Adelgundis Jaegerschmid, a Benedictine nun, about her memories of Husserl. I asked for the author's address and later visited her in Freiburg. It turned out that she had been a friend of Edith Stein. In fact, twenty-four of the letters that Edith Stein wrote to her have been published [in *Self-Portrait in Letters*]. Since a friendship soon developed between Sr. Adelgundis and myself, I often heard a great deal about Edith Stein.

I was much impressed at the time that between the two World Wars quite a few German-Jewish thinkers had dealt with Christianity in various ways. Edith Stein was only one, even if a somewhat unusual case. I wrote to Sr. Waltraud Herbstrith of the Tübingen Carmel, who has published a great deal about Edith Stein and has probably been the foremost champion of her beatification, to ask for her advice and help.

Sr. Waltraud sent me the third edition of her book *Das wahre Gesicht Edith Steins* (The True Face of Edith Stein) in which I found two statements by Edith Stein that upset me a great deal. The first appeared to be taken from the Benedictine monthly *Erbe und Auftrag* (Legacy and Task), published by the Archabbey of Beuron. In it Father Paulus Gordan, to my knowledge himself of Jewish descent, wrote the following in 1962:

> True, we must say today that [Edith Stein's] high-minded and shocking statements (such as on the day of the synagogue burnings: "That is the shadow of the cross that falls upon my people! Oh, if they would only realize! That is the fulfillment of the curse which my people have called down upon themselves!") betray a not fully clarified theology and are defined by preformulated ideas which, however, she has not appropriated as her own.[1]

In Sr. Waltraud's book we find only the alleged words of Edith Stein—without the restrictive remarks (pp. 195-96). Indeed she continues the discussion over several pages. She writes that Israel did not respect the Lord and: "Like Cain, it killed Abel and thus became unsettled and homeless."[2] I answered in a letter (dated July 9, 1980):

> This was, for many centuries, I suppose, the accepted interpretation of history in the Christian West. Secularized and vulgarized, it became a foundation for Nazism. Since nine of my closest relatives fell victim to this demon, such a sentence affects and hurts me deeply. It inevitably drives a wedge between Judaism and Christianity, which no expression of love for the Jewish people can remove.

In her reply of July 14, 1980 Sr. Waltraud wrote,

> It is good that you remind me of such things, because, despite all affection for Jews, we are often still tied to a certain

system of thought, without noticing it.... That is how it was for Edith Stein, too. She was a convert, and even though she did not tolerate criticism of her Jewish people, she had accepted phrases such as "unbelief of the Jews," etc.

That was the second statement by Edith Stein to which I took exception and which later on became a crucial point in the discussion concerning her beatification, especially because, as far as I know, the authenticity of the first Stein quotation has not yet been completely settled. Sr. Waltraud continues in her letter:

> The book *In Search of God* (the earlier title was *The True Face of Edith Stein*) has been revised several times, because nowadays one cannot write any more as I used to write as a young nun. However, the sentence you quote from the old edition, "It is the shadow of the cross..." (pp. 195-196), has remained so far. It does not originate directly with Edith Stein, but with her first biographer, Sr. Teresia Renata Posselt. Its style is totally Posselt.... The fourth edition is due in two months. I am now omitting this passage by Posselt.[3]

In a letter of July 24, 1980, I try to explain that, in my view, it is not necessary to stylize Edith Stein in any way, for her life and her conversion are impressive and convincing, even for a non-Catholic....

Of course, even Sr. Waltraud cannot eliminate that sentence from the handwritten last will of Edith Stein dated July 9, 1939, which reads:

> I ask the Lord to accept my life and death to his honor and glorification, for all the intentions of the Sacred Hearts of Jesus and Mary and the church, especially for the preservation, sanctification and perfection of our Holy Order, particularly the Carmels of Cologne and Echt, for the expiation of the unbelief of the Jewish people and so that the Lord may be welcomed by his own people and his kingdom come in majesty.

Sr. Waltraud had reprinted a facsimile of the page in Edith Stein's will on which this sentence appears, opposite the foreword, up to and including the fifth edition of her book. In the sixth edition this facsimile has been omitted. Already in 1983 she had written to me: "Here Edith Stein is under the influence of a preconciliar theology, especially as a convert." If the Vatican had shown a similar opinion, in my view an essential argument against the beatification of Edith Stein would have become invalid. Between May 1983 and May 1986 I had no reason to occupy myself with Edith Stein. I spent the Spring of 1986 in the United States with my wife. On that occasion we attended a dinner given for us by the Chairman of the Secretariat for Catholic-Jewish Relations of the National Conference of Catholic Bishops in Washington, DC. At the end of the affair I was given the most important documents that had been prepared either by the Vatican Commission for Religious Relations with the Jews or the corresponding Commission of the American Conference of Bishops. I used them as the basis for an essay that appeared in *Commonweal* in September 1986. Two statements are especially gratifying to me. First, the 1985 *Notes on the Correct Way to Present Jews and Judaism in the Preaching and Catechesis of the Roman Catholic Church* declare that "Christian sinners are more to blame for the death of Christ than those few Jews who brought it about—they indeed 'knew not what they did' (cf. Lk 23:34)," and second, the above-mentioned document confirms that the "permanence of Israel...is a historic fact and a sign to be interpreted within God's design" (para. 22 and 25). I quote further from the address of the pope in the Synagogue in Rome, that "each of our religions...wishes to be recognized and respected in its own identity, beyond any syncretism and any ambiguous appropriation,"[4] and that "'the Lord will judge each one according to his own works,' Jews and Christians alike (cf. Rom 2:6)."[5] Since these and several other statements that I consider gratifying had been criticized by representatives of some Jewish organizations, because the Holocaust had not been adequately dealt with and a recognition of Israel by the Vatican had not been promised, I enumerated the reasons why I do not consider this criticism valid. I concluded my essay with another quotation from the 1985 *Notes* document, which says that "the people of God of the Old and the New Testament are tending toward a like end in the future: the coming or return of the Messiah—even if they start from two different points of view."[6]

...Upon my return to Germany in May 1986, I learned from my friend, the Benedictine nun, that Edith Stein was to be beatified in May of the following year. I wrote (on the twenty-third of the same month) to Cardinal Ratzinger that, in view of Edith Stein's statement indicating that she wished to atone for the unbelief of the Jews, the danger existed that the beatification would mean a setback for the relations between Christians and Jews. I continued as follows: "Since Edith Stein's death was just as involuntary as that of many of my relatives, it can actually only be her baptism that led to her beatification." On September 1, I received the following message from Dr. Josef Clemens, Cardinal Ratzinger's assistant: "Be assured that your concern has received careful attention. His Eminence thanks you for your concern and asks me to give you his best wishes."

It was surely a coincidence that a few days later I received a circular from the Cologne Carmel (dated September 8) from which I want to quote excerpts here.

> Certainly most of you have read...about the impending beatification of our Sister [Teresa] Benedicta of the Cross—Edith Stein. The pope, so we were informed, would beatify her during his second visit to the Federal Republic on May 1, in Cologne. In fact, however, the negotiations that must precede every beatification and that, for Edith Stein, have been pending since 1972, are not yet concluded. The last phase of this process will begin on October 28; the final decision is not likely to come before the beginning of next year, we were told.
>
> What does this last phase deal with? Among other things it concerns the question whether or not Edith Stein may be given the title of martyr. At first this question was totally ignored in the beatification process. Instead the procedure for non-martyrs was followed, where the "heroicity" of every Christian virtue must be proven.... Besides it is a condition that prior to beatification of non-martyrs a "miracle" must have occurred in response to their intercession. Well, it is true that upon Edith Stein's intercession much has occurred that is miraculous; but a medically verified yet medically inexplicable event of healing has not been found up to now. Therefore the postulator of the process decided to reopen the question of martyrdom anew. Edith Stein has often been called a martyr, even long before the start of the beatification process; but that was meant

colloquially.... The decisive characteristic [is] "to bear witness
for Christ by suffering the death penalty"; thus martyrdom was
defined already in early Christian times.

The author of the circular, Sr. Maria Amata Neyer, called to
our attention that the "surrender of life... 'as witness of faith' and
'for Christ's sake' cannot be fixed definitively for all time and for
all places, but must be decided for every such martyr in particular
and after considering all the circumstances." She then describes
how the deportation of Jews baptized in the Catholic faith, among
them Edith Stein, was an act of vengeance against the Dutch bishops for their public protest against the persecution of the Jews.
Later in the circular, Sr. Maria Amata asks for patience:

> Should the proceedings be concluded in time, then Edith
> Stein's beatification will take place on May 1 within the solemn
> papal Mass in the Cologne stadium. The Vicar General of the
> Archbishopric of Cologne stated the other day that all other
> considerations are premature for the time being. We must ask
> you, dear readers, to watch for information in the press at the
> appropriate time.

The church was having difficulty finding valid reasons for the
long-planned beatification. This is clearly evident from the tone
and argumentation of a letter that the postulator of the *causa*, Dominican Father Ambrosius Eszer, Professor at the Angelicum in
Rome, wrote on November 8, 1986 to James Raphael Baaden, an
American Jewish writer living in England. Baaden, who had occupied himself with studying Edith Stein in preparation for a book,
had written to the Congregation concerned with the canonization,
asking for clarification about whether Edith Stein died for being a
Jew or a Catholic. He believed himself to have proof that she died
as a Jew; therefore he asked how it was possible to beatify her as a
Christian. On March 20, 1987, the *National Catholic Reporter ...* published an essay [by Peter Hebblethwaite] that included the most
important portions of Father Eszer's reply to Mr. Baaden. Father
Eszer writes, among other things, that Mr. Baaden is, of course, free
to defend his viewpoint; however, the Catholic Church is sovereign
in matters of faith and morals and "does not depend on interfer-
ences from outside" (p. 25). He continues:

> You are not the only Jew who feels uneasy about the pos-
> sible declaration of Edith Stein as a martyr and of her eventual
> beatification. She was a Catholic like Sts. Peter and Paul and
> many other Catholic saints and in her spiritual testament she
> offered her life not only for peace but also for the conversion
> of all Jews to the Catholic church.

The good Father appears not to have understood that Peter
and Paul did not offer their life and death as atonement for the
unbelief of the Jews; besides he seems not to have heard about the
declaration *Nostra Aetate* nor about the approach to the relationship
between the church and Jews therein set aside. On the contrary he
notes that "elsewhere Edith Stein speaks of the 'fault' of the Jews"
(because they did not become Catholics) and adds: "at least this is
the meaning I see in this phrase, and it is the more benign interpretation." The *National Catholic Reporter* comments: "One shudders
to think what the less benign interpretation might be." For me
there is no doubt: The interpretation of the "final solution" as punishment for the execution of Christ by the Jews.

Since Edith Stein, just like millions of people who, in contrast
to her, remained faithful to their Judaism, did not go to her death
voluntarily, but was barbarously murdered by the henchmen of the
regime as a member of a so-called inferior race, only two arguments
can be valid for her status as a martyr: first, the attitude of her
murderers; and second, her attitude in the face of impending
death. Father Eszer holds to the first argument. For the church that
person counts as a martyr who is killed out of hatred for the
church—*odium fidei*. He reasons that Edith Stein belonged to the
300 Jews who had converted to Catholicism and were living in Holland, whom the authorities dragged into the gas chambers to revenge themselves on the Catholic bishops who, despite a warning,
publicly read a pastoral letter against the persecution of the Jews.
To these bishops I express my profoundest gratitude and my deepest respect....

It is understandable that the postulator must insist in his strat-
egy that Edith Stein died as a Catholic. When a Jewish speaker
maintained in a lecture in the Cologne Carmel that Edith Stein has
always remained a daughter of Israel (an expression that later on
Pope John Paul II used as well to smooth the rough waters), Father

Eszer called this "absolutely wrong"; in such a statement he saw his *causa* endangered.

James Raphael Baaden writes that Edith Stein's death was, no doubt, accelerated by the courageous act of the bishops, but in no way caused by it. The cause was her affiliation with what the National Socialists call the "Jewish race." From their standpoint, her conversion was secondary. About the motives for her conversion, by the way, even the family of Edith Stein does not agree (a fact irrelevant for the beatification process). Her niece, journalist Susanne M. Batzdorff, writes in the *Aufbau* of May 8, 1987.

> In the family, however, there was always speculation whether a personal crisis or a bitter human disappointment might not have played a role in this. In later years, when questioned about this, she smiled and said, "That's my secret."

At any rate, Father Eszer, too, knows about a correspondence between Edith Stein and the philosopher Roman Ingarden, who also belonged to the Husserl circle. Baaden thinks that Father Eszer had only seen the part of their correspondence published in 1962, a small selection of the 150 letters that are in possession of Roman Ingarden's son, a teacher in Torun, Poland [later published in 1991 as Volume XIV of Stein's *Werke*]. Father Eszer says about this:

> As far as I could find out, this correspondence contains no obstacle against the declaration of Edith's heroic virtues, for their relationship soon ended. She obviously loved him, but later on they discussed only scholarly subjects. Even if indeed she loved him, it would not be a sin.

The fact that in 1932 she wrote that she saw no doctrinal reason that women could not be ordained as priests, likewise was not regarded as an obstacle to her beatification—or was perhaps overlooked.

...After her baptism Edith Stein did not hesitate to call herself Jewish when this declaration of solidarity with the Jewish people really counted. Cardinal Höffner spoke of her "heroic readiness," referring to Edith Stein's words to her sister Rosa, when they were arrested on August 2, 1942, "Come, we are going for our people."

It is hard for me to comprehend what she meant by the phrase "for our people." Like millions of Jews she was arrested, against her will, solely because of her membership in a so-called race. Like millions of Jews she tried, even after her imprisonment, to save her life. Her niece writes (in the *Aufbau* of May 8, 1987):

> Up to the last moment she tried to further her emigration, and, even from Westerbork, asked her prioress to do her utmost in this matter. Even from the freight car transporting her eastward, she managed to smuggle scribbled notes or oral messages to various people, a clear sign that she wanted to enable others to trace her route of deportation." [7]

Certainly well-intentioned but ambiguous is the plaque in the Cologne Carmel that reads: "She died as a martyr for her people and for her faith." Her people, I suppose, are the Jews, her faith, I suppose, is Catholicism. The American Catholic journal *America* (of January 10, 1987), however, translates this: "She died for her people and their faith." That does not seem correct, for she was beatified as a Catholic, not as a Jew....

Her conversion to Catholicism meant, in the words of her niece Susanne Batzdorff (cf. *Aufbau*, May 8, 1987) "that she was abandoning her Jewish people, her Jewish family." "By becoming a Catholic," writes Mrs. Batzdorff elsewhere, "she had abandoned her people. By entering a cloister, she was proclaiming to the outside world her desire to dissociate herself from the Jewish people. Despite our love for her, a rift had opened that could never be bridged" (*New York Times*, April 12, 1987).[8] Her 84-year-old mother suffered especially because she would never see her daughter any more. Added to that was the fact that she left her people once and for all just in the year of disaster, 1933. Let us remember once more that her will, in which she speaks of the unbelief of the Jewish people, was written in 1939, hence more than a year after the so-called *Reichskristallnacht*. Her niece adds that now her letters to her family "were signed with her new name 'Benedicta,' for us a further sign of distancing herself from her former self, from the name that her Jewish parents had given her" (Ibid.).

I myself had learned of the final decision about the beatification of Edith Stein from a newspaper item dated February 10, 1987, which indicated that the *Deutsche Bundespost* would issue a postage stamp on the occasion of the beatification of Edith Stein. I sat down and wrote to Cardinal Höffner:

> Those of us who, in spite of everything, returned to Germany, to make peace and to help those of different faiths with their work and in their day-to-day existence, but also in order to return to one's own and together confront an inane, secularized world in the service of the one God, must feel the manner of decision and the triumphalism of the church that can be expected, as a deadly blow against everything that people of good will have attempted to do against all the unnameable odds. It may be that I am the oldest, or even the only survivor of a once existing German-Jewish culture; the last, therefore, who can lift up his voice in the name of reverence toward the violated ones.... Therefore, dear Cardinal, be humane, be Christian. Seek out ways to sow love and friendship instead of more and more conflict, bitterness and injustice."

...I wish I could end my presentation here. Unfortunately there exist also within Jewish circles tendencies similar to those of the *ecclesia triumphans;* to be more specific, organizations that turn the idea of Jewish chosenness and its meaning in the economy of salvation into a purely earthly self-righteousness. I am thinking of the interpretation of the Holocaust as an exclusive property of the Jewish people, as a theological concept, which turns the chosenness with reference to the messianic era into a contemporary political statement. That seems to me to explain the opposition of some Jewish organizations to the construction of a place of worship in Auschwitz by six Sisters of the Carmelite Order.[9] Likewise the reaction of many Jews to the reception of the president of the Austrian Federation by the pope appears to me to be an aspect of the same complex. Even the attitude of the representatives of the Central Council of German Jews during their meeting with the pope seems to me to show a similar tendency: While the beatification of Edith Stein does not appear to have been discussed, the gentlemen expressed their request that the Vatican recognize at long last the State of Israel, a quid pro quo that characterizes the entire wretchedness of our situation.

I would think that the situation of the Western World has become so precarious, whether because of internal or external developments, that we can neither afford the luxury of an *ecclesia triumphans* nor of a self-righteous Judaism. A dialectic of our salvation histories, a mutual supplementation or even strengthening, is today not only a fascinating theological topic, but to my way of thinking a necessity in the spiritual and material struggle for survival. This requires both Jewish and Christian self-criticism. Our neighbors can very well help us accomplish this. Thus I see the pope's intention and many of his words as a hopeful sign. At the same time I see the opinion of Cardinal Ratzinger, recently expressed in an interview with the Italian Catholic journal *Il Sabato* (Oct. 24, 1987) as an obstacle. Concerning Edith Stein, he writes: "From a Jewish heritage she moved to a new and different heritage, yet, by entering into unity with Christ, she entered into the real heart of Judaism." Here the German-Jewish philosopher Franz Rosenzweig, who died in 1929, appears to come closer to the truth and to create a clearer basis for our common efforts, when he writes to a friend: "Judaism and Christianity exclude one another, but they supplement each other."

Lecture in the Carmelite monastery of Mainz during the Edith Stein celebrations from October 28, 1987 to December 7, 1987

Edith Stein: Sign of Contradiction, Sign of Reconciliation

by Jan H. Nota, SJ

Chancellor Konrad Adenauer justified the munificent German assistance to the State of Israel during his term with the words that, although you can't help the dead to live again, you have the duty to help the living.

In the stadium in Cologne on May 1, 1987, when I was asked to say a few words to the huge number of people—approximately 75,000—I experienced how the dead live on even after Auschwitz. This crowd of people had gathered for a woman, Edith Stein, who had become so dear to me, who had suffered unspeakably both physically and spiritually at the hands of people who called themselves German, yet who wanted to rob her of her membership in the German people. "I shall remain German," she said to me in 1942 in the monastery in Echt, and she wanted me to acknowledge that. I answered her: "Absolutely." That was not long before her horrible death.

And now the pope had traveled from Rome to Cologne to tell the many people from numerous lands, but especially those from Germany, in the name of the church: Edith Stein is with God forever; she is blessed, venerable—she can help us here on earth. She is a martyr—a witness for God's presence in a world where for many people God seems to be absent.

Until her death Edith Stein witnessed to her faithfulness to the God of Israel who revealed himself in Jesus. Until her death she affirmed her belief in the church as the one body of Jesus Christ.

Jan H. Nota, SJ, *was a professor of philosophy in Holland, Canada, and the United States.*

The human multitude in the Cologne stadium was grateful and happy that on this May morning the church was honoring "one of ours." As I listened to the pope's carefully chosen words, I had the impression that a true reconciliation between Jews and Germans, between Jews and Christians, was possible. That is what Edith Stein really ought to be: a sign, a symbol of reconciliation. In her the "daughter of Israel," the "daughter of the Church," and the daughter of Germany meet in a living synthesis.

In my talk I further said that Edith Stein can also be seen as a sign of contradiction. Just as Jesus Christ for many people is a sign of contradiction, Edith Stein, too, experienced with pain the distress that her beloved family could not understand her entry into the Catholic Church. In a pluralistic society such conflicts will always have to be dealt with.

Right after the beatification, Edith Stein became a "public figure," as her niece Mrs. Susanne Batzdorff expressed it. This public aspect of her witness also had the effect that her person, the meaning of her words, can be interpreted in diverse ways. Some of Edith Stein's words are also being reinterpreted, e.g. her last recorded words to her sister Rosa, as the SS were arresting them, "Come, we are going for our people." It was said that only one woman in Echt heard these words, and the testimony of a woman is unreliable. I myself knew this woman, Maria Delsing, well. She was a friend to the Carmel in Echt and to Edith Stein. Sr. Stanislaus of the Carmel of Echt told me that she, too, heard Edith Stein speak these last words on leaving the monastery.

Some Christians and Jews understood these words as anti-Jewish. They should not be understood that way, but rather as emerging from Edith Stein's often demonstrated attitude of solidarity with persons who were weaker, or threatened, or discriminated against. Edith Stein believed in the fruitfulness of redemptive suffering, as we find it expressed in St. Paul's Letter to the Colossians (1:24). Paul sees his own suffering as completion or supplementation of Christ's suffering. Edith Stein, in her adoration of the heart of Jesus, was filled with the idea of sharing in the suffering of Jesus, longing for co-redemption. With her "last words" she wanted to console her distraught sister Rosa and encourage her on their final way of the cross. Even after these last words, Edith

Stein tried everything possible, even from the concentration camp Westerbork, to escape to Switzerland. But she suspected that she would not succeed in this. Since all opportunities for helping her persecuted brothers and sisters were cut off for her, she wanted to offer God her life for those condemned to death.

Today, Jews and Christians should communicate with one another more intensely in order to understand each other's thoughts and feelings better. I believe I can find even in Karl Marx something of the redemptive aspect of suffering. In 1844 Marx spoke of the redemptive role of the proletariat. He said that the suffering of the proletariat had not only redemptive power for themselves but also for all of humanity.

While our Jewish friends interpret the role of the suffering servant in Isaiah 53 with respect to the entire Jewish people of God, the Christians identify the fate of Jesus Christ with the servant of God. It is high time that Christians and Jews in particular get to understand one another better. That is true especially for the interpretation of Edith Stein's fate, who, even after her conversion, regarded herself as Jewish. Edith Stein wrote, "We can only know a person if that person reveals himself to us. And even then our knowledge remains incomplete. Only a knowledge guided by love can penetrate into the mystery of the person."

We often say lightly, "I know my friend completely." Basically that is the end of any friendship. The other's personhood runs the risk of becoming an object and thus ceases being a person. For me the beatification of Edith Stein is not an end but the beginning of a dialogue between Christians and Jews. Our Jewish friends rightly say that Edith Stein's death is a challenge to the Christian churches to give up their anti-Jewish prejudices, which weakened their opposition to Nazi anti-Semitism. Edith Stein is not only the victim of brutal Nazis; her death was caused in part by Christians' excessive fear for their own lives while their Jewish brothers and sisters were murdered next door.

The conflict between Christians and Jews can only be reconciled when we Christians learn to take the religion of our Jewish friends seriously, to believe that God did not cancel his covenant with them. Pope John Paul II encouraged such reconciliation in the Synagogue of Rome in 1986. And our Jewish brothers and sisters must learn to abandon their hitherto justified fear of Christians: They will realize that they are being taken seriously as the root stock of the church of Christ. Edith Stein saw this conflict very clearly, as well as the impossibility of achieving reconciliation in the atmosphere prevailing in Germany between the two world wars. For herself she could solve this conflict only by placing it in the context of the suffering of Christ. In the torture of her innocent people she saw the suffering of the innocent Son of God. And so she hoped for both—victims and murderers—salvation from the just God.

Thoughts About a Picture

by Martin Cunz

The shortest trip ever taken by the pope was the one from the Vatican across the Tiber to the synagogue that stands in the old ghetto of Rome. It was also his longest trip, lasting almost 2000 years. I hardly dare to imagine how much bloodshed and Christian arrogance toward the Jews could have been prevented and how much good could have occurred if the Bishop of Rome had dared to take that step across the Tiber earlier—just fifty years earlier, when hatred against Jews by persons who, after all, had been baptized, was about to extinguish European Jewry! What would have happened if Pius XI had crossed the Tiber, embraced the rabbi and said: "You are our elder brothers!"

The image of the encounter between the Roman Rabbi and the Roman Bishop is a symbol. It shows what it's all about when Christians and Jews approach one another today:

1) If Christians of all denominations seek a dialogue with Jews today, that means first and foremost an expression of return and atonement. For centuries, Christians believed that the Jews ought to convert to Christ and the church. Today many Christians are discovering that we ourselves must return to the God of the Jews to whom we have access in Jesus Christ.

2) In the return to the God of the Jews many Christians become aware that the centuries-old Christian contempt of the Jews was not only a crime against the Jews. We have broken away from Jesus Christ. It is he whom we have denied. We reproached the Jews

Martin Cunz *is a parish priest and director of the Foundation for the Church and Judaism, in Zürich, Switzerland.*

for having crucified Christ, and we did not notice that it was we ourselves who were forever crucifying him in the persons of the Jews!

3) The therapy for the Church's anti-Jewish malady consists in learning to approach the Jews and in letting them tell us who we are. The point of this is not just to replace the negative image of the Jews by a positive image. The Jews are just as imperfect as we ourselves. Rather the point is to take the Jews seriously, just as they are, as a part of our own faith, even with their weaknesses, where applicable. We have need of the testament of faith, so that we may bear witness to the same God.

4) Christians are learning to ask Jews: "What does it actually mean to you to be a world religion? Isaiah says, after all, that the people Israel is a light unto the nations! What can we learn from you for our own faith? What is it that only you and no one else can give the world?" The Jews will have to learn to answer such questions, because heretofore they were hardly ever asked of them in earnest.

5) Our access to the Jews can only be through Jesus Christ. That means that we must learn to see our Lord and Master amid the Jewish people. Jesus is not the enemy of the Jews. Rather he lives, speaks, fights, loves, dies, and rises with his people, not against them. That has consequences for our Bible interpretation and teaching.

6) The goal of the dialogue between Christians and Jews cannot, as in the case of the Christian churches, be "unity." True, we are children of one Father like the two lost sons in the parable. The only "unity" that is possible between us, however, is the one God of Israel. Because he is the one, we can and must go our separate ways, for he has called us to do so.

7) The key word for dialogue therefore is not "unity" but "diversity." The different nature of the Jews is for us a proof for the One God, who is simply different from us. The most beautiful fruit

of our encounter would be if we could praise God for the fact that the other exists and in his vocation is faithful to God.

The image of the encounter between the pope and the rabbi of Rome awakens in me all these thoughts and hopes. It is an icon of brotherhood between Christians and Jews.

From Mirjam: Christliche Zeitschrift für die Frau *[Zürich] 69/4 (April 1988): 142.*

Rabbi Elio Toaff and Pope John Paul II
(Rome, May 13, 1986)

The Jews Did Not Want to Bring Burnt Offerings

by Ernst Ludwig Ehrlich

Holocaust or Shoah? A discussion is taking place with good reason over which of these two terms should be applied to the mass murder of the Jews. Apparently Elie Wiesel first introduced the expression "Holocaust" (Hebrew *ola*, i.e. burnt offering) into our usage, but he later moved away from it and now uses the term "Shoah." This word appears in Isaiah 47:11 and means "disaster."

One might ask what reasons speak against a concept that connects this mass murder with the Biblical expression for "sacrifice", no matter what history the word "ola" in particular may have had within the Hebrew Bible. Theological questions are not paramount here, or at least should be regarded as secondary in importance. First, the issue is that millions of Jews, of individuals, who until then appeared only to share a common humanity with others, were murdered solely because they were Jews. This occurred with the help of many who participated in one way or another. This year we recall the 50th anniversary of the Jewish pogrom of November 9, 1938. At that time everyone saw the synagogues aflame, Jewish businesses demolished, and Jewish men deported. Therefore it is simply senseless to try—often without even noticing it—by means of semantic acrobatics to exonerate people of that time from their responsibility.

Ernst Ludwig Ehrlich, Ph.D., *is the European director of B'nai B'rith, in Geneva, Switzerland. He fled Nazi persecution under difficult circumstances.*

A Passage From Isaiah

The Jews who had been plundered and murdered by the Nazis did not want to bring a "sacrifice," neither a sin offering, a burnt offering, nor any other kind of offering! These millions of murdered Jews wanted to live. If they were religious, they wanted to serve their God as living Jews, not dead ones. If they called upon the name of God in the extermination camps and prayed, they were not offering themselves to God as a sacrifice, but crying out from instinctual piety. This also fits in with Jewish rabbinic tradition, where the passage from the Book of Isaiah was not understood in the sense of a particular person or people dying as expiation. On the contrary, Genesis 22, the story of how Isaac is not sacrificed, is the most emphatic polemic against any form of human sacrifice: God does not want it, cannot want it!

By the way, it is characteristic that in the passage from Isaiah from which the word "shoah" is taken, the concept of disaster as expiation is rejected (Is 47:11).

Hence there is nothing mysterious to be solved or to be utilized in one way or another in the face of the murder of millions of Jews, culpably caused, or at least facilitated, by thousands of bystanders, bureaucrats, profiteers, opportunists, and finally also murderers. That also held true for Edith Stein. She did not wish to die but had tried, with all the means at her disposal, to arrange for her escape to Switzerland. Her last written message does not deal with a putative sacrificial death but with the hope of receiving the Swiss visa after all. It was denied her, and even if it had arrived at the last moment, the Nazi murderers would still have deported her. The negotiations had dragged on much too long, through no fault of Edith Stein, due to the delays in obtaining the most essential documents from Rome and elsewhere. Even after everything had been collected, she was denied the visa. Edith Stein wanted to live; one must not suppress her will to live nor her urgent desire to get into a Swiss monastery.

No observant Jew had the intent of bringing a burnt offering. At long last, one ought to stop attributing to the murdered Jews religious concepts that are not in accord with Judaism. That way one does not honor their memory, but tries instead to introduce a creeping missionary theology, as if this horrible murder might have had meaning after all, and what's more, a meaning derived from Christian theology. There is, after all, a vast difference, whether one perseveres in one's faith in God, remains true to God, or is obsessed by the concept of "holocaust," which was absolutely foreign to these Jews.

The Pope Says "Shoah" Too

"Shoah" has no religious dimension, unless one inquires into the theological ethics of those who proclaim, upon seeing the Nazis' crimes against the Jews: "The curse has been horribly fulfilled, even to the present day." The problem we are here dealing with is the preamble to the "Shoah." Concerning this, Pope John Paul II spoke of "correcting a false religious view of the Jewish people, which in the course of history was one of the causes that contributed to misunderstanding and persecution" (Mainz, November 17, 1980). And the United Synod's resolution (November 22, 1975) states:

> We are the land whose most recent political history is darkened by the attempt to extinguish the Jewish people systematically. And we were, despite exemplary behavior of specific individuals and groups, generally a religious community that lived on with its back to the fate of this persecuted Jewish people. We let our view focus too strongly on the threat to our own institutions, and we reacted with silence to the crimes against Jews and Judaism.

That would indeed be a subject for Catholics to think about in view of the pogrom against the Jews in the year 1938. The question of which term to use in view of the human failure to confront mass murder is secondary. We are of the opinion that the term "holocaust" is inappropriate; the word "shoah" describes the event more accurately. Pope John Paul II, who has shown on various occasions that he knows how to respect the sensitivity of the Jews, uses the term "shoah" on principle. Perhaps some day we will owe it to the pope that at least Catholics will connect this term with the Jewish genocide. Then, perhaps the Hebrew word will come to stand for Jewish genocide and the term's meaning will be clear. In any case, one should not avoid a historic responsibility by attributing to the Jews a "holocaust theology" that was and is absolutely foreign to them. We cannot prevent others from exploiting Edith Stein for theological purposes; Jews and Judaism, however, should be left out of it, if at all possible.

First published in
Christ in der Gegenwart *(Christ Today) 40 (1988): 62.*

Addendum September 15, 1992

The pope's beatification of Edith Stein in Cologne was not used for anti-Jewish purposes, as many people, especially Jews, presumed. On the contrary: Probably never before had a person of rank cited the crimes of the *Shoah* so insistently as the pope did on this occasion. No takeover of the Jews by the church occurred, but Edith Stein's Jewish fate, just like that of all other Jewish martyrs, was stated most impressively. Since the pope's entire homily was shown on German television, the events of the *Shoah* could be transmitted to millions of people. It is part of the tragic events of our time that such statements by the pope are ignored by Jews and suppressed by Catholics. The insistence of his sermon, especially in connection with the *Shoah,* and his engagement during his talk demonstrated that this pope from Cracow, only a few kilometers from Auschwitz, understood the deep meaning of the *Shoah* for the Jewish people. His homily at the beatification of Edith Stein is an impressive testimony.

Prof. Ernst Ludwig Ehrlich

Of Saints and Martyrs

by Menahem Benhayim

E dith Stein has been well known in Jewish-Catholic circles for many years. The Edith Stein Guild, organized after the Second World War, has been trying for years to promote Edith Stein's canonization. Besides, the Guild has promoted solidarity among Jewish Catholics as well as Jewish identity within the church.

Edith Stein, the German-Jewish nun, was murdered in Auschwitz together with her sister Rosa. Her beatification...appears to Jewish Catholics and their friends to be a great achievement. During a celebration in Cologne, the pope himself acknowledged her as a "great daughter of Israel" who "remained faithful to her people in loyalty and love" and who at the same time was a devout Catholic. In a sense she became a further dramatic symbol of the Jewish tragedy in Christian Europe, and an insistent answer to the revisionist lie that the Holocaust was a Jewish invention, that allegedly no one was gassed at Auschwitz.

The Israeli media reported on the beatification in detail, but the reaction was not enthusiastic. Rabbi David Rosen, a moderate Orthodox rabbi originally from Ireland, a veteran in interfaith concerns, remarked bitterly: "I suppose there are people who believe that we should be grateful." His statement reflected the feelings of several Israeli commentators that the whole affair was tasteless and served only to hush up the Catholic Church's guilty conscience, which it must have in view of its failure during the war and its contribution to the history of European anti-Semitism that reached its zenith with the Holocaust.

The tension was certainly not diminished by the fact that the church honored a victim of the Holocaust who—according to the

---

Menahem Benhayim *is a journalist in Jerusalem, Israel.*

general view of the Jews—had deserted and had once declared that she was sacrificing her life to God for her Jewish people and for its sin of unbelief concerning Jesus. The references to Edith Stein herself were surprisingly free from bitterness. At worst she was portrayed as a pitiable victim of false hope that the church would rescue her from the Nazi terror.

There were interviews with relatives, especially with an older niece, Anni Meyer, who knew her rather well and who now lives in Israel. By and large her statements gave the positive impression of a "unique individual whom we all loved"... She states that, even after her conversion to Catholicism, Edith Stein attended the synagogue with her deeply religious mother on Yom Kippur. Besides, Edith Stein, she says, published a book about Jewish family life in which she condemned the growing anti-Semitism during the Weimar Republic.[1] According to her niece she tried desperately to shake up the church: In vain she tried to get in touch with the Vatican and Pius XI, to urge opposition to anti-Semitism that raged during the Hitler regime. In this connection the radical Catholic theologian Hans Küng determined that during the entire Nazi rule no German bishop dared to defend the Jews publicly. In Israel and elsewhere the beatification provoked condemnations of the Catholic Church for its alleged complicity with the Nazi regime and for its failure to aid the Steins and other Jewish Catholics as well as the entire Jewish population during the War.

Upon the arrival of the Gestapo in the monastery in which Edith and Rosa Stein had sought refuge, it is reported that Edith said to her sister, as they were being led away for deportation to Auschwitz, "Come, we are going for our people." This shows the strong sense of solidarity with the Jewish people that she maintained all her life. Some Jewish authors therefore see her rather as a Jewish martyr, due to Christian malice, than a future Catholic saint.

"According to Jewish law she remains a Jew, as she was from birth, and according to her remarks en route to Auschwitz she was aware of her origins to the last moment," a Jewish Orthodox author commented. A German soldier reports that he saw "a special glow" in her eyes as she, still wearing the habit of her order, was transported eastward to her death.[2] Her Israeli niece Anni Meyer remembered that no one had such eyes as her aunt Edith.

From The Hebrew Catholic *(September/November 1987): 90ff.*

Edith Stein and Freiburg

by Hugo Ott

It was a rather untroubled time (1916) when Edith Stein got to know Freiburg and soon became familiar with this southern German landscape and, yes, even got to feel somewhat at home. Rather untroubled, though the war continued, intensified, and claimed casualties in her circle of relatives and friends. The hope for a German victory gradually disappeared as the major battles in the West failed to bring about a turn of fortunes.

In July of 1916 Edith Stein, a twenty-four-year-old from Breslau, had come to this southwest corner of Germany for no other reason than that her teacher Edmund Husserl had been called from Göttingen to Freiburg. She would have to take the oral doctoral examinations there, and if she wanted to pass with distinction, she would have to get to know the professors somewhat. She also wanted to be close to the revered master Edmund Husserl so that he might write the required report and set in motion the proceedings. The custodian of the Faculty of Philosophy, who would transmit the doctoral dissertation from one professor to another, had to receive the obligatory tip, so that the deadline would be met, because classes resumed in Breslau on August 6, 1916.

Therefore it was fortunate that Edith Stein could find accommodations at one of the most beautiful spots in the city of Freiburg, out in Günterstal. This would be the quiet corner for her to prepare for her examinations, but it was also an escape hatch to the Black Forest that lured her to go on outings during the hot summer. Ah, this splendid villa, built in the style of a Tuscan country estate, painted in the rich yellow hue of the southern sun! Again and again the young philosopher gazed at the Wolgemuth house

---

Hugo Ott *is a professor of economics and sociology in Freiburg.*

with its beautiful garden, where she could philosophize so nicely, unaware that it would become St. Lioba Monastery a few years later, a place of retreat for her.

The best present the brand-new Ph.D. brought back home to her mother in the east, besides her diploma, was Husserl's offer to work with him as his private assistant. True, the salary was very modest, almost not worth mentioning, since the unworldly scholar assumed that the Jewish girl from Silesia was well-to-do. True, the proud mother Auguste, an efficient businesswoman and widow, was willing to provide so that her youngest child need not suffer deprivation, but could get ahead in academia, surely an aim worth striving for! Now it was necessary to find a permanent residence in Freiburg, preferably in the vicinity of Husserl's apartment in Unterwiehre, the new part of town. Many beautiful middle class homes had been built there during the pre-war years.

The widow Theresia Keller ran a guest house at Goethestrasse 63, on the third and fourth floor. She charged reasonable prices, since the house was a bit noisy; the leisurely Höllental train crossed Loretto Strasse only a short distance away, and the tracks ran behind the house. The train signals and the creaking of the double barriers punctuated the day. Edith Stein moved to this idyllic spot in October 1916, energetically burying herself in the Master's manuscripts, organizing them, submitting to his work schedule as much as possible, accompanying him on daily walks up to the Hilda Tower, discussing, but even more listening to the logical thinker's monologues, and learning. When the wind stood in the southwest, one could hear the dull rumbling from the Vosges Mountains battlefront, frozen in place since the summer of 1914, with fierce battling over each spot. Sudden flashes from the battlefield could be seen from the crest of the Vosges at nightfall during the winter of 1916–1917. It was not purely idyllic. Edith Stein learned from the station mistress that huge troop movements had begun.

Not purely idyllic, since collaboration with the revered Master became more and more difficult, until it grew intolerable. How could Husserl know that his highly praised disciple aimed higher and aspired to teach philosophy at a university? That could not end well and at last it demanded the brief and painful step that Edith Stein took in the spring of 1918.

She had remained faithful to her landlady and had moved with her to Zasius Street 24 at the end of 1917. She lived there until the war ended and the confusion of the postwar weeks erupted over this landscape, too. It would be best to go home again. There was nothing to keep her in Freiburg any more—at least for now. And yet, after the severe disappointments, after a reorientation in her innermost personal life, this city acquired a new quality for Edith Stein. There was the Master, whom she loyally revered as before, even though their personal contact was interrupted for many years. There were also familiar people from the phenomenologist circle, but above all, there was the monastery of St. Lioba in Günterstal, which had been established in the mid-twenties. Thus a spiritual-biographical triangle gradually appeared, among Speyer, the place where Edith Stein taught school; Beuron, the wellspring of her liturgical life; and Freiburg. Again and again she stopped there on her way to Beuron for the religious festivals.

And again it seemed as if her hopes to qualify for an academic career would materialize. In 1931–1932 she applied for a university appointment. The signs looked favorable and yet turned out to be deceptive. As a fallback there was an assured lectureship at the Pedagogical Academy in Münster—but that was, after all, not a university. These intensive weeks during the winter of 1931–1932 were at the same time her farewell to a city and a landscape where Edith Stein could have lived an academic life. No one could know that it was to be a farewell forever. Edith Stein celebrated Easter in Beuron in 1933 one more time—the last time. In her beloved Danube valley she could gather strength for the difficult times that had just arisen for German Jews through Hitler's ascent to power. When on Good Friday 1933 she arrived in Beuron, the ominous "law for the restitution of the civil service"[1] had been passed: It was to affect her teaching position in Münster. The only possible road for her now led into the seclusion of Carmel, into strict enclosure. Intellectually and spiritually she remained connected with Freiburg, the shrunken world of Edmund Husserl, and St. Lioba in Günterstal. In her prayers she was present at the sickbed of her teacher, whose forsakenness touched her deeply. Her Carmelite asceticism prevented her from giving vent to her indignation.

During the early days of August 1942, when the locked transport train moved south from Holland with its human cargo destined for death, the philosopher Edith Stein, the Carmelite Teresa Benedicta a Cruce, slipped a note through the small barred window during a stop at the station of Schifferstadt, not far from Speyer, an area well known to her. By mysterious means it reached the hands of Sr. Placida Laubhardt, a Breslau compatriot, Benedictine nun in Günterstal, who still lives there. "En route ad orientem," it read—"On the way to the East," toward the sunrise, driven out of the land of the setting sun, the occident that had lost its honor, back to the origins of light, full of anticipation that the abyss of existence would simultaneously be the beginning. The ramp of Auschwitz was located in the land of origin of Edith Stein's ancestors, the Eastern landscape was familiar to her blood. With her sister she was going back there for her people, to death.

Address at the official dedicationof the memorial tablet (below)
for Edith Stein in Freiburg, at Goethestrasse 63, May 5, 1987

Companion in Human Fate

by Joachim Köhler

In his Lenten pastoral letter on the occasion of the beatification of Edith Stein, the Archbishop of Cologne, Joseph Cardinal Höffner, spoke emphatically: "The beatification does not make of Edith Stein a remote, non-historic being. She stands before us, human like us, a companion in our human fate."[1]

I read that letter with a great deal of suspense. My expectations were directed toward learning something from it about the process of canonization, about the conditions by which persons can become holy in this world, how the everyday, the coincidental, the historical—in short, the circumstances in which we as human beings are always entangled—can become the means for our sanctification. The saints, the Cardinal continues, "are meant to give us an example of Christian life in the here and now."[2] Toward this end, Edith Stein proclaims "a fourfold message,"[3] which the Cardinal considers very significant, particularly for our time. Using four quotations by the Carmelite, the pastoral letter refers back to episodes from her life, but in the end it is a statement about holiness.

Edith Stein's Fourfold Message

1) Under the motto "My longing for truth was one single prayer," Edith Stein is described as a seeker who surmounted the various stages of her life without any problem. Looking back on her university studies, during which she "joined a socialist women's group demanding emancipation,"[4] she is said to have spoken about the sin of radical unbelief. As a highly gifted philosopher, she is said

Joachim Köhler *is a professor of medieval and modern church history at Tübingen, Germany.*

to have believed that "modern science, especially psychology and philosophy, had found the magic formula by which all problems of man and the world could be solved."[5] Since Edith Stein was not satisfied with superficial answers, this phase of her search for knowledge and truth changed when she came to know Adolf Reinach's widow. Reinach was a university friend who was killed in the war in 1917. The pastoral letter then cites the famous quotation that describes the young assistant's first encounter with the cross: "It was at this moment that my unbelief broke down."[6]

This is an important contour in Edith Stein's life: "She stands before us as a human being like ourselves."[7] Suddenly we have second thoughts: Does not this summary of her life convey a lesson? Is it the real life of the student, the assistant, the religious that runs such a clear course, or is it an interpretation of the course of her life to which Edith Stein herself contributed, an interpretation of her own life, inspired by the doctrine of perfection?

Indeed: The two essential quotations from this first paragraph of the Lenten pastoral are interpretations that she expressed in her reflections about her life. Her first biographer, Sr. Teresia Renata Posselt, introduces these quotations with an imprecise word "later." She even questions whether Edith Stein "ever prayed for the grace of faith. She herself said later: 'My longing for truth was a prayer in itself.'"[8]

I don't intend to cast doubt on the fact that Edith Stein expressed herself in these or similar words, but this quotation has been handed down by the Mistress of Novices, Sr. Teresia Renata Posselt, who had her own way of playing on words and her own power of expression and has thus, as her first biographer, contributed considerably to the received view of Edith Stein.[9]

Concerning the second quotation, which tells of the first encounter with the cross in connection with the widow Anna Reinach, Sr. Teresia Renata Posselt says: "This revelation which Sr. Benedicta made to a priest only a short time before her death, she concluded with the words, 'Therefore at my clothing I could express no other desire than that of being called in the Order *of the Cross*.'"[10] One ought to give thought to what may have moved Edith Stein in her innermost self so "shortly before her death," and how an extraordinary situation can influence and change one's interpretation of one's own life.

That holds true especially for that quotation with which the Lenten letter expresses the young student's renunciation of Socialist and emancipatory temptations. The monastery in Echt possesses notations made by Edith Stein in connection with conferences held during spiritual exercises, which P. Johannes Hirschmann had given from September 3 to 7, 1941. On the third day, after the eighth conference, she wrote: "State of my soul prior to conversion: Sin of radical unbelief. Salvation purely by God's mercy, without personal merit. Remember this often to become humble." [11]

We might wonder whether this quotation does justice to Edith Stein's total personality, since by its fixed chronology and spiritual dimension it could omit certain biographic traits. Emancipation of woman was important to the student, the assistant, and the instructor, and she expressed such thoughts in her lectures and writings prior to her entry into Carmel. These ideas don't disappear in Edith Stein's cloistered existence. The Cardinal hoped that "many young people could find themselves in Edith Stein," by rediscovering those ideas.[12]

2) The awareness that God dwelled within her is the second message that the cardinal transmits to us with the quotation "God within us, and we in him, that is our share in the kingdom of God." [13] Doubtless Edith Stein lived in these mystical traditions that were developed in Pauline theology and in the course of history. The remark that this awareness was "for Edith Stein a great consolation, especially at difficult moments," [14] offers an opportunity to speak once more of this awareness as a vivid experience in the context of the life of the Carmelite.

3) It is the vocation of the nun "to stand before God for all." [15] The Cardinal places this quotation, from a letter that Edith Stein wrote on May 14, 1934 from the Cologne Carmel to her college friend Fritz Kaufmann, as a motto above the third message of Edith Stein. Höffner has reinterpreted the saying "God in us, we in him," to apply to the individual, "You in me, I in you" [16] and determined that the realization of this motto is to be found in the nun's answer to God's call. Then the cardinal develops the idea of sin and sin offering, as Edith Stein consciously claimed it as her own since about 1939. The cardinal contrasts it with the present-day situation, saying

"Nowadays some people don't like to hear the word 'expiation.' They demand protests and the use of force."[17] Was the idea of expiation in such a radical form not a consequence of the fact that in the time of National Socialism the church did not take up the challenge of Edith Stein for solidarity of Christians with the Jews who had to suffer persecution? For, before Edith Stein offered herself as a sin offering "for her threatened and humiliated Jewish people,"[18] she had taken several steps to call the attention of the church, and those in positions of responsibility in the church, to the fate that was to engulf Jews and Christians alike. But this message was not understood at that time.

4) "Wedded to the Lord in the sign of the cross"—this sentence, which Cardinal Höffner chose as motto for his fourth message, is taken from the language of mysticism and is an expression of nuns on a very high spiritual level. This quotation is from a letter of Edith Stein to a friend, the Ursuline Mother Petra Brüning in Dorsten. The letter was written on December 9, 1938 in Köln-Lindenthal.[19] Here, too, we may ask whether this idea expresses "the valid style of Christian being" here and now,[20] for the Lenten pastoral letter is not directed to religious, but to parishioners. In connection with this, Edith Stein's course of suffering is described. After *Kristallnacht* Edith Stein had to leave the Cologne Carmel. "In order not to endanger the Cologne Carmel, she arranged to be taken to Holland during New Year's night 1938, where the Carmel of Echt welcomed her affectionately."[21] In 1941, the Dutch Catholic bishops protested, together with representatives of the Protestant churches of Holland, against the deportation of the Jews. "Edith Stein had to die, because the Nazi rulers wanted to take revenge against the Catholic bishops who had publicly defended the rights and dignity of every person, including the Jews."[22] At this point in the Lenten pastoral message there is a reference to the joint pastoral letter of the German bishops of August 19, 1943, about the Ten Commandments as a law of life for the nations, and the following sentence is quoted:

> Killing is evil in itself, even when it is allegedly done for the public good; to guiltless and defenseless retarded or mentally ill, incurable, or mortally injured people, those with hereditary

illnesses or newborn infants with birth defects, guiltless hostages and unarmed prisoners of war or other prisoners, or persons of different race or origin.[23]

Apparently this quotation is meant to give the reader the impression that the German episcopate stood up for the Jews just as courageously as the Dutch bishops. In reality this pastoral letter of August 19, 1943 was a belated and last-minute proclamation of the entire episcopate in the years of Hitler's regime, which came about only because the majority of the German bishops had disregarded the concerns of Cardinal Adolf Bertram, the chairman of the Conference of Bishops in Fulda. All earlier demonstrations of episcopal unity, "over which a struggle had been going on for months, with much seriousness, anxiety and hope," came to "a lamentable end."[24]

Father Ludwig Volk, the most knowledgeable concerning the sources about the bishops during the Nazi period, has pointed out that Bertram, in an earlier text intended for publication, had by his own deletions, eliminated:

> ...that which could have made the Lenten letter (of Passion Sunday 1943) into a document of solidarity. Thus, however, the proclamation was deprived of its singular character and that remarkable quality extinguished that would have elevated it to an eminent sign of dissent, pointing the way in an hour of breakdown of law and oppression of the church.[25]

Even if the Lenten pastoral letter of the Cologne cardinal tries to sketch the stages in Edith Stein's life, there remain gaps in the portrayal, which finally create the impression that Edith Stein was an extraordinary human being, and not a human being like us. The "substance" of history on which saints thrive, the historical basis on which persons become saints is not so straightforward that we could distinguish good from evil without any trouble. In the case of Edith Stein that might mean that the difficulties that were placed in her path should be sought only outside of the church, in the godlessness of her student days, in the hubris of rational knowledge, in the ideology and brutal power politics of the Nazis. History is not that simple. God writes straight with crooked lines. Meticulous historical research shows that a "Catholic unity" existed neither in the time of the Weimar Republic nor during the Third Reich, even though one can read about it in documents of the time and in sworn statements of today. The contemporary historical background is very diffuse. But only against this diffuse background can we put the statements of Edith Stein in their proper perspective; only thus can we fully comprehend her actions and activities, her readiness for expiation and suffering and her martyrdom. To recognize Edith Stein as a "companion in human fate" we must read her biography in its historical context. In the following pages, a few facets from the life of Edith Stein are used to illustrate the rich, multilayered, differentiated life of this Carmelite, in order to clarify the conditions for sainthood.

Edith Stein—A Political Person

Edith Stein was a political person, and she remained so in her thinking even when she withdrew from the world. The withdrawal into Carmel was not a withdrawal into a pious niche. The withdrawal had been forced on her by the "coup." Carmel became a place of self-realization for her. Not for a moment did she acknowledge the Hitler regime in order to save her religious life. On the contrary: solidarity with the sufferers became one of the strongest motives for her life in the convent. An essay by Sr. Waltraud Herbstrith, titled "A German Patriot," sheds more light on the issue.[26]

Before she entered Carmel, Edith Stein occupied herself with the issue of women's rights—definitely in an emancipatory sense. In a lecture before professional women she pointed out women's political significance in public life:

> The postwar years have demonstrated with mounting clarity that just as private life and public life are intertwined with one another for better or for worse, so is the life of each particular nation and state with that of the others.... The nations of Europe that engaged in a life and death struggle with one another, fell together. For all of them the hard facts of poverty make them realize that only together they can rise again.[27]

Edith Stein demanded that women participate in politics. She welcomed the fact that an international women's petition dated February 6, 1932, demanded that many contemporary women should see the cause of peace and understanding among nations as their cause.[28]

The background of these political statements can be elucidated if one looks at Edith Stein's contacts with the archabbot of Beuron, Raphael Walzer. First, however, the archabbot would have to be removed from the twilight in which he is generally regarded, when one connects him to the Benedictine abbots Ildefons Herwegen in Maria Laach and Albert Schmitt in Grüssau.[29] In his political insight into the events surrounding the Nazi rise to power in 1933, Walzer differed from those abbots who were not unfriendly toward the National Socialist movement. His political astuteness became his undoing. He had to resign as archabbot. Raphael Walzer, for his part, had contact with Eugen Bolz, the President of the State of Württemberg from whom he got information about the political and economic events at the end of the Weimar Republic. The church did not appreciate this concern for politics, and from 1933 on it was generally condemned as "political Catholicism." When we read up on Raphael Walzer's statements about Edith Stein,[30] however, we won't notice anything of his political astuteness. That has to do with the fate of Raphael Walzer, whose life ought to be reevaluated.

Fateful Solidarity with the Jewish People

After her entry into Carmel Edith Stein felt fatefully tied to her family and her Jewish people. This solidarity is an essential ingredient in her attitude of sacrifice and expiation. This solidarity is part of her personality; it clarifies her idea of sacrifice. It remains to be investigated whether Jewish traditions play a part in this aspect of Stein's character. In considering Edith Stein's sacrificial attitude, one must acknowledge that there were also victims who did not have much time to reflect, who were carried off by the brute force of National Socialism as by a natural disaster. National Socialism is often portrayed as though it erupted over Germany like a catastrophe of nature and buried many victims under its force. The way in which Edith Stein saw herself as a sacrifice has nothing to do with such thinking. Few people recognized as clearly as she that this catastrophe was caused by human beings: it was a catastrophe that was bound to develop from insignificant beginnings. We can only understand her statements about offering herself as a voluntary sacrifice if we explain this clearsightedness, this sober sense, this political astuteness. The fate of Edith Stein renders absurd all attempts to separate political resistance and religious belief. Edith Stein's statements about having taken the sacrifice upon herself consciously and voluntarily are important because they correct the superficial interpretation of her entry into the convent as a flight from danger. Edith Stein's letters are a wonderful testimony to her concern for her family: "My brothers and sisters and their children...are in great trouble. I must pray that they find a home on earth as well as in eternity,"[31] she wrote to one of her acquaintances on August 12, 1938. Powerless and deeply concerned because she could not help, she worried about each single member of her family.

> My brothers and sisters are also very much in need of prayers. The sister who remained in Breslau [Elfriede Tworoger] was transplanted to the country where, with eleven other ladies, she is housed in an attic room and obliged to an eight-hour work shift. She is assigned to a sewing room. My eldest brother [Paul] and his wife live with the expectation of a similar compulsory action. So far all the attempts made by our relatives in America to get them over there have been in vain. They report the facts without complaint.[32]

Images from the Old Testament rise within her to interpret her solidarity with her family:

> [I trust] in the Lord's having accepted my life for all of them [relatives]. I keep having to think of Queen Esther who was taken from among her people precisely that she might represent them before the king. I am a very poor and powerless little Esther, but the King who chose me is infinitely great and merciful. That is such a great comfort.[33]

The thought of sacrifice finds its final completion in her religious name. In 1938 Edith Stein confesses that she had chosen her religious name "a Cruce" (of the Cross) already as a postulant:

> I received it exactly as I requested it. By the cross I understood the destiny of God's people which, even at that time, began to announce itself. I thought that those who recognized it as the cross of Christ had to take it upon themselves in the name of all. Certainly, today I know more of what it means to be wedded to the Lord in the sign of the Cross. Of course, one can never comprehend it, for it is a mystery.[34]

The text of the sacrificial offering, which Edith Stein wrote down for the prioress of the Carmel in Echt on Passion Sunday 1939, has to be read against the background of the flight from Cologne and the uncertain future:

> Dear Mother, please, will [you] allow me to offer myself to the heart of Jesus as a sacrifice of propitiation for true peace, that the dominion of the Antichrist may collapse, if possible, without a new world war, and that a new order may be established? I would like it [my request] granted this very day because it is the twelfth hour. I know that I am a nothing, but Jesus desires it, and surely he will call many others to do likewise in these days.[35]

An Initiative for the Rescue of the Jews

In her essay of December 18, 1938, "How I Came to the Cologne Carmel," Edith Stein reports a mishap that she experienced in 1933. She had forgotten her house key and could not get into the Collegium Marianum where she was living. A Münster teacher offered to let her spend the night in his house. While his wife made the bed, the host began to relate "what American newspapers had reported concerning cruelties to which Jews had been subjected. They were unconfirmed reports," says Edith Stein. She continues:

> True, I had heard of rigorous measures against the Jews be-
> fore. But now a light dawned in my brain that once again God
> had put a heavy hand upon His people and that the fate of this
> people would also be mine. I did not allow the man who sat
> opposite me to notice what was going on inside of me. Appar-
> ently he did not know about my Jewish descent. In similar
> cases, I would usually enlighten the others immediately. This
> time I did not do it. It would have seemed to me like a breach
> of their hospitality if I had disturbed their night's rest by such
> a revelation.[36]

That was not a game of hide-and-seek, but consideration.
Immediately thereafter Edith Stein traveled to Beuron, just as she
had done every year since 1928. There she celebrated Holy Week
with the Benedictine monks. "This time," she reports in 1938, "a
special reason drew me there. During the past weeks I had constantly given thought to whether I could do something about the
plight of the Jews. Finally I had made a plan to travel to Rome and
to ask the Holy Father in a private audience for an encyclical."[37]
Edith Stein, however, never had a chance to get to see the pope.
The Holy Year was being celebrated. She abandoned the trip and
instead submitted her request to the Holy Father in writing. In her
report of 1938 she stated: "I know that my letter was delivered to
the Holy Father unopened; some time thereafter I received his
blessing for myself and for my relatives. Nothing else happened."[38]
And she adds, from the perspective of 1938: "Later on I often
wondered whether this letter might have come to his mind once
in a while. For in the years that followed, that which I had predicted for the future of the Catholics in Germany came true step
by step."[39]

The German Bishops and the Jewish Problem

The pope, the German bishops, and German Catholics
altogether were very far from such sensitive observations and from
realizing that their actions might deter disaster for Jews and Catholics alike. On March 31, 1933, the director of the Deutsche Bank,
Oscar Wassermann, went to see Cardinal Bertram, the chairman

of the Fulda Conference of Bishops, with a letter of recommendation from Bernhard Lichtenberg, the Canon of Berlin. He requested that the episcopate intervene with the Reich president and with the Reich government to rescind the boycott that had been instituted against all Jewish businesses. In a circular to the rest of the bishops Bertram communicated his misgivings about this intervention:

> My misgivings concern the fact that: 1) this concerns an economic conflict in a sphere which is not closely related to church interests; 2) This step appears as an intervention in a matter that does not directly touch upon the episcopate's responsibility, while the episcopate has good reasons to restrict itself to its own area of responsibility.[40]

We can save ourselves the trouble of enumerating the third and fourth objections. Instead, let us look at the conduct of the archbishop of Munich, Cardinal Michael Faulhaber. The bishop of Augsburg requested that he grant an audience to a certain Justizrat Hofner: "Nowadays these good people are literally clinging to us," Bishop Kumpfmüller wrote to Cardinal Faulhaber in 1933, "If only one could intervene more effectively! They believe the bishops are still the most likely to get results."[41] The reply of the cardinal of Munich was unambiguous:

> I explained to an intellectually eminent, serious Catholic of Jewish birth that at baptism one is expressly told that faith is valuable for eternal life but that no one is supposed to expect earthly advantages from baptism. In spite of that, nowadays people are peddling their pity for the converted Jews from door to door, and I wouldn't think of making a special appeal to the Reich Chancellor on this subject. Therefore I ask that you advise Justizrat Hofner against paying me a visit. Right now we have to put so many fundamental matters in order that we can't possibly make an issue of every single prisoner or person whose job is in jeopardy.[42]

On the other hand, Cardinal Faulhaber had sharply opposed the so-called "atrocity propaganda" abroad. On March 30, 1933, he had written to Cardinal Mundelein in Chicago:

The false reports about bloody atrocities in Germany that
have appeared in American and other foreign newspapers,
and the attacks against the new regime in Germany because of
its fight against Communism have caused the German government to resort to countermeasures. Starting April 1, they are
introducing a strict boycott against all Jewish businesses....
The foreign newspaper correspondents did not consider the
difficulties for German Jews that have resulted from their
newspaper reports. I ask Your Eminence to use all your influence, so that the foreign newspapers which, up to now, have
reported atrocities, make a statement that they have become
convinced of the untenable character of their earlier reports.[43]

Two weeks later Faulhaber could no longer defend the new
regime so straightforwardly. On April 11, 1933, he had received a
letter from Dominican priest Franziskus Stratmann, a university
chaplain in Berlin, which informed him of the cruel reality.
Stratmann reported that:

...especially personnel policy and the persecution of the Jews
makes a mockery of any concept of justice. A barbaric, unprecedented spiritual and material expropriation is being conducted against tens of thousands of innocent, defenseless, and
powerless people, and no authoritative voice is opposing it in
public. It is said that the bishops protested against the expropriation of the aristocrats; why do they keep silent about this
much worse offense?... Dreadful economic, bodily, and psychological abuses occur every day, mainly against Jews and
descendants of Jews. Probably 80% of what is called atrocity
propaganda from abroad is directed against real atrocities.
Every acquaintance with whom one talks about it can testify to
particular cases. I myself have seen, here in St. Norbert Hospital, where I am the chaplain, the bare upper torso of a Jewish
businessman, which showed the gruesome traces of abuse.
This gentleman, who served in the army for four years and was
severely wounded in action, and who was not at all involved in
politics, was beaten with whips and leather thongs, together
with other Jews, on Boycott Day in an SA [i.e., *Sturm-Abteilung*
(storm trooper)] clubhouse for hours, just because he was Jewish. Very reliable people have related numerous similar cases.[44]

Two things in this report are remarkable: 1) that the bishops protested when the nobility were dispossessed during the Weimar Republic; and 2) that, as early as 1933, the persecutions of the Jews were not all that secret.

However, this letter did not cause Cardinal Faulhaber to make a noticeable correction. On the contrary, Faulhaber's previously quoted remarks and the statement that, at the moment, more important matters had to be transacted, were written ten days after Stratmann wrote the cardinal.

There is a theological root to the bishops' inability to show solidarity with the Jews in the face of their persecution. Cardinal Faulhaber, who had been professor of Old Testament in Strassburg prior to his nomination as archbishop of Munich, took the position in his famous 1933 advent sermons in the Munich Cathedral, that the neo-pagan attacks of National Socialism should not rob us of the Old Testament. These sermons, however, did not cause a change in attitude toward living Jews. Faulhaber even postulated a theological disinheritance of the Jews:

> At that time the curtain in the Temple in Zion tore and with it the covenant between the Lord and his people. The Daughter of Zion received her letter of divorce, and since then, eternal Ahasuer[45] wanders restlessly through the world.... These books are not written by the Jews, they are inspired by the spirit of God and are therefore divine words and divine books.... A dislike of the Jews of today must not be transferred to the books of pre-Christian Judaism.[46]

Behind such utterances lie the ideas that the church is the true Israel, and that because the Jews have no future, they also have no history. Such utterances helped prepare the way for the elimination of the Jews. Thus the defense mechanism of the Catholic community was weakened. Therefore a solidarity among the persecuted could not arise. Although, since 1936, the Catholic Church considered itself a persecuted church, the bishops continued to distance themselves theologically from the Jews. According to the pastoral letters of 1939 by Archbishop Gröber of Freiburg and by Bishop Hilfrich of Limburg, the Jewish people are considered guilty of deicide. Since the day of the crucifixion that people allegedly stands under a curse. Such differentiations led to conflicts of conscience. "Spiritual resistance on the inside, obedience on the outside."[47] The Catholic Church accepted the bearer of governmental power even in the totalitarian state and obeyed him as its lawful sovereign. As an organized entity the Catholic community did not wish to take risks on behalf of other groups.

An Encyclical Against Racism and Anti-Semitism

In her notes of the year 1938, "How I Came to the Cologne Carmel," Edith Stein recorded the following remark: "For in the years that followed, what I had predicted for the future of the Catholics in Germany came true step by step."[48]

Despite the escalation of the persecution of Jews, the initiative of the Roman Curia to take a public stand on the madness of racism and on anti-Semitism petered out...[49]

The Example of the Dutch Bishops

From the very beginning, the Dutch Church and Dutch Catholics clearly distanced themselves from National Socialism. In a pastoral letter of February 2, 1934, the bishops strongly warned the faithful against the dangers emanating from the National Socialist movement. They forbade church functionaries to become active in the National Socialist movement. They wrote:

> Though it may be true that the Fascist and National Socialist parties in our country do not directly advocate the totalitarian state, we must point out several great dangers which emanate from these parties... [The Fascist and National Socialist parties] place practically unlimited power into the hands of a few people who offer no guarantee, cannot offer a guarantee that the rightful demands of the Catholic Church will be respected.... Whoever strives to empower a Fascist or National Socialist party is not sufficiently conscious of his sacred duty.... Whoever thinks that he must follow his own views despite these our warning words, should know that he will have to take responsibility before God and his conscience for his shortsighted

presumption.... The bishops cannot and will not permit persons who perform functions that are directly under their jurisdiction, or as representatives of Catholic Action, to be active in behalf of National Socialism or Fascism or to join one of these groups. We therefore forbid membership or active participation to our priests and religious leaders of Catholic organizations or Catholic institutions, as well as all who work in the Catholic school system or are under the jurisdiction of the bishops.[50]

On May 10, 1940, Hitler's armies attacked Luxembourg, Holland, Belgium, and France. Germany's so-called "Western Offensive" lasted only a few weeks. Holland was beaten in five days. At first the occupation forces hoped to find friends or even allies [in Holland]. Hitler permitted Dutch prisoners of war to return to civilian life. The German civil supervisory administration proceeded very carefully at first. It guarded against provoking the general secretaries who carried out government business in place of the ministers who had gone into exile.

When the occupiers began to enforce the Nazi ideology by bringing the press and politics into line, the climate changed. In October 1940 the first anti-Semitic measures started. Registration of all 150,000 Dutch Jews immediately provoked official protest from the Catholic bishops. Violence against the Jews began in February 1941. Self-defense groups were organized in Jewish neighborhoods. When, after the murder of an SA man, raids were carried out and Jews were mishandled and arrested, armament, rail and shipbuilding firms were paralyzed by strikes.

The bishops also pushed their resistance against the National Socialists by declaring that in future they would deny the sacraments to members of the Nazi movement and their umbrella organizations. The pastoral letter was to be read on August 3, 1941. Threats by the Gestapo against Archbishop DeJong were in vain.

In September 1941, Reichskommissar Seyss-Inquart decreed that henceforth Jewish children could be taught only by Jewish teachers. Therefore, Jewish children were to be removed from their previous schools and to be taught in their own Jewish schools. In the name of all bishops, Archbishop DeJong protested against the exclusion of "non-Aryan" children from Catholic parochial schools. He forbade Catholic school principals to carry out the decree.

From the beginning, the persecution of the Jews had united the Christian churches in Holland for joint action. In February 1942, a joint commission of Catholic and Protestant churches submitted a memorandum to the Reichskommissar condemning the terror of the occupation forces. In it they protested against the imprisonment and deportation of numerous Jews and against the large number of fatalities among the deported. For March 22, 1942, a joint pastoral letter of all churches was to be prepared. Although the Netherlands-Reformed Church yielded to the threats of the security police and did not have the letter read, it protested massively against the restrictions of its rights.

Despite all protests by the population and the churches, the measures against the Jews were intensified. When Jews were ordered to wear the yellow star, Dutch fellow-citizens showed their sympathy with the Jews by wearing yellow flowers in their buttonholes. Posters challenged the Dutch to show their respect to Jews wearing the Jewish star. At least three priests were arrested for wearing the Jewish star.

The first deportations began in July 1942, in an easterly direction. Two days after the deportations began, the church sent a telegram of protest to the Reichskommissar. Thereupon, his representative promised that converted Jews who had belonged to a church prior to January 1, 1941, would not be deported. The churches were not satisfied with this exemption. They decided to go public with this protest. The telegram of protest sent to Seyss-Inquart on July 11 was included verbatim in the pastoral letter. Seyss-Inquart, who had been informed earlier of the contents of the pastoral letter, requested the head of the General Synod of the Netherlands-Reformed Church not to mention the telegram. The Netherlands-Reformed Church was willing to make this concession. In all Catholic and a few other Dutch churches, however, the pastoral letter including the telegram text was read on July 26:

> The undersigned Dutch churches, already deeply shaken by the measures against the Jews in the Netherlands by which they are excluded from participation in normal national life, have become aware with horror of the new regulations by which men, women, and children and entire families are to be

deported to the territory of the German Reich and areas under Germany's jurisdiction. The suffering that this will cause tens of thousands of people, the knowledge that these measures contradict the deepest moral conscience of the Dutch people, but above all the infringement these measures constitute against God's commandment of justice and mercy, compel the churches to implore you not to carry out these measures. In addition, as far as Christians of Jewish origin are concerned it behooves us to make this urgent request because of the fact that by these measures their participation in the life of the church is being cut off.[51]

This declaration is followed by a prayer for the Jews. On the following Sunday a large number of Catholic Jews were arrested and deported. The best-known victim was Edith Stein. The Nazis called this measure a retribution for the pastoral letter. The Protestant non-Aryans—approximately 9,000—were not deported.

The assertion that the resistance to National Socialism and the protest against the persecution of the Jews had not changed the situation, as the example of Holland shows, distorts history.

The detailed portrayal of events in Holland has shown that the situation of the Catholic Church in Holland cannot be compared to that in Germany; with the occupation of Holland, if not before, it should have become clear to the public worldwide that the occupiers used different measures in occupied territories than they did in the Reich. Edith Stein's attempts to get to Switzerland are to be understood against this background. Finally it is inconceivable that the rights of the Carmelite Order could have been placed above human rights.

Hagiography Without Contemporary History?

A glance at the history of that time has revealed human, all-too-human glimpses. It became apparent how Edith Stein, "a human being just like us" matured into her great task. No stage may be skipped here if we wish to continue to experience her as a "companion in human fate." Every detail is important.

To a terrifying extent, however, when we contemplate details of this history, we find Ernst Ludwig Ehrlich's 1984 statement to be confirmed:

> Jews and Catholics were too far apart, spiritually and humanly, to generate solidarity in the face of the Jews' persecution.... Only the downfall of Hitler prevented Christian eyes from being forced open to the Jewish-Christian problem.[52]

Only the catastrophe opened eyes. Did it really do so? In the first Stein biography under the chapter heading: "Edith Stein—A Saint?" Sr. Teresia Renata Posselt cites the following report about a teacher and an answered prayer. According to the teacher, it was "a very remarkable report": She had held a novena for Sr. Teresa Benedicta a Cruce (Edith Stein) and on that occasion lit a candle in the Cologne Carmel for a man who stood before a court of law.

> It was a former school inspector, my superior, who as a former Nazi stood before a denazification court for the third time. Since 1945, he had already served three years in an internment camp and for two years had literally starved because he received not one penny of a salary or pension. The proceedings were to decide once and for all whether he would ever get a pension or remain a welfare recipient for life.[53]

Since this former Nazi was a Protestant, the teacher was hesitant to let him know about her pious efforts. Finally she wrote to him: "As a visible expression of my caring and good wishes for you, a candle is being lit in the Carmel of Cologne on August 29. May its quiet light illuminate the Nuremberg proceedings."[54] The teacher's report continues:

> This letter reached the hands of the defense attorney. He copied the sentence and quoted it publicly as the last sentence in his defense address. It is so strange to imagine this sentence spoken during a public proceeding—and its effect is even stranger: The defendant burst into tears—everyone was moved. From then on the hearing turned in his favor. In half an hour all obstacles had been removed. Even though he was district leader and had been found guilty in two prior trials,

he was designated a "fellow-traveler" and will shortly receive his pension. How marvelous that Sr. Benedicta has helped a Nazi, of all people.[55]

...Edith Stein herself had a different perspective on history. On August 28, 1939, Edith Stein wrote the following lines to the philosopher Peter Wust in Münster, who had fallen ill with cancer of the larynx and subsequently died of this disease:

> I was deeply moved that the suffering involves for you the very organs with which so many sins are committed today. It seems to me like a call to make a particular kind of reparation. Such a call is an extraordinary grace. I believe that such suffering, when it is accepted with a willing heart and carried to the end, is reckoned before God as a true martyrdom. It is in this sense that I remember you before the Lord. I beg him for strength also for your dear relatives, for whom the sacrifice is surely even harder than for you yourself.[56]

This letter is perhaps one of the most important messages to all who wish to venerate Edith Stein as a Blessed. If we seek a "Christian lifestyle valid here and now," then that must be, following this message, "like an invitation to a labor of reflection and mourning."[57]

Monument in Echt bearing the names
of Edith and Rosa Stein

Sister Edith Stein:
A Rabbi Reacts

by Nancy Fuchs-Kreimer

Edith Stein was an extraordinary philosopher and mystic who died at Auschwltz at the age of 51. Although she faced lifelong discrimination as both a woman and a Jew, she was able to establish herself as an accomplished German academic—the prize student and assistant to the great phenomenologist Edmund Husserl. In Germany today, the name "Edith Stein" is everywhere: schools, libraries and streets bear her name.

By all accounts, Stein was a woman with a deep and luminous soul. "From the moment I met her, I knew: here is someone truly great," said a Dutch official at the Nazis' Westerbork camp, echoing an almost universal sentiment. "Talking with her was like...journeying into another world."

Hundreds of people pilgrimaged to Stein for spiritual guidance. "I find great happiness," Stein wrote, "whenever someone arrives here all worn out and battered, and then goes away with a measure of consolation." A friend corroborates Stein's sentiment: "The more wretched a person was, the more pleasure [Edith] felt in seeking him out as one of God's favorites."

Still, Stein's life-choices complicate a Jewish effort to understand her, because not only was she an adult convert to Catholicism, but in 1933 she became a nun in the Carmelite order. The Catholic Church (interpreting Stein's martyrdom at Auschwitz in its own fashion) recently beatified her, and in time, she may be canonized.

I found myself reading a recent biography (written by another Carmelite sister), *Edith Stein: A Biography,* by Waltraud

Nancy Fuchs-Kreimer *is a Reconstructionist rabbi with a Ph.D. in Jewish-Christian relations.*

159

Herbstrith (San Francisco: Harper & Row, 1985), with a confusing mix of emotions. On the one hand, I felt proud of this intellectual, spiritually gifted woman. On the other, as someone seeking Jewish women role models, I felt abandoned and betrayed. Her baptism in particular—in an era of such extreme Jewish vulnerability—feels almost like an act of treachery.

Why *did* Edith Stein turn to Christianity? As the eleventh child of a family headed by a pious Jewish woman who was widowed shortly after Edith's birth, Stein and her family struggled against enormous financial and emotional odds. Like her daughter after her, Stein's mother had a strength-giving faith in God that sustained her through difficulties.

As an adult, Stein—a devoted daughter, sister and aunt— struggled for many years with the wrenching incompatibility of the joy she found in Christianity and the pain she was causing her family. Even after her conversion, she loyally attended Jewish holiday services with her family; she wrote loving, weekly letters to her mother. Although the intensity of the bond between Stein and her mother raises more questions than it resolves, this biographer would have us dismiss the hypothesis that Stein left Judaism in order to separate from her family-of-origin.

Converts from Judaism often wish to abandon what they perceive as a narrow and parochial community, but this was not the case for Stein. She always considered herself a proud member of the Jewish people and she admired traditional Jewish life. Immediately upon entering the convent, Stein began her autobiography with the purpose, she said, of educating readers about Judaism and thus combatting anti-Semitism.

In 1933, Stein requested a private papal audience (it was declined) in the hopes of convincing the Pope to take action on behalf of Jews, and she referred to herself (using a Jewish metaphor long after she became a Christian) as being like "Queen Esther, separated from her people just so she could intercede before the King." While this role was not the catalyst for her conversion, it certainly underscores that Stein was not fleeing Jewish identity. When Stein and her biological sister (also a convert) were taken from the convent to Westerbork, she said, "Come, Rosa, we are going for our people."

As a university student, Stein, enchanted with secularism, studied psychology and philosophy and gave up Jewish religious practice. Soon, however, she found herself among a circle of university intellectuals who were questioning the orthodoxies of science, rationality and philosophy. The first religious books to capture her adult interest were by medieval Catholics, beginning with the mysticism of Teresa of Avila, whose autobiography Stein discovered on a friend's shelf and stayed up all night to read.

Personal encounters were also important factors in her jouney towards Catholicism. Once she visited an empty cathedral into which a lone woman entered, Stein wrote, "as if to talk to a friend." A meeting with a young, grieving Catholic widow revealed to Stein how "the Cross triumphs over the sting of death." Finally, the cloistered life of the Carmelite sisters was immensely attractive to her. The structure of contemplation and work made her "radiantly happy," providing her with the "transcendent tranquility" that she sought.

There is a school of thought that holds Christianity to be a religion of love and interiority, and Judaism more strictly a religion of law and duties. Was Stein drawn then to the Church because of these "Christian" qualities? It appears not. For Stein, the love she felt for God and the interior depths she cultivated came to fruition through a commitment to a highly exacting regime of law (that of the nuns), as well as specific daily acts of kindness and devotion in the private and public sphere. In fact, Stein's very life teaches how inadequate this alleged dichotomy is.

On the subject of death, Stein clearly preferred a Christian view over a Jewish one. Three years before her death, she wrote, "I joyfully accept in advance the death which God has appointed for me"—an attitude towards death that is uncongenial to Judaism's "life" orientation. True, Stein's biographer may well have exaggerated the extent to which Stein's martyrdom was voluntary. Also true, Judaism has a concept of *kiddush hashem* (dying to sanctify God). Nevertheless, I believe Stein was correct in understanding that her own approach to death was more consonant with Christianity than with Judaism.

The question that remains for me as a Jew is whether and how Stein sought spiritual nourishment from Judaism before she

turned to Christianity. Unfortunately, this question is not important to Stein's biographer, so we have little information on the matter. We do know that Stein wrote to an Orthodox Jewish friend asking whether he believed in a personal God and that the man's answer—brief and lacking in emotional content ("God is Spirit—
there is nothing more to be said")—felt to Stein "as if I had been
given a stone instead of bread!"

But did she seek further in Judaism? Did she read the Baal
Shem Tov or Maimonides? Did she know of Martin Buber? Did she
attend the Frankfurt Lehrhaus where a brilliant renaissance of Jewish learning was occurring at the very same time as her conversion?
This we don't know.

I suspect that Stein's being a woman had something to do
with the direction of her spiritual journey. When Franz Rosenzweig
was a young philosopher about to abandon Judaism (according to
the theory of Nahum Glatzer), he visited an Orthodox *shul* on the
eve of Yom Kippur and was awakened to the spiritual depth of his
native religion. But would Franz Rosenzweig have remained a Jew
if he had been hurried upstairs to sit behind a *mehitza* that fateful
night? Frankly, I doubt it.

It seems hardly a coincidence that the book that decisively
turned Stein toward faith was written by a woman—Teresa of Avila.
Does a female author of similar stature exist within the Jewish spiritual canon? No. The life with women to which Stein was ultimately
attracted—the paradoxically restricted and liberated life of the
cloistered nun—has no parallel in the Jewish world. The tremendous focus on family which is so characteristic of Jewish life may
have made it even more difficult for a single, 30-year-old, female
philosopher to find adequate models within Judaism.

Still, this is not to say that there were no options for an intellectually brilliant, spiritually ambitious woman within Judaism of
Stein's time, even less to imply that there are no such options today.

What does Edith Stein's story leave me feeling, as a Jewish
woman, a rabbi and a scholar of Jewish-Christian relations? On the
one hand, here is someone who courageously follows what she
takes to be her vocation from God, and who (even allowing for
hagiography) clearly brings godliness into this world. A co-prisoner
at Auschwitz wrote, "It was her complete calm and self-possession

that marked Stein out. She went among the women like an angel, comforting, helping and consoling them," and a novice at Stein's convent remarked that, "At Mass, she seemed to participate as if she were offering herself on the altar." Before such testimonies, I can only be humble.

On the other hand, I am angry when a Jew chooses not to continue to struggle with the civilization into which she was born, however difficult she may find it. I don't understand why Stein didn't wrestle longer and harder with this complicated blessing of Jewishness. And I feel sad and cheated that her profound work as a translator, philosopher, inspirational writer and spiritual director enhanced another tradition and not mine. Judaism needs every great spirit we have to help us in the task of religious renewal. Stories such as Stein's make me feel more committed than ever to ensuring that Jews, particularly women, not be hindered in experiencing the riches of our faith.

Though Stein can never be a role model for me as a Jewish woman, she is still someone from whom I can learn. Her writings about women's roles (suggesting that as we move into the public sphere we stay conscious of our uniquely feminine capabilities) prefigure the most current feminist thought. I am fascinated by Stein's very intense and extensive prayer life; I am intrigued by her career as a spiritual counselor. I would like to know more about that role, and about the way in which we can incorporate some of its functions into contemporary Judaism.

Stein can, after all, in certain ways, be a teacher to us. Though she found her bread elsewhere, we can use some of her leaven in our own Jewish lives.

This article is reprinted with permission from the Winter 1991 issue of Lilith: The Independent Jewish Women's Magazine. *The magazine's subscription and editorial address is 250 West 57th Street, New York, NY 10107 (Phone: 212-757-0818).*

ERINNERE DICH-VERGISS ES NICHT
IM GEDENKEN AN
EDITH STEIN
JÜDIN - PHILOSOPHIN - PÄDAGOGIN
KARMELITIN - MÄRTYRIN
ERMORDET IN AUSCHWITZ-BIRKENAU
AM 9. AUGUST 1942
LEBTE VOM 14.10.1933 BIS 31.12.1938
IM KARMEL KÖLN-LINDENTAL
DÜRENER STR. 89
PFARRE CHRISTI AUFERSTEHUNG
AM 1.5.1987 VON PAPST JOH. PAUL II
SELIGGESPROCHEN IN KÖLN

Memorial plaque in Cologne, Germany

Edith Stein and
Catholic-Jewish Relations
by Eugene J. Fisher

On April 24, 1987, the Bishops' Committee for Ecumenical and Interreligious Affairs of the National Conference of Catholic Bishops (USA) issued a brief "Advisory on the Implications for Catholic-Jewish Relations of the Beatification of Edith Stein." It was addressed to the Catholic community of the United States but formed in response to very serious concerns being raised about the beatification by our Jewish partners in dialogue.[1] To understand what was (and is) at stake in this most sensitive of issues, one needs to see it in the context of the many painful and symbolically powerful events of those years.

It must be recalled at the outset that it was not until the late 1970's that the word "Holocaust" first entered the working vocabulary of most Western languages as a reference to the genocidal attack on the Jews by the Nazis. Before then, although appearing in the work of Eli Wiesel and other pioneers of Holocaust literature, it had been reserved for all practical purposes to professionals in the field and to those actively engaged in Jewish-Christian dialogue.[2] It was in this period, too, that Holocaust survivors first began in large numbers to emerge to tell their long-repressed stories.

The 1980's were in some ways a time of great pain and vulnerability for the Jewish people. Many younger Jews learned for the first time in any detail what had really happened to their parents, grandparents and other relatives during World War II. It had been too painful to be told for three decades, and now had to be told with urgency as the survivor generation began to die out. Into this

Eugene J. Fisher *is Associate Director of the Secretariat for Ecumenical and Interreligious Affairs of the National Conference of Catholic Bishops, Washington, DC.*

mix of raw sensitivities and deep anxiety that the witness could be
lost came the Holocaust deniers, spreading their obscene notion
that the murder of two-thirds of European Jewry had never happened, that it was all just a Jewish and/or Zionist propaganda attack on the good name of the non-Jewish (which is to say largely
Christian) peoples of Europe. While the successes of the denial
movement were quantitatively minor, the very fact that it existed
and had managed to snare a number of otherwise quite reputable
academic and media institutions into taking it seriously as a question
to debate had a profoundly chilling effect on the Jewish community.

Nor was this the only emotionally charged event of the period. On May 13, 1986, Pope John Paul II, continuing his papally
unprecedented quest for reconciliation between the Catholic
Church and the Jewish People, became the first pope ever to visit
the Great Synagogue of Rome, and not just visit, but to pray with its
rabbi and congregation, listening intently to a Jewish homily on the
meaning of Genesis 17 (God's eternal covenant with Abraham,
Sarah, and their descendants). The pope's personal solidarity with
the Jewish survivors of the Holocaust was expressed by the presence
of a large contingent in the congregation, sitting together and
wearing their blue and grey concentration camp uniforms. The
pope, reflecting on a year that saw also the assemblage of leaders
of the great world religions at Assisi on October 27, 1986,[4] concluded the year by lifting up his visit to the synagogue as an "event
that transcends the limits of the year, since it is measured in centuries and millennia in the history of this city and this Church. *I thank
Divine Providence that I was able to visit our 'elder brothers' in the faith
of Abraham in their Roman Synagogue!* Blessed be the God of our
fathers! The God of Peace!"[5]

As 1987 opened, a new period of more positive relations between Jews and Catholics appeared to be on the horizon. It was
announced that preparations were under way for an extraordinary
meeting between representatives of the world's largest Jewish community and the pope during his visit to the United States in September of 1987. Indeed, the pope had decided to begin his visit to
these shores with the meeting with national Jewish leaders in Miami, thus making it and the meeting with ecumenical Christian
leaders later that day the very keystones of the trip.

But the pain associated with the healing of a trauma so vast
and profound as that suffered by the Jewish people during the

Holocaust can intensify even as the healing process proceeds. The announcement of the beatification of Edith Stein was one of a series of events that greatly exacerbated the pain and illustrated how much still needs to be done to bring about a measure of reconciliation between Jews and Catholics after the Shoah. For during this period, also, the controversy over the establishment of a cloistered Carmelite convent in an abandoned theater adjacent to Auschwitz was reaching a crescendo. And during the summer of 1987, just weeks before the scheduled meeting between the pope and Jewish leaders in Miami, the pope received in audience the president of a traditionally Catholic country, Kurt Waldheim, the former General Secretary of the United Nations whose lies about his unsavory Nazi past had recently been revealed.

The Auschwitz convent controversy was not to be resolved until 1993, when the pope personally intervened to ask the nuns to move to a new building that had been built for them a short, but saving distance away. In the meantime, Rabbi Avi Weiss and a few of his students had nearly destroyed the agreed resolution with an ill-advised breach of the convent wall and sit-in on the front porch of the convent itself, precipitating a perhaps equally ill-advised public response by Cardinal Josef Glemp, the primate of Poland. One can add to this volatile mix the general sense of unease left in the Jewish community after the Christian President of the United States, Ronald Reagan, and the Christian President of Germany, Helmut Kohl, met in a cemetery in Bitburg containing the remains of Nazi executioners of Jews to offer a gesture of forgiveness to each other for what Christians had done to Jews during the War. One can also add the misunderstanding precipitated by remarks made by one of Israel's greatest friends in the Church, Cardinal John O'Connor of New York, when in 1989 he was asked by a reporter for his feelings after visiting Yad VaShem in Jerusalem. Deeply moved, the Cardinal resorted to Catholic terminology to describe his feelings, was misunderstood, and was blasted in a virtually unprecedented joint Jewish statement issued on the Sabbath as he was flying home from Israel.

It is not coincidental that all of the great controversies between Jews and Catholics of the late 1980s and early 1990s revolved, like a hurricane spinning on its axis, around the Holocaust. Profoundly religious symbolism, such as nuns at prayer and the cross at Auschwitz, the meaning of "forgiveness" and the pope as the "Holy

Father" for Catholics and a symbol of Christian misdeeds for Jews, became almost inextricably entangled as event after event sparked hurtful rhetoric from both sides of what should have been a dialogue.[6] Jewish reaction to Edith Stein and Catholic reactions to the expressions of Jewish concern thus need to be understood within this larger picture. They need also to be placed in the perspective of the tremendous progress on the part of the Catholic Church in implementing in its liturgy and classrooms the renewed vision of its understanding of Jews and Judaism begun by the Second Vatican Council's declaration, "Nostra Aetate" in 1965.[7]

Briefly put, since they are spelled out elsewhere in this volume, Jewish statements on the beatification and, now, declaration of sainthood of Edith Stein revolved around two central concerns. On the one hand was the concern that declaring a Jewish convert (note: *not a convert from Judaism,* since she had stopped practicing her faith long before her conversion!) to be a saint might precipitate Catholics to launch massive efforts to convert other Jews. We have seen just recently the understandably emotional response of the organized Jewish community to the resolution adopted by the Southern Baptist Convention during its 1996 meeting in New Orleans. That resolution, efforts for which seem to have been spearheaded by so-called[8] Messianic Jewish congregations within the Southern Baptist fold, raised for most Jews medieval and more recent memories of Christian efforts to convert Jews that, once launched, almost inevitably lead to abuses and even to forced conversions, too often resulting in Jewish martyrdom at the hands of fanatic Christians.

The second Jewish concern lay in the nature of the Holocaust and in how it is to be remembered by future generations. This is the fear that by pointing such a bright spotlight on a Christian victim of the Holocaust, the Catholic Church might be in some way trying to turn itself, in history's memory, into its chief victim, thus at once glossing over the historical culpability of so many Christians in the deed and, in effect, appropriating the Holocaust as primarily an event of Christian martyrdom. Both of these concerns are present in Jewish reactions to the sanctification of Edith Stein just as they were at her beatification. Both were addressed by the pope at the beatification and in subsequent papal references to her over the years since then. Both were also addressed by the April 24, 1987, statement of the National Conference of Catholic Bishops' Ecumenical and Interreligious Committee (BCEIA). Here, since it is important to establish a benchmark to judge whether Catholic teaching materials have been responsive to legitimate Jewish concerns such as these, is what the Bishops' Committee on Ecumenical and Interreligious Affairs said:

> We see the beatification of Edith Stein as a unique occasion for joint Catholic-Jewish reflection and reconciliation. In honoring Edith Stein, the Church wishes to honor all the six million Jewish victims of the Shoah. Christian veneration of Edith Stein does not lessen but rather strengthens our need to preserve and honor the memory of the six million.
>
> Catholic veneration of Edith Stein will necessarily contribute to a continuing and deepened examination of conscience regarding sins of commission and omission perpetrated by Christians against Jews during the dark years of World War II, as well as reflection on those Christians who risked their very lives to save their Jewish brothers and sisters. Indeed, it was in retaliation for a public letter by the Dutch Catholic Bishops protesting the deportation of Jews that Edith Stein was picked up by the Nazis and sent to Auschwitz. Through the beatification of Edith Stein the Church calls all Christians today to join with the Jewish people in opposing any and all forms of anti-Semitism.
>
> Catholic respect for the integrity of Judaism and for the ongoing validity of God's irrevocable covenant with the Jewish people is solidly founded on our faith in the unshakeable faithfulness of God's own word. Therefore, in no way can the beatification of Edith Stein be understood by Catholics as giving impetus to unwarranted proselytizing among the Jewish community. On the contrary, it urges us to ponder the continuing religious significance of Jewish traditions, with which we have so much in common, and to approach Jews not as potential "objects" of conversion but rather as bearers of a unique witness to the Name of the One God, the God of Israel. As the Holy Father declared during his visit to the Rome Synagogue: "Jews and Christians are the trustees and witnesses of an ethic marked by the Ten Commandments, in the observance of which man finds his truth and freedom' (April 13, 1986). Celebration of Edith Stein's own witness can only serve to enhance the Church's sense of the significance of the 'spiritual bonds' (*Nostra Aetate*, no. 4) which link us to the Jewish people.

In my experience watching the devotion to Edith Stein in the Church over the last decade since the beatification, the basic guidelines developed by the BCEIA have been well observed. There has never been any hint of an organized conversionary effort using her name being developed among Catholics.[9] Nor have the educational and devotional materials that have been developed around Blessed Edith Stein sought in any way to diminish the Jewish reality of the Shoah. Rather, they stress that the Nazis who killed her did so because she was a Jew, no more and no less than the rest of the six million. They stress that the killers of Edith Stein and, by extension, the perpetrators of the Holocaust were, by and large, baptized Christians even if it cannot be said that they were practicing Christianity in perpetrating mass murder. They stress the guilt of Christians and call all to repentance, even as they point to the saintliness of the life and death of Edith Stein.

A decade may not be a long time in the life of the church or the Jewish people. But it may be sufficient to begin to have an idea of how the Church in future generations will understand her, not as a figure of Christian triumph, but as a goad to Christian humility.

Finally, as I have tried to show here, Saint Edith Stein is herself but one of many modes of self-reflection that the church has and will set up for herself in the wake of "the century of the Shoah." Already declared Blessed, for example, is Bernard Lichtenberg, the Rector of the Catholic Cathedral in Berlin, who Sunday after Sunday rose to preach against anti-Semitism despite warnings from the Gestapo, who was arrested and mistreated so badly that he died on the way to internment in Dachau. He is a clear model for how Catholics should act in such times though, again, far too few followed his example.

Will the sanctification of Edith Stein be good in the long run for Catholic-Jewish relations? I believe I have reason to hope that it will. But it will not erase the pain and the ambiguity—moral, historical, and symbolic—that encrusts the heart of the dialogue at this pregnant point in time.

Dr. Eugene J. Fisher
Washington, DC, 1997
This article was written especially for the
English-language edition of Never Forget.

The Canonization of Edith Stein
by Daniel F. Polish

As the church celebrates the canonization of Edith Stein we hear expressed the hope that she will serve as a bridge to Catholic-Jewish understanding. I fear she will not do that. I do hope that she will serve another, no less useful, purpose: as witness to the very real differences of perspective that still characterize these two communities of faith.

Whereas at one time, the focus of the discussion about Edith Stein was on the question of whether it was prudent or proper for the Catholic Church to beatify her, or later to canonize her, the question to be asked today is in what light she will now be viewed by the church, and in what terms presented by it.

The central irony of what has become the *problem* of Edith Stein would have no more than personal ramifications were it not for the role in which the Catholic Church has chosen to cast her. Her beatification, and now canonization, have caused this personal dilemma to be thrown into the arena of public discussion and debate. It serves to highlight one of the many areas of significant disagreement between the Catholic Church and the Jewish understanding. Thus, while we cannot embrace the notion that Edith Stein will serve as a bridge, we can see the occasion of her canonization as opening a door to significant discourse. For if this moment offers us the opportunity to explore this area, it will have served constructive purposes.

At the heart of the dilemma posed by Edith Stein is a terrible paradox and a question. The paradox is that while for Hitler there

Rabbi Daniel F. Polish *is the rabbi of Vassar Temple in Poughkeepsie, NY. His article on the beatification of Edith Stein in the October, 1987, issue of* Ecumenical Trends *won a Catholic Press Association Award.*

was no way one could cease to be a Jew, from a Jewish perspective one can choose to leave Jewish life. The question is one posed to the Catholic Church. Put most starkly, it is which understanding of Jewish identity will it choose to embrace: that of Edith Stein's murderers, or that of the Jewish people themselves?

To elaborate on this paradox, it is clear that in the eyes of those who executed her, Edith Stein was a Jew. For them she died as a Jew. She came from a Jewish family, and was thus deemed to be racially Jewish. To the Nazis, it made no difference that Edith Stein had converted to Christianity. To Jewish self-understanding, on the other hand, that fact made all the difference. While a nonpracticing, even nonbelieving, Jew is considered to be Jewish, one who embraces another faith is understood by Jewish teaching as renouncing Jewish faith and must, as a consequence, be considered no longer a Jew. Thus the painful paradox and the dilemma that while Edith Stein died precisely because the tormentors of the Jews considered her to be Jewish, to those in the midst of whom she suffered and died she cannot have been deemed a Jew at all.

The Catholic Church in choosing to canonize Edith Stein for her death among the Jews of Auschwitz seems to be rejecting the Jewish community's definition of itself and not respecting the boundaries that that community has established for itself. I find it suggestive that many Christian discussions of the life, work, and role of Edith Stein make use of the phrase "Jewish-Christian" to describe her, while that phrase appears in absolutely none of the Jewish discussions. This disparity is far from accidental and in no way incidental. It leads us to the heart of why Edith Stein's canonization is so problematic to the Jewish community.

Implicit in the Christian comfortableness with the locution "Jewish-Christian" seems to be the belief that one can embrace Christian faith and remain, in some way, part of the Jewish people. From the perspective of Jewish self-understanding, this is an impossibility. One cannot be a Jew and a Christian. To Jews the phrase "Jewish-Christian" is an oxymoron. The sadness of Edith Stein's family at her conversion to Catholicism, the sense of abandonment and betrayal that they expressed, and emotions that attend such perception characterize what Jews will commonly feel about any person who has chosen the same path Edith Stein did. Not lovely emotions, perhaps, but humanly understandable. They underscore the boundaries that a Jew transgresses when he or she chooses to become a Christian.

Whatever religious choices Edith Stein made for herself must be respected, as her family ultimately came to do, as her own personal affair. The use to which the Catholic Church puts this personal decision transforms it into a subject of public discourse.

The employment of the phrase "Jewish-Christian" to describe Edith Stein, especially in light of the exalted place in the Catholic Church to which she has now been elevated, suggests to some that there is a programmatic purpose to which her memory is being put. More than one skeptical voice within the church itself has noted that the church seems to have a saint drawn from the ranks of every ethnic and national group from which it wants to elicit loyalty and devotion. Irish, Italian, Polish, Gypsy groupings each have their respective "voice at the table." Against such a background, unpleasant as it may be to articulate so baldly, is it possible to ask if Edith Stein might not be intended as a vehicle by which Jews could be made to feel comfortable within the body of the church?

The perpetuation of the concept "Jewish-Christian," and the elevation of Edith Stein to serve as its incarnation, raises uncomfortable associations for Jews who remember the relentless efforts of the Catholic Church throughout much of our shared history to entice, bully, extort, seduce, or legislate Jews to leave the faith of their ancestors and embrace Catholicism.

At this time when the church has taken such strides away from accusations of deicide, the doctrine of supersession, and the practice of spiritual imperialism, such a role for Edith Stein seems an anomaly. It seems more of a piece with efforts in other sectors of the Christian community to mount energetic efforts to "win Jewish souls." Christianity is, after all, from its beginnings, a missionary movement. It has always had a genius, absent in Judaism, for marketing itself—packaging its teachings to make them attractive or palatable to various "market sectors." If Jews feel reluctance or guilt at leaving the Jewish people, is it too far-fetched to imagine a church, endowed with such a genius for marketing, consciously or unconsciously, intentionally or accidentally, reframing its identity and proffering the notion that one can believe as a Christian without ceasing to be a Jew?

The locution of "Jewish-Christian" is more easily understood as serving the purposes of such a program than by any other explanation for its usage. Could there be any wonder that it causes Jews unease and concern? One can understand the Jewish reaction, then, to the canonization of Edith Stein when she is held up as the embodiment of this category.

If the motivations of the church are as innocent as it claims, if it truly wants to take advantage of Edith Stein's canonization to signal its enduring respect and love for the Jewish people—its commitment to the validity of their independent religious path—I would be bold enough to put forward a suggestion. The suspicion and pain raised by this matter will not be resolved until the church takes the theologically complicated step of officially disavowing the need or value of Jewish conversion to Christianity and taking the action it has heretofore been unwilling to embrace, of officially renouncing all programs of mission to the Jews on its own behalf or by any Christian body. Granted, this would require a very different self-definition than the church has had in the past. It may, however, be a way of self-understanding that is emerging for all religious traditions in this time of cultural interpenetration.

In any case, absent such actions, a cloud of suspicion will always hang over the church's motives in choosing Edith Stein for canonization. Along with those suspicions will be the presumption that in focusing its anguish about the Shoah on the fate of one saint, it is seeking to avoid coming to terms with its own role in creating a culture of Jew-hatred in Europe, and its complicity, in some measure, with the fearsome events of the Shoah itself. It also leaves in the air a presumption that the church seeks to cast the tragic events of the Shoah in its own terms, and put them, ultimately, to the service of its own purposes.[1]

Rather than serving as a bridge between these two communities of faith, the canonization of Edith Stein, in evoking widely disparate interpretations, threatens to underscore remaining issues that divide them. Unless addressed constructively this event may well have the effect of moving them further apart and reversing the positive and fruitful strides that have been made in recent years. For the death of Edith Stein, who was born a Jew and died a Christian (which was, in personal terms, a tragedy), to have the effect of further alienating Jews and Christians from one another compounds her tragedy exponentially.

On one issue Jews and Christians will agree. The paradox of the Christian Edith Stein, being done to death because her persecutors considered her to be a Jew, teaches a terrible lesson about the consequences of group hatred. None can afford to stand by impassively when any group is singled out for abuse. Edith Stein's death reminds us what happens when group hatred is unleashed. Once set to its murderous task, the *golem* of contempt, distrust, and hatred cannot be kept under control, nor its energies focused. It takes a course of its own devising that none could predict or even imagine.[2] That a Catholic nun should die among the Jews of Auschwitz is a cautionary symbol to which all can respond. Perhaps from such a shared understanding some modicum of hope may be derived. The light of such a moment will not shine as bright as some might imagine or wish, but it can light the way to a more hopeful future.

Rabbi Daniel F. Polish
October, 1997
This article was written especially for the
English-language edition of Never Forget.

Victor J. Donovan, CP, receiving the Edith Stein Award
October 15, 1960, Roosevelt Hotel, New York City

l.r.: Erna Biberstein (Edith Stein's sister), Victor J. Donovan, CP,
and Sol Rosenbaum (president of the Edith Stein Guild)

Edith Stein and the Edith Stein Guild
by Victor J. Donovan, CP

The question has often been asked: What effect will the canonization of Edith Stein have on Jewish-Christian relations in this country? I will leave that to the sociologists to answer. My purpose in writing is simply to testify to the effects I have seen in speaking as a member of the Edith Stein Guild of America. The work of the Guild has brought me into contact with both Jews and Christians. I can vouch that many men and women have asked more and more often for information on this Carmelite nun who offered her life at Auschwitz.

She has also been to me what Beatrice was to Dante in guiding him through the various regions of *Paradiso,* after having seen *Inferno* and *Purgatorio.* In my ninety years I too have seen the equivalent *Inferno* and *Purgatorio* in Jewish-Christian relations in the years prior to World War II. People were so suspicious of motives then that when rabbis and priests were observed talking together in public, many wondered who was trying to "convert" whom.

Pope John XXIII is often credited with having changed such an attitude of fear between Jews and Catholics. He astounded the world by introducing himself to a group of Jewish visitors to the Vatican in five simple words: "I am Joseph, your brother!" This marked a new beginning in the church's relationship with the synagogue. The pope went on to convoke the Second Vatican Council that same year. The changes wrought by that council are still being felt thirty-five years later.

What was Edith Stein's contribution to the changes in the church? Ultimately, only God knows. However, we should not forget that she wrote a letter to an earlier pope, Pius XI, in an attempt

---

Victor J. Donovan, CP, *is a Passionist priest and a founder of the Edith Stein Guild in New York.*

to have action taken on behalf of her people. She urged him to issue an encyclical condemning Nazi anti-Semitism. She was later assured that her appeal had been received by His Holiness. Her letter remained a long time in the Vatican files. It acted like a silent reminder to later historians of what might have been.

The world today knows the awful price paid because so little attention was given to her warnings: millions of lives lost, thousands of hospitals built to care for the permanently disabled, cities destroyed, only to be rebuilt at an astronomical cost to later generations.

My first experience of Edith Stein's influence came only after I had glimpsed what it meant to be a Jewish refugee. On August 25, 1939, while another priest and myself were studying the German language in a monastery near Regensburg, we received official notification from the American Consul General in Munich to "depart from Germany immediately." War was imminent. Long lines of flatcars weighed down with tanks, guns, and trucks were moving toward the Polish border.

We wasted no time, boarding the first train for Zürich, Switzerland. War broke out within a few days, on September 1, 1939. We returned to our monastery in Rome, where we stayed until the following spring. We then caught the S.S. Washington in one of the last sailings from Genoa to New York. Space was at a premium. We doubled up to make room for all the Jewish refugees who had bought passage. They were willing to put up with anything in order to escape the Nazis.

I made friends with some who spoke English. They gave me my first lessons in what it meant to be a Jew in Germany under Hitler. Their descriptions of the November 9 *pogrom,* called *Kristallnacht* because of all the broken glass covering the streets, were terrifying. That night marked the end of any hope for Jewish survival in Nazi Germany. Jewish stores and homes were shattered. Synagogues were set aflame. The sacred scrolls were dragged from the tabernacles and strewn about the streets. When rabbis tried to rescue their sacred scrolls, they were clubbed down. The police stood idly by, while firemen kept watch lest Christian property be burned.

By the time the S.S. Washington docked in New York harbor, I knew that I had made a most unusual five-day retreat. It did not consist in sermons given by an eloquent missionary, but in a collection of stories told by Jewish refugees who spoke with deepest emotion. I felt akin to St. Paul on the road to Damascus, hearing the words: "Saul! Saul! Why are you persecuting me?" The cry "Why are you persecuting me?" still rings out today; only the names have changed.

The resolution I made at the close of my "retreat" was to seek ways of passing my experience on to others. Knowledge was not enough. A personal interest in individual people was needed. Books gave bare statistics about the suffering of European Jews, with numbers rising horrifically until they reached six million dead. But nothing affected me as powerfully as these individual stories, among them Edith Stein's.

She and I seemed to be following paths that would soon converge. I was sent to the Catholic University of America in Washington, DC, to gather material for a course in Sacred Scripture for first-year seminarians. The course was supposed to include study of the first five books of the Hebrew Bible, known as the *Torah* (or the *Pentateuch* in Christian circles). This required some elementary knowledge of the Hebrew language. Needless to say, I sought divine intervention!

Thus, on August 18, 1942, began twenty-two years of teaching in the field of Jewish history. Later I would learn that this was less than a fortnight after the deaths of Edith Stein and her sister Rosa at Auschwitz on August 9. Some called it pure coincidence. I prefer to agree with the rabbi who once said: "There is no such thing as pure coincidence with God. Coincidence is God's way of manifesting his will in human affairs."

From time to time, as I taught the course, I invited Jewish neighbors to come and speak with our seminarians. There seemed to be a mutual interest in learning more about each other. I also accepted invitations to join Jewish families on such occasions as Passover seders and weddings. The students always greeted my return with numerous questions. I shared with them what I had learned. This method showed good results at examination time. They may have failed to memorize the Hebrew alphabet, but they had learned to look upon the Jewish people not as strangers but as friends.

We ran the risk of being misunderstood in those days, prior to the outreach of Pope John XXIII. Several times I was reported as denying my faith because I had taken part in a seder supper with a Jewish family. That I encouraged my students to do the same was a double fault. Conditions improved slightly after the halfway mark of the twentieth century. Christian churches showed more serious efforts at ecumenism, and also began to involve their Jewish neighbors.

American Catholic interest in the Jews made several strides forward in 1955. First, the Edith Stein Guild of America was founded, in an upper room of an apartment in Jackson Heights, New York. Then came the American editions of Hilda Graef's *The Scholar and the Cross*, and John Oesterreicher's *Walls Are Crumbling: Seven Jewish Philosophers Discover Christ*. Both books opened new channels in Catholic-Jewish relations, and both contained the first serious studies in English of Edith Stein, who died as a Discalced Carmelite nun, Sr. Teresa Benedicta of the Cross, in the concentration camp of Auschwitz.

Of these events, the founding of the Guild was to prove most beneficial. The small founding group of fifteen men and women became living words of truth. They knew that anti-Semitism was a moral sickness that thrived on ignorance. They had agreed on three simple objectives: 1) to foster a better understanding among Catholics of their Jewish heritage (as the pope had said, "we are all spiritual Semites"); 2) To create a better understanding between Catholics and Jews; and 3) to promote the canonization of Edith Stein as a patron and guide in Jewish-Catholic relations.

Convert-making was not included among our objectives (though we were sometimes accused of fostering it). One of the great advocates of reconciliation between Jews and Catholics, the late Rabbi Marc Tannenbaum, had this to say of the Guild in 1987, when he received its "Man of the Year" award: "There is no question of the conversion of anyone with the Edith Stein Guild. Their only questions are: 'Do Christians really take the Gospel seriously?' and "Do Jews really take the Torah seriously?'" Indeed, the only conversion the Edith Stein Guild has been guilty of fostering is the conversion of all people from hatred to love.

The Guild has continued for over forty years to carry on its work of opening people's eyes to see how evil propaganda has poisoned people's minds. Shameful documents like the "Protocols of the Elders of Zion" have been exposed as fraudulent time and time again, yet continue to appear in the most unlikely places. Too often do we decry such slanders but do little about them, and too seldom do we hold ourselves accountable.

The Edith Stein Guild has made use of every possible means to create good relations, including newspapers, radio, television, the internet, videos, slide shows, and (perhaps most effective) public lectures. As cofounder of the Guild I am often invited to speak of our work. I once received an invitation to speak in the synagogue of my home town, to a senior class in comparative religion. My theme was reconciliation between Jews and Catholics. I was only five minutes into my talk when the intercom system broke in noisily with: "Emergency! Emergency at St. Bernadette's! Rabbi Simchas, you are wanted! Emergency!" The rabbi responded immediately, leaving me startled and confused. The students saw how perplexed I was, and explained that every Wednesday afternoon a class of Jewish children crossed the street to attend Hebrew class in one of St. Bernadette's classrooms made available to them by the local pastor. The synagogue needed the extra space.

This was a good example, I felt, of how far we have come in tearing down walls that separate us, and building bridges that unite us. I wrote about this incident in an article for *Priest* magazine, entitled "Getting Across the Street." But Pope John Paul II later outdid me on April 13, 1986, by "getting across 2000 years" in his visit to the synagogue in Rome. His visit, and his staying to worship with the rabbi and his congregation, was an historic occasion. He was setting an example for others to follow. Fostering better relations was no longer something reserved to theologians and scholars, but brought down to the grassroots level. The Edith Stein Guild felt vindicated for all the years we had been advocating a deeper religious dialogue with the Jews.

Many years have passed, and many similar experiences have been stored in my memory. I felt sure that God would eventually reveal the task he intended me to fulfill. To my delight, like Elisha when he prayed for a "double portion" of Elijah's spirit (2 Kgs 2:9),

I was blessed with a "double portion" of Edith Stein, in the person of her sister Erna and her favorite niece Susanne Batzdorff.

Erna's friendliness made it easy to imagine what Edith must have been like. Her soft Silesian accent sounded as if it were coming all the way from Breslau. She was eager to answer all my questions about Edith's love for children, family, and friends. Her face shone with pleasure as she met people who had visited the nuns of the Carmelite convent in Cologne, Germany, where Edith had lived. October 15, 1960, was a day I have long remembered, when Erna stood by my side at the Hotel Roosevelt in New York City as I received the Edith Stein Guild Award for that year. She gave me a broad, understanding smile when I told her she was there as a "stand-in" for her youngest sister, Edith. (As children, they were often mistaken for twins.)

Susanne Batzdorff, Erna's daughter and Edith's favorite niece, was the image of her mother in many ways. She never raised her voice. She spoke slowly and deliberately. She inherited her mother's office of self-appointed family spokesperson and reviewer of articles and books written by her Catholic aunt. She was a faithful guardian of her Jewish religion and would not allow any hagiographical exaggeration of her aunt's Jewish piety. She loved to write verses about Edith, whom she referred to affectionately as "Tante." There was always a note of sadness when she brought up the question of Edith's conversion and entrance into the Carmelite convent.

Susanne deserves everyone's praise for the long hours she has spent translating her aunt's German writings into English. It has been a labor of love. This present volume bears witness to her exacting work. She has been an inspiration to me, even though she has never failed to correct carelessness in my research. Rank and seniority matter little to her.

Our hope for the future of Jewish-Christian relations rests a great deal on the role we assign Edith Stein. Is she to be a bridge, reaching from Christian to Jewish shore? Or will she be a barrier, like the Berlin Wall, keeping Jews and Christians apart? The symbol of a bridge reminds me of a lesson that the late Rabbi Joseph Lichten once taught me. He told me about a pond in Massachussetts to which the native Americans had given a name of twelve syllables, too many for me to remember. But the English translation ran, "We fish on our side of the pond, you fish on your side, and nobody fishes in the middle!" The rabbi used that free translation as an image of what Jewish-Christian relations were like when he was a boy. Perhaps today, in the spirit of Edith Stein, we can make our own paraphrase: "We Christians dialogue with each other on our side, you Jews dialogue together on your side, and we all come together in the middle to dialogue about reconciliation, to make plans, and to pray that our future together will be free of anti-Semitism and racism."

Perhaps Edith Stein can be the bridge from which to do our dialogical fishing. She touches both shores. It is our job to keep all the access roads open, to remove all roadblocks, and to clean away the graffiti of hate and misunderstanding. The greatest bridges built by human ingenuity only link one city to another. Edith Stein helps us join earth to heaven, offering glory to God in the highest and peace on earth to people of good will.

Victor J. Donovan, CP
Holy Family Monastery, West Hartford, CT
This article was written especially for the
English-language edition of Never Forget.

l.r.: Dr. Ronald Kleinman, Simeon Tomás Fernández, OCD, John Sullivan, OCD, on June 6, 1996, the day Dr. Kleinman gave testimony to the Vatican Congregation's medical board.

The Canonization Miracle
And Its Investigation
by Kieran Kavanaugh, OCD

Before canonizing anyone as a saint, the Catholic Church normally requires evidence not only of that person's heroic virtue, but also of one or more miracles attributable to the candidate. The reputation for sanctity itself, in the Catholic view, results from the direct movement of God to inspire the faithful to believe that a particular servant of God is worthy of imitation and intercession—thus worthy of being considered a saint. But in addition to the human investigation and judgment concerning the individual's heroic virtue, a sign from God is sought. The miracle provides evidence that the candidate's renown for sanctity is authentic and of divine origin. Obviously the miracle must come through the intercession of the candidate.

The number of miracles required for beatification and canonization has diminished over the years. The Apostolic Constitution *Divinus Perfectionis Magister* ("Divine Teacher and Model of Perfection"), which went into effect on January 25, 1983, lightened the miracle requirement to a total of two: one for beatification and one more for canonization.

Once a cause has reached the point at which only a miracle is needed to advance it, nothing further can be done, humanly speaking, but to pray and wait for the miracle. The waiting may go on and on and never come to an end, since the next phase no longer depends on human effort. What can be done, and is done, by the promoters of a cause is to encourage the faithful to pray to the servant of God or blessed for a miracle (usually a physical healing), as

Kieran Kavanaugh, OCD, *is a noted authority on Carmelite spirituality, and served as vice-postulator for the canonization of Edith Stein.*

a sign that God works or continues to work through the intercession of the candidate. Since the process by which the church investigates a miracle is scarcely known, it may be helpful to explain in some detail the events and procedures that led to the approval of the miracle needed for Blessed Edith Stein's canonization.

The Illness and Sudden Recovery of Benedicta McCarthy

As earlier essays have indicated, the long and exacting investigation into the heroicity of virtue practiced by Edith Stein resulted in a positive judgment by the church. On January 26, 1987, in the presence of the Holy Father, John Paul II, the Decree confirming both the heroic degree of virtue and the martyrdom of Edith Stein was read. On May 1, 1987, Pope John Paul II beatified Edith Stein as a martyr in Cologne, Germany.

Some six weeks before the beatification, Father Emmanuel Charles McCarthy, a priest of the Melkite rite (which permits the ordination of married men), and his wife Mary, parents of twelve children, returned home on the evening of March 20 after a retreat in Rome. It was the first time they had left the children for any more than a few hours in almost twenty years of marriage. The two oldest college-age children were at home on vacation sharing the duties of caring for the younger children. When the parents arrived home, some of the children came out to meet them and informed them that the youngest child, Benedicta, was sick and that Kristin, the oldest daughter, was with her at Cardinal Cushing Hospital in Brockton, Massachusetts.

When Benedicta, who was two and a half years old, arrived at the hospital it was first thought that she had spinal meningitis. She was semi-conscious and limp. While the different tests were being carried out, acetaminophen was discovered in her blood, something that was not being looked for or even suspected. According to Mrs. McCarthy's report of what she heard from other doctors, Benedicta had more than sixteen times toxicity level in her blood, and her liver was five times the normal size. Because of her critical condition, Benedicta was transferred by ambulance to

Massachusetts General Hospital in Boston where she could receive the best treatment. Benedicta's condition looked so bad the next day (Saturday) that the McCarthys feared she was dying. Her kidneys were also beginning to fail. In the middle of Saturday night the phone rang. It was the hospital saying that Benedicta now had an infection that made her case even more serious, if that were possible. The next day Mrs. McCarthy found that Benedicta had been given a paralyzer (muscle relaxant) so that she could be put on a breathing machine. She had suffered a rough night and the doctors had been in and out of her room working on her. A transplant team of doctors came to speak with Mrs. McCarthy. They informed her that Benedicta was in critical condition and had urgent need of a liver transplant, and that if they had a compatible liver available they would proceed with a transplant at once. There was no liver available, but they had put Benedicta on the highest priority across the nation to receive one. They explained to Mrs. McCarthy that there was only a 50% survival rate with a transplant and that if Benedicta did survive, she would have to be on medication for the rest of her life.

The day before, Mrs. McCarthy had been speaking on the telephone to her sister, Teresa Smit, about Benedicta's condition. It was her sister who asked if Benedicta hadn't been named after a woman recently proposed for beatification. Benedicta had been born on August 9, the day of Edith Stein's death, which is now the feast of Teresa Benedicta of the Cross. Teresa Smit then suggested that they pray to Edith Stein, Benedicta's patron. When this was mentioned to Fr. McCarthy, he concurred that the family should pray to Edith Stein for Benedicta's cure.

On Sunday afternoon, March 22, about 5 P.M., Mrs. McCarthy put her hands over the area of Benedicta's abdomen where her liver was located and prayed, "Dear Heavenly Father, in the name of your Son, Jesus Christ, through the intercession of Edith Stein, if it be according to your will for your greater glory, may Benedicta's liver return to normal size and normal functioning. Amen." She repeated this prayer one or two more times. All the McCarthy's solicitous friends, calling to ask about Benedicta, were requested to pray to Edith Stein for the little child's cure.

When Mrs. McCarthy arrived at the hospital on Monday, a couple of doctors from the transplant team stopped to tell her that there was a change in Benedicta's liver and that if a liver were to become available at that moment, they would hesitate to transplant it. The doctors felt they should wait at least twenty-four hours to see the status of Benedicta's liver before they did the transplant. By the end of the week, Benedicta had completely recovered. Several of the doctors and nurses were amazed. "It's a miracle," more than one said. Benedicta left the hospital without a single prescription.

Public Interest in the Cure

News of the extraordinary recovery reached a reporter from the Maine Catholic weekly, *Church World.* At first Fr. McCarthy hesitated to provide information, fearing what the consequences of such publicity might be. But Mrs. McCarthy felt favorable toward allowing publication of the story. The remarkable account appeared in the Maine paper on May 14, 1987. It was later published in *The Catholic Digest* (October 1988) and in *Carmelite Digest* (Winter 1988).

The Carmelite Digest also published an article ("Asterisk to a Miracle," 1988), written by Fr. McCarthy, about how the only other patient in the pediatric intensive care unit when Benedicta was brought in was a little boy, unconscious and dying of a heart problem. After learning about Benedicta's condition, the boy's mother offered her son's liver for a transplant for Benedicta, which was not possible because of the condition of the child's liver. At about 5 P.M. on Saturday, Benedicta went completely unconscious and her "numbers," which were the figures of the dying when she arrived, kept going down. At about 8 P.M. the little boy's grandfather came over to Fr. McCarthy and in a low voice asked: "Father would you do us a favor? We have decided to let 'our little fellow' go home to God tonight. Would you mind coming over and saying a final prayer for him?" While Fr. McCarthy was praying over the little boy he felt inspired to anoint him. Afterward the grandfather said "You know, Father, it's odd you should be here saying the final prayer for 'our little fellow.' Because you know, we're a Jewish family. But when my son married my daughter-in-law years ago, she was a Catholic. So when our little boy was born she went out and had him baptized."

In April of 1991, when I traveled to Rome for our general chapter, Fr. Simeon Tomás Fernández, our postulator-general for the causes of saints, asked to speak with me. He knew I was living in Boston at the time. People interested in the cause of Blessed Edith Stein had been sending him news about the miraculous cure, and he had begun gathering information about it. He showed me the folders of material that he had collected. They contained all the medical records, reports of the events written by Fr. McCarthy and Mrs. McCarthy, and the articles that had appeared in the press. He wanted my opinion of the materials, for it seemed to him, as it did to me after reading them, that the cure was worth investigating. But I had no qualification as either a nurse or a doctor, and was without experience in working for the causes of saints.

The Investigation of a Presumed Miracle

Fr. Simeon asked me to assist him by taking on the position of vice-postulator for the investigation of the miracle. Miracles must be investigated in the diocese in which they occur, and the presumed miracle took place in the archdiocese of Boston where I was residing. In August of that year, Fr. Simeon came to Boston and taught me the procedures that must be followed in the inquiry into a presumed miracle. He had exceptional experience in dealing with the Congregation for the Causes of Saints. As postulator for ninety-two causes throughout the world, not all of them Carmelite, he had steered many of them to a successful conclusion. Not only did he have the practical skills but he had remarkable determination and persistence, qualities necessary for a postulator.

After my mini-course, the first thing to be done was to compose a letter to Cardinal Bernard Law of Boston petitioning him to open a tribunal to investigate the cure. In this letter we had to give our reasons for thinking the cure of Benedicta was miraculous and worth investigating. Through the director of intensive care and pediatric nursing services, we had by that time found the doctor who was the attending physician in Benedicta's case. Dr. Donald J. Medearis wrote in a letter to the director that he was enclosing a letter from Dr. Ronald Kleinman. He said that Dr. Kleinman was the expert and that he agreed with Dr. Kleinman's judgment of the case after reviewing the chart. Dr. Ronald E. Kleinman in that enclosed letter of April 22, 1991 explained in medical terminology what happened in Benedicta's case and in the end concluded: "All in all I would say that her recovery was remarkable. Awesome or miraculous would also be appropriate descriptors. As you can see from the notes in the chart, we were fully prepared for liver transplantation at the time; expecting that she probably would not recover liver function."

One of the serious hurdles in the investigation of a presumed miracle is to find a doctor willing to come forward and make statements or cooperate in an inquiry. What proved fortunate was Dr. Kleinman's distinguished position as associate professor of pediatrics at Harvard Medical School. Then, in August of 1991, *U.S. News & World Report* published a study conducted to ascertain the ten best hospitals in the nation. Massachusetts General Hospital ranked number three among the top ten, surpassed only by Johns Hopkins Hospital and the Mayo Clinic.

At the beginning of September, I received a call from the judicial vicar of the Boston archdiocese, Msgr. Robert P. Deeley, saying that the cardinal had told him to contact me about initiating the investigation and setting up a tribunal.

In establishing a tribunal, the local bishop, having judicial power in his own diocese, usually delegates a judge to take his place, who in this case was Msgr. Robert P. Deeley. Besides a judge, the tribunal needs a promoter of justice (who must also be a priest) and a notary. Fr. Michael Smith Foster was appointed the promoter of justice and Loretta Celucci the notary. A doctor also must be appointed either by the bishop or the delegate judge, preferably by the bishop. The doctor must assist at the interrogatory sessions especially to help in dealing with the medical facts. James F. McDonough, M.D., agreed to serve in this position and was named by the cardinal to the tribunal.

My duties at this time consisted of gathering witnesses and preparing the questions that needed to be asked. In the investigation of a presumed miracle it must be established that a miracle truly took place and that the miracle occurred through the intercession of the Servant of God or Blessed whose cause is being promoted. While looking for help with the drafting of the medical questions, I discovered that when little Benedicta was in the throes of the crisis the housestaff at Mass General Hospital made several phone calls to experts on acetaminophen overdose at the Rocky Mountain Poison Center. The experts there advised that in three to five days there would be a resolution of the hepatic injury. They held that if Benedicta survived this period she would have a histologically normal liver in thirty days.

I thought this meant the end of the road for our inquiry since we had here an explanation for Benedicta's cure. But I soon learned that during the investigation into a presumed miracle it is not unusual to receive conflicting opinions, especially before all the information has been collected. The diocesan inquiry is a fact-finding one. In consulting Dr. Kleinman further we learned that although the information from the Poison Center was correct, it did not apply in Benedicta's case. I then continued preparing the list of questions for the witnesses. When the list was finished, the promoter of justice, as required, studied the questions, made the changes he thought opportune, and signed them. The scope of the interrogatory was to ascertain: a) the seriousness of the illness; b) the occurrence of a sudden cure, unexplainable through medical science; and c) whether the cure could be attributed to the intercession of Blessed Edith Stein.

We then arranged an opening session at which the cardinal was present along with all the members of the tribunal. The purposes of the opening session are to confirm the members of the tribunal, have each take an oath to fulfill his or her duties faithfully, receive a list of the witnesses presented by the postulator, and indicate the time and place for beginning the interrogation of the witnesses. The chancellor read the letter of request by the postulator that an inquiry into the presumed miracle be made and the decree of the cardinal by which he appointed the tribunal. Everyone then accepted the office to which he or she was named, and took an oath to fulfill this office faithfully and diligently.

At this opening session Cardinal Law told us of an aunt of his who had been a Discalced Carmelite nun and had prayed for his vocation. He was interested in the cause of Edith Stein and favored

our taking time away from many other pressing matters to carry out
the investigative work as best we could.

We had to be careful to follow all the procedures exactly because when an inquiry is ultimately finished and sent to Rome, the
first thing examined is whether all the procedures were followed
correctly. If they were not, the cause cannot move forward until the
matter is remedied.

I had gathered all the medical records; a summary of them
was also made. Since the handwriting of the doctors and nurses on
the daily charts would be illegible to European doctors, it was necessary to have this handwritten material typed out by someone familiar with medical charts. Fortunately, among the Discalced
Carmelite nuns in Danvers, Massachusetts (outside Boston) were
five nurses. They quickly prepared for us a typed copy of the handwritten notes.

In the second session all documents (medical records, personal testimonies, and so on) are presented by the vice-postulator.
At the invitation of the delegate judge I had to take an oath that I
was delivering without interpolation or falsification all the documents in my possession relative to the presumed miraculous cure,
and then sign it. The notary had to certify every page of every document with her seal. Minutes had to be kept for each session; any
further documents submitted are put at the end of the session. The
witnesses were then called in one at a time. Each was made aware
of the seriousness of the inquiry and asked to take an oath, swear-
ing on a bible: "In the name of God. Amen. I [name] swear to tell
the truth, the whole truth, and nothing but the truth regarding all
that I will be asked about concerning the presumed miracle attributed to the intercession of Blessed Edith Stein. So help me God."

When the interrogation was finished, the witness could add,
delete, correct, or modify. When ready to approve the account,
each witness took another oath to confirm the truth of what was
declared ("I swear to have told the truth in what was declared") and
signed his or her name.

During the interrogations, the judge, the promoter of justice,
and the doctor may ask questions. The secretary must note who
asked the question. The witnesses may also prepare some written
material they may want to submit. I presented eight witnesses. Besides the witnesses presented by the postulator, at least two others

had to be presented (ex officio) by the judge; this brought the total number to ten.

It was clear from hearing the family witnesses that they thought Benedicta was near death and that a cure was sought for her through the intercession of Edith Stein. Of course, from the medical viewpoint, the key witness was going to be Dr. Kleinman. When Benedicta McCarthy arrived at Massachusetts General Hospital, he was the physician responsible for patients admitted to children's services with gastrointestinal liver problems. In his testimony he declared that he was Jewish and that he had never heard of Edith Stein. He pointed out that when Benedicta was brought to the emergency room, she showed signs and symptoms indicating that a significant part of her liver had been seriously injured and wasn't functioning adequately. In fact this evolved to such a point that she was not only in liver failure, but in kidney failure, and in a coma. She was close to death. He was aware that most children under the age of five recover even from very serious acetaminophen poisoning. The reason Benedicta's case was unique was that she, unlike most children, went into multi-organ system failure. It was at that moment that a team of doctors began to consider the liver transplant. And then Benedicta started to recover spontaneously. Her kidney function improved. Her sensorium cleared, she awoke, and then gradually her liver function improved as well. The recovery was permanent and no further treatments were necessary. Doctor McDonough then asked Dr. Kleinman, "In your estimation do you think that her recovery was something extraordinary?" Dr. Kleinman answered, "Yes, it was extraordinary." The questioning went on with terminology that was beyond me: metabolytes, encephalopathy, bilirubin, excitatory inhibitory transmitters, transaminase. As to whether the acetylcysteine administered could have been effective in Benedicta's recovery, Dr. Kleinman pointed out that this treatment wasn't begun early enough to be effective and that the child's disease would not have progressed as it did if it had been. And to the follow-up question, "It [the recovery] all seemed to have happened within a period of twenty-four hours?" Dr. Kleinman answered, "That's right. Yes."

Another requisite in the process was that two physicians be appointed to examine Benedicta and give a report on her present state of health. After examining Benedicta both doctors testified that she was in good health and functioning at a level appropriate for her age. They found no physical evidence or residual effects of her toxic acetaminophen ingestion.

The Study in Rome

According to the procedure, after all the evidence is received, two certified copies of the process must be delivered to the Congregation for the Causes of Saints. In a closing session, at which the cardinal was present, the notary presented both the original acts and the two certified copies of the process. The promoter of justice declared that he had no objection to either the original copy of the process or the copies made from it. The cardinal and the delegate judge declared the integrity and authenticity of both the original and the copies. The original process, closed and sealed, is conserved in the curial archives of the archdiocese. The certified copies of the same, closed, sealed, and signed on the outside by the cardinal, were consigned to the vice-postulator that he might present them to the Congregation for the Causes of Saints. I delivered a package of two authentic copies to the Apostolic Nunciature in Washington, D.C., for delivery to the congregation. The boxes with the original acts and the copies to be sent to Rome were sealed with wax and the diocesan seal.

At the closing session when the cardinal asked Dr. McDonough if he had an opinion from the investigation about the cure, the doctor answered that he thought that the cure could be approved as a miracle. The secretaries said that it was a miracle they got all the work done the way it was supposed to be done. This closing session took place on April 26, 1993. Delivered by diplomatic pouch to the Vatican, the process was opened there and studied to ascertain whether everything was validly done. Once the materials were approved, the testimony had to be translated into Italian and a summary of the most relevant facts of the whole case presented along with a copy of the whole process in what is called the *positio*. The huge oversized volume came to 768 pages.

Not until January 1995, a little less than two years later, did I receive word of the outcome. It is the custom of the Congregation to give the *positio* to two doctors to examine. If one out of the two favors the miraculous nature of the cure, the *positio* is given to three other doctors. Two out of these three doctors must approve.

Fr. Simeon informed me that the first two doctor consultors to whom the *positio* had been given voted negatively on the miracle. They were of the opinion that since Benedicta had received the proper treatment and that 95% of children recover from an overdose of acetaminophen poisoning if treated properly, Benedicta's cure was naturally explainable. Fr. Simeon asked me to translate the negative reports of the doctor consultors so that he could send them to Drs. Kleinman and McDonough for their opinions and written comments.

Drs. Kleinman and McDonough agreed to write their opinions regarding the conclusions of the doctor consultors in Rome. In his response Dr. Kleinman pointed out carefully the many reasons why Benedicta did not belong in the category of those 95% who recover but to the 5% of acetaminophen poisonings that progress to death. Dr. McDonough in his response explained how he had consulted with many experts in the field and had come to concur with Dr. Kleinman.

These responses were so impressive that the consulting doctors in Rome desired to clarify some further points and discuss the entire case with Dr. Kleinman. Dr. Kleinman flew to Rome in early June 1996 and met with a team of five Italian doctors who interrogated him about the case. He said "it was no piece of cake." In these discussions questions arose about how Benedicta got the Tylenol and when. As a consequence, Msgr. Deeley and I were asked to take some further sworn testimony from one of the McCarthys who had some recollections in this regard. Because some in the family had the flu, the Tylenol had been taken down from a safe place where it had been stowed on Wednesday. It was extra-strength Tylenol, it had been in reach of Benedicta, and empty wrappers were seen close to the package. Her sickness began on Wednesday night. Her older sisters thought she had the flu, but no one gave her any Tylenol. This testimony was sent to Rome at the beginning of October 1996.

On January 16, 1997, a meeting of five doctor consultants was held to examine the entire case in the light of Dr. Kleinman's clarifications and this new information. Now it was clear that Benedicta belonged to the 5% who do not recover from an overdose of acetaminophen. The dosage had gone sixteen times beyond the toxicity level and the acetylcysteine was administered too late to be effective in her cure. In addition, Benedicta could have also had the flu, which would have added to the seriousness of her condition. This time all five doctors gave similar opinions and the vote came out unanimous in favor of the medically unexplainable character of the cure.

Clearly the McCarthys and their friends had prayed to Edith Stein for the cure. No one thought the theologians would find any difficulty in their examination of the case. And this proved so; on February 25, 1997, the theologian consultors of the Congregation approved the miracle. On March 25, 1997, Pope John Paul II approved the miracle for the canonization.

Both the causes of Louis and Zélie Martin, St. Thérèse of Lisieux's parents, and of Blessed Elizabeth of the Trinity have many enthusiastic supporters among Carmelites and others. But all that can be done is to wait and pray until God through a miracle gives his sign to go forward to the next stage, either beatification or canonization. Other reports of cures through the intercession of Edith Stein were received, and if the cure of Benedicta McCarthy had not been approved, the postulator would have had to investigate these to see if any of them had merit enough to warrant an official inquiry. However, I am happy that the cure of Benedicta McCarthy has been accepted by the church as miraculous because investigating a presumed miracle and obtaining its approval is, to quote Dr. Kleinman, "no piece of cake."

Washington, DC, 1998
This article was written especially for the
English-language edition of Never Forget.

Part II

*A Great, Exceptional Personality:
Edith Stein Remembered*

Martin Honecker, Freiburg

Max Müller

My Reminiscences of Edith Stein

Freiburg, 1988

In 1931, on behalf of my advisor, the philosopher Martin Honecker, I had three conversations with the philosopher Edith Stein, to discuss with her her qualification to teach at a university. Both Professor Heinrich Finke, whom Edith Stein had approached through a reference from Sr. Adelgundis Jaegerschmid, and Edmund Husserl were in agreement with Edith Stein's wishes. Martin Heidegger, too, is said to have reacted positively. I was at the time academic assistant to Honecker. He was an absolutely honest person, upright and responsible. Honecker surely spoke to Edith Stein repeatedly; I had only supplementary discussions with her....

When I met Edith Stein, she was very attractively dressed. She appeared to me full of joy, feminine, charming, and full of hope for a university career. She appeared delicate, but not small. Her facial traits were balanced, her expression not pessimistic. Her eyes were especially expressive. I was very disturbed when I learned two years later that she had entered "the strictest women's order in the church." It did not seem to me to suit her *joie de vivre*.

Honecker had given Edith Stein hope for a *habilitation,* but had told her that both his doctoral candidates, Gustav Siewerth and myself, must not suffer disadvantage as a result. Realistically, that meant that Edith Stein would have to wait at least two to three years. Since she had no salary after leaving Speyer, Honecker tried to find her a fellowship through the Görres Society, where he was a General Secretary of long standing. He also suggested that she prepare a major scholarly work for her *habilitation.* Edith Stein called this work *Act and Potency.* It was to be an examination of phenomenology and Catholic philosophy. Edith Stein saw this work as her special task at the university.

Max Müller *is a professor of philosophy in Freiburg, and cofounder of the Christian Democratic Union (CDU).*

Edith Stein asked me about possibilities within the philosophy department. Siewerth and I, at the time, had almost completed our doctoral dissertations and wanted to become university lecturers after that. Edith Stein, therefore, was in third place. When one considers in retrospect that after Hitler's assumption of power, from 1933 to 1935, there was a cessation of all new admissions to the faculty in Freiburg, this would have been an additional unfavorable factor for Edith Stein. As a Jew she had no chance after 1933 anyway. In 1936, admission to *habilitation* was reopened, and both Siewerth and I were able to obtain favorable habilitations. Heidegger was Second Examiner for both of us and gave his approval for both. But what good did it do me when Heidegger testified to my good character and teaching talent and philosophically excellent achievements, but characterized me as questionable with regard to the ruling ideology of National Socialism?

When I talked to Edith Stein in my parents' apartment, we discussed the exciting work of the day, Heidegger's *Being and Time*. I remember that Edith Stein said it was "a magnificent work, but very foreign to me." Later on she wrote an empathic but very critical analysis of Heidegger's existential philosophy as a supplement to her main opus, *Finite and Eternal Being*.

Husserl called Heidegger his most ingenious disciple. Although he realized that Heidegger's thinking led away from his own, he proposed him in 1928 as successor for his teaching position in Freiburg. At first, Alexander Pfänder of Munich was under consideration. But already in 1930, in his postscript to his *Ideas,* Husserl decisively rejected Heidegger's work. Objectively seen, therefore, the break originated with Husserl.

After 1933, Husserl was isolated from the university. On occasion, Honecker asked me to visit him [i.e., Husser], so that his connection to the department would not cease. During these conversations, Husserl appeared to me cheerful and relaxed. Outwardly, at least, he had coped with the unquestionably shocking events of 1933. He took daily walks in the Sternwald with his private assistant Eugen Fink, who remained loyal to him under the Nazis. Husserl avoided political topics. His wife Malwine, on the other hand, appeared worried to me. She did not tolerate the anti-Semitic discrimination against her husband well, especially since they had lost a son for the German fatherland in World War I.

One cannot say that Heidegger acted directly against Husserl during the Nazi period or that books were burned in Freiburg. However, in the second edition of *Being and Time* his dedication to his former teacher was removed. That happened, however, against Heidegger's wishes, as the publisher Borgmeyer confirmed. Most of the faculty members did not dare to visit Husserl or attend his funeral.

The phenomenologist Fritz Kaufmann was a wonderful man. He had been admitted as a university lecturer under Husserl in 1927. As a Jew, he, too, had no opportunity in the Third Reich. Later, Kaufmann emigrated to the United States. My contact with him continued even after the Second World War. He came ever closer to religion. I had great esteem for Hans Lipps, phenomenologist and physician, but I knew him only through his writings. Someone wrote a doctoral dissertation under my supervision on the philosophy of yet another friend of Edith Stein, the phenomenologist Roman Ingarden from Cracow. Ingarden's transcendental realism was closer to the realism of Edith Stein than to the transcendental idealism of Husserl.

In 1928 Heidegger published Husserl's *Lectures Concerning the Inner Consciousness of Time.* This work had been prepared by Edith Stein, but her name was not mentioned. Heidegger deliberately issued this work of Husserl one year after the publication of his own work *Being and Time* in order to show the difference between his analyses of time and Husserl's. Husserl spoke of "inner consciousness of time," of the "flow of time," of "the transcendental and universal ego." Heidegger's concept of time was, for Husserl, no longer transcendental/phenomenological, but existential/anthropological.

Anthony Mertens

My Reminiscences of Edith Stein

Bruges, 1988
...During my university vacations, I sometimes took small gifts and money to the Roermond Carmel at my mother's request. At such times I spoke with Mother Antonia, an intelligent, amiable and very pious nun. I complained to her that I had to pursue—in my view—senseless studies, while all around us conflicts of universal historical significance assailed us: Bolshevism, National Socialism, religious conflicts. It was the time of the Sudeten Crisis, around 1938, the Munich Agreement, the so-called *Reichskristallnacht,* and the Austrian *Anschluss.*

It must have been spring of 1939 when Sr. Antonia encouraged me at the grille of the speakroom with the following words, "Dear friend, in this difficult time I cannot give you advice with your problems and frustrations. Go to the Carmelite convent in Echt. For the last few months, a very well-educated and learned sister by the name of Teresia Benedicta has been living there. She is a convert from Judaism and a philosopher and comes from the Carmel Cologne-Lindenthal. She is better informed than a peasant girl like myself. When you get a chance, remember me to the prioress of Echt and ask her to speak to Sr. Teresia Benedicta."

In this simple way it began. I had never heard of Edith Stein, the philosopher and Husserl disciple, for as I found out, Edith Stein had assumed the name of Sr. Teresia Benedicta in Carmel. What did we Catholic students know of German philosophers? We read Nietzsche, a bit of Feuerbach and Marx, but the Christian philosophers who were of importance to us came from France: Maritain, Gilson, Garrigou-Lagrange, Bergson, and later, of course, de Lubac, Danielou, and Congar. We knew very little about Germany. At the university we had heard of Husserl, Scheler, and even Heidegger, but our actual knowledge of them was very modest.

Anthony Mertens *is a journalist and publisher in Bruges, Belgium.*

Rahner, Küng, and Przywara were too young as yet. True, I recall discussions about Guardini, Muckermann, Wust, K. Pfleger's book *Minds that Struggle with Christ,* and C. Schmitt. Our real interest, however, was inspired more by Paris than Berlin, Munich, or Vienna.

So, during my vacations in the summer of 1939, I bicycled twenty kilometers from my village to Echt to meet the learned Carmelite, Sr. Teresia Benedicta a Cruce, in the modest monastery that was situated in a quiet village street.... I announced myself to Mother Prioress.... I told her my wish to have a conversation with the learned nun who had found refuge in this convent several months ago. The prioress was friendly, she smiled and said simply: "Let's call Sr. Benedicta right away. During the hours between prayer times she is busy with her research work. Right now she is translating a *tractatus* by St. John of the Cross from Old Spanish." Then the prioress disappeared for a few minutes. When she returned, she had with her a fellow-sister who was veiled like herself. The sisters wore a thin, almost transparent fabric in front of their faces. After the usual greeting of "Praised be Jesus Christ," both seated themselves behind the grille.

From summer 1939 until summer 1942 I talked with her about a dozen times in increasingly friendly manner about the religious and ideological problems that occupied me then. They touched us both deeply. When we first met, I did not know who Edith Stein was. Her name meant nothing to me. Gradually I realized that she was an excellent translator of theological and philosophical works by Cardinal Newman, Thomas Aquinas, John of the Cross, and Teresa of Avila. Soon she also became known to me as a religious educator. My admiration for her grew increasingly, as did our joyous friendship.

In our first encounters, the prioress was present during our conversations. Half joking, half participating, she joined in our conversation. After about the second or third conversation, I asked, "Dear Sr. Benedicta, may I see your face, for it is annoying to me not to know what you look like." Sr. Benedicta looked at her prioress as if to ask her. "But of course," answered the prioress. Sr. Benedicta pushed the veil aside and looked at me as if I were an expert in photography. She smiled and called to the prioress: "Now

you, too, must remove your veil; Mr. Mertens wants to see you too."
She did so, and a few critical remarks followed. Both sisters looked
at each other pleasantly. Then they also looked at me pleasantly, as
if they wanted to say, "Well, young man, what do you think of us?"
Edith Stein's face was round and pale. She had dark eyes that
looked around keenly. She did not appear sad, but wise. When she
had something to criticize, a hint of aggression would appear,
which, however, was overcome by a quick smile. In subsequent encounters with Edith Stein, she remained without a veil, even when
I spoke with her alone. She was about fifty years old at that time.

In a talk with Sr. Benedicta, I once complained that I had to
spend my precious life in senseless, useless studies in such historical times. Excitedly she replied that I should not talk nonsense.
Millions of young men had to sacrifice their lives in a senseless war,
while I had the luxury of delving into the meaningful study of European culture. She was annoyed at me, got up and asked the prioress—in a sort of ritual childlike obedience—whether she might
quickly go to her cell to get a pamphlet. Sr. Benedicta returned
after a few minutes and passed me a brown booklet through the
wooden turnstile. It was a philosophical essay titled "Investigations
Concerning the State," written by Dr. Edith Stein and published in
Munich in 1925. Sr. Benedicta said: "I give you this essay as a memento of our discussion. Read it carefully. You will see how interesting the various aspects of law can be." It seemed to me, a future
jurist, as if she wanted to say to me: "If I could delve into this spe-
cialized subject at that time, as a young philosopher, what are you
so upset about, young man?"

I still have this memento. It stands beside the Edith Stein bi-
ographies and translations by her that I have collected since 1945.
The two or three typed letters from Edith Stein unfortunately got
lost in the battles during the winter of 1944–1945 in Limburg. At
that time we did not know what had happened to Edith Stein's unpublished works, but fortunately these manuscripts were saved in
an almost miraculous manner and brought to the Husserl Archives
in Louvain. Later these papers were taken to Brussels....

My vacation visits to the Carmel of Echt were abruptly terminated in the summer of 1942. At the start of that tragic year the
Wannsee Conference took place in Berlin, at which the Nazis decided

to kill all the Jews in Eastern European camps. Thus the converted German Jews in various Dutch monasteries were threatened. The Dutch episcopate's protest against the deportation of Jews was answered by the arrest of several dozen converted Jewish religious.

Of course I had found out who Sr. Benedicta was through our conversations "behind the grille," and had learned the course of her academic and religious development that led to her entry into the Cologne Carmel in 1933. Sr. Benedicta told me of her friendship with the families of Husserl, Conrad-Martius, Koyré, Scheler, the noted author Gertrud von Le Fort, with the monks of the Abbey of Beuron. Formerly she had gone to Beuron for regular retreats. She told me about her visits to Paris, Prague, etc.

I recall especially her stories about her family history that took place mostly in Breslau. To my question about her mother's reaction to her entry into Carmel she mentioned that the farewell from her mother was one of the most upsetting events in her life. Her mother was a great woman.... Only after the war was I able to read the moving description that Sr. Benedicta wrote down for her prioress in Cologne for her last Christmas in the Cologne Carmel in 1938....

Toward the end of my studies at the University of Nijmegen, I became engaged to a friend who had studied philosophy and archaeology in Paris, Rome and Freiburg (Switzerland) prior to 1940. In Freiburg (Switzerland), she had become friends with the daughter of the Swiss President Philipp Etter. Of course I told my fiancée of my encounters with Sr. Benedicta in the Carmel of Echt. When in 1942 the menace against the Jews in the Netherlands increased, I was happy to learn that they had applied for admission to Switzerland or Spain for Sr. Benedicta and her sister Rosa who worked at the gate in the Carmel of Echt. The sisters were to be brought to safety abroad. In Holland the Italian and Swiss consulates were still open at that time. Now and then emigrations could still be successfully arranged via these institutions, even in the midst of war. After several urgent queries, a Carmelite monastery in Switzerland, Le Paquier, offered to accept Sr. Benedicta until the end of the war. My fiancée wrote an emergency message to her friend, the daughter of the President of Switzerland, and to the Italian Consul in the Hague.

When an answer came at last, several weeks later, it was too late anyway. The hostile measures by the Nazis against the converted Jews led to a quick and deadly end. The Nazis came for Edith Stein on Sunday afternoon, August 2, 1942. Sr. Benedicta was summoned out of chapel during prayers by the security police, arrested, and deported with her sister Rosa. Via two transit camps, both arrived in Auschwitz only a week later. They were gassed a few hours after their arrival.

Many years later, in late autumn of 1972, thirty years after the death of Edith Stein, I visited the Auschwitz death camp. At the same time [I visited] the deserted, empty spot where camp Birkenau was once located. At the edge of this area simple memorial tablets can be found bearing the names of the European nations from which people were deported and gassed. I placed a bunch of flowers on the stone that recalled the dead from the Netherlands, to remember Edith Stein with the lonesome prayer of a grateful distant friend from long ago.

Heinrich Spaemann

Witness to the Presence of God:
A Portrait of Edith Stein

Cologne, 1987

With very important and very balanced individuals, the first impression is often the unforgettable one, because they are not splintered; their entire being is present, as otherwise only in children. What has remained with me from my first encounter with Edith Stein is the impression of someone very simple, plain, clear, childlike, serene. At the same time she was obviously a human being characterized by intellect and responsible living. Her eyes were quiet and attentive, radiant but without overeagerness, as is the case with very inward and serene individuals. She did not talk a lot and not fast. Round about her there was a beautiful silence.

From "Witness to the Presence of God: A Portrait of Edith Stein."
Westdeutscher Rundfunk *(April 17, 1987): 32.*

Überlingen, 1988

...I met Rosa Stein at the entrance to the Cologne Carmel on several occasions. She was a plain, simple woman and, insofar as one can say without knowing her more closely, one of those poor ones who are called blessed in the Sermon on the Mount. I was present at her baptism in Köln-Hohenlind, at Elisabeth Hospital. Sr. Benedicta (Edith Stein) was also present, at least from afar, from one of the side galleries of the chapel. She was ill at the time.[1] Thus it could be arranged that she could witness the holy event, seeing and hearing it, even though from a distance.

Heinrich Spaemann *is a parish priest, author, and spiritual director of the Psychiatric Clinic in Oberlingen.*

I was very surprised that Rosa, who, after all, went along to Echt and to Auschwitz, was not beatified simultaneously with her sister. Surely, at the time, hers was still a "first love" [of God]....

Heinrich Maria Janssen

Encounter with Edith Stein in 1932

Hildesheim, 1987

During my theology studies, while preparing for my ordination as a priest, I had an encounter with Edith Stein...at the German Institute for Scientific Pedagogy. This was a meeting place for students and teachers who were dedicated to Christian educational principles. Edith Stein worked there, too, as a lecturer. She had only recently come to the Institute in Münster from Speyer.

Prof. Rosenmöller had invited several students from his seminar in religious philosophy. Among the guests was Edith Stein. Someone asked me to talk about my dissertation, which was on the question: "How does unemployment limit the integration of a young person into society?" The great economic crises of that time—1932—had caused six million people to be without jobs in Germany alone.... The task I had set myself was not an easy one, especially since no literature was as yet available on this topic. During our conversation it became clear that in answering the problem, I had only examined and dealt with male youth. Edith Stein saw this as wrong; hence she considered my paper only a partial response. She stressed the fact—and I clearly remember this—that the thesis needed supplementing. The stated problem would need to be dealt with from the perspective of female youth as well; unemployment causes considerable problems to girls as well, and they had to be examined.

The work had been turned in. I confess that I was embarrassed by Edith Stein's criticism and became a bit unsure. I did not add to my research, because Prof. Weber did not object to the omission and judged the work in a positive manner.

Very Rev. Heinrich Maria Janssen *was bishop of Hildesheim, Germany, from 1957 to 1982.*

I remember that as a lecturer at the German Institute for Scientific Pedagogy, Edith Stein was mostly interested in the education of girls and women and that she was vitally interested in a quality professional education and professional opportunities for women. According to her own words these can never be achieved through "high-handed struggle against nature and limits set by nature, but only through humble submission to divine order."

Bruno Thiebes

Excerpts from a Letter to Sr. Waltraud

Speyer, December 28, 1987

...The year before my ordination as a priest on June 26, 1930, I attended the seminary for priests here. Occasionally I saw Dr. Edith Stein in the convent church St. Magdalena, but she never spoke to me. In May 1930 we nine deacons held our trial sermons on Tuesdays and Fridays during the May devotions. Dr. Edith Stein listened to us in the convent church. Next morning she sent flowers to the seminary for each of us in appreciation. We were impressed, since even then Edith Stein already had a reputation as an exceptional personality. Unfortunately I lacked the foresight to keep the bouquet as something precious. At any rate she surely achieved her purpose; she encouraged and showed her solidarity with us future priests.

Now a few eyewitnesses who know Blessed Edith Stein personally: In the convent St. Magdalena itself and its branches thirty-six sisters are now alive who knew her and talked with her. Twelve of these were her students....

The oldest priest here is Dean Emeritus of the cathedral Dr. Philipp Weindel, Speyer. He was chaplain of the cathedral from 1927 to 1929. He had occasional conversations with Dr. Edith Stein. On September 17, 1927, he was sitting in his confessional. Vicar General Joseph Schwind occupied the adjacent confessional. Dr. Weindel heard the muffled sound of a fall and went to look: Vicar General Schwind had collapsed and fallen from his confessional. Dr. Weindel looked after the victim, together with others who were present in the cathedral. A few minutes later, Dr. Edith Stein hurried over from St. Magdalen's, greatly worried about her father confessor. She accompanied him as he was taken to his apartment right next to the cathedral, but Schwind had already died in the cathedral.

Bruno Thiebes *is a dean of the cathedral in Speyer, Germany.*

There are several elderly women teachers living in our diocese who were Blessed Edith's students at St. Magdalen's and who have preserved a deep veneration over the years, especially now.

When the beatification process began, in our diocese the then canon and official Dr. Alois Heck was charged with arranging for the questioning of people from our diocese and with the writing of the reports. At that time additional eyewitnesses were still alive....

An especially important eyewitness is retired parish priest Ferdinand Meckes.... This is the priest who witnessed the transport train to Auschwitz pass through the train station in Schifferstadt on August 7, 1942. He stood on the platform as the train arrived. The first and last cars of the long train were passenger cars for the supervisory personnel; all the other cars were windowless freight cars. Through a chink, a pair of eyes were visible. When a male voice called out "Schifferstadt," some movement within the car was audible. Another pair of eyes appeared at the chink. A woman's voice asked the priest whether he was from Speyer. When he said yes, the voice asked to remember her to the priests in the seminary and Canon Lauer (who was then instructor of religion at St. Magdalena.) It was evidently Dr. Edith Stein's voice.

The train started to move, a note flew out of the chink bearing the handwritten name Dr. Edith Stein.[1]

Fr. Meckes gave the note to two women teachers who were also waiting on the platform for a train to Speyer. They recognized the handwriting of their former teacher Dr. Edith Stein and kept the note. We have not been able to find out anything so far regarding its further whereabouts. Station master Fouquet of Schifferstadt was also on the platform at the time; he observed and heard the exchange between Edith Stein and Father Meckes....

Philipp Weindel

Speyer, 1988

...I knew Dr. Edith Stein personally. Her father confessor and spiritual mentor was Vicar General Canon Schwind. His confessional in the cathedral was near mine. Suddenly I heard a noise, and when I looked out from my confessional, Prelate Schwind had fallen from his confessional. He had suffered a stroke. My fellow chaplain on the other side aisle also heard the noise and came over. We carried the severely ill prelate to a bench, where he died after a few minutes. Soon thereafter, Dr. Stein entered the cathedral; she had heard about the stroke of her father confessor. My fellow chaplain and I carried the dead man [he had expired in the meantime] to his apartment, and Dr. Stein accompanied us.

I knew Dr. Stein. She had given several lectures in the city, some of which I attended. Her manner was very reticent and shy. In the town she was a much respected personality. However, I did not know her well.

A nephew of Prelate Schwind, who put his papers in order after his death, told me that he had burned the correspondence between Edith Stein and his uncle. At that time one could not foresee that Dr. Edith Stein would some day be raised to the honors of the altars....

Philipp Weindel *is a doctor of theology and a dean of the cathedral in Speyer, Germany.*

Berta Hümpfner

Waigolshausen, 1988
...Before me lie six books, among them two written by you, which I have read with great joy and profound emotion. This great woman, who appeared so inconspicuous and modest, was my German teacher for two years in the teacher's college. During the German lessons, we clearly recognized what great intellectual gifts this woman had, how she was able to make the classical authors relevant, or to discuss our compositions with us. She was always totally involved. I especially remember one personal experience. At the examination, four topics were offered for us to choose from for the German essay. Of twenty-eight students, I was one of two who chose the topic: *Ich bin kein ausgeklügelt Buch, Ich bin ein Mensch mit seinem Widerspruch* (I am no cleverly contrived book; I am a human being with human inconsistencies).

After four hours, we had to turn our work in. I felt right away that I had not succeeded. I had always had a B in German; this mark was now in danger. Indeed I got a C. After the lesson, Dr. Stein came to me, tapped me on the shoulder and said that for the orals I should be prepared to interpret a few passages from Goethe's *Faust*. She must have noticed my great disappointment and helplessness, but it went all right. I got my usual grade.

Sometimes she took us to the theater. She negotiated with the sisters, accompanied us in person, sacrificed her scarce leisure time, and was happy to give us pleasure. Dr. Stein was simply our great role model. Therefore, even though I no longer lived in the Palatinate, but between Würzburg and Schweinfurt, I kept up with events in her life. I collected newspaper clippings and books about her life. I am seventy-five years old now, and I am privileged to experience this wonderful woman's beatification. For that I thank God....

Berta Hümpfner *is a teacher in Waigolshausen, Germany.*

Ludwig Martin

Otto Borgmeyer:
Edith Stein's Publisher in Breslau

Karlsruhe, 1988

Edith Stein had difficulties finding a publisher for her translation of Thomas [Aquinas]. The publisher Borgmeyer was interested in it and edited both volumes in 1930 and 1931. When the Cologne Carmel charged Edith Stein with preparing "Potency and Act," her *Habilitationsschrift* [second dissertation, written for the university where one will teach —TRANS.] for publication as *Finite and Eternal Being*, Borgmeyer was again the only one in Nazi Germany who dared to consider publishing it. Despite Gestapo surveillance of his firm, he tried until 1937 to publish the work. But publication came to a standstill, since Edith Stein and the prioress of the Cologne Carmel, Sr. Teresia Renata Posselt, refused to publish the work under a different author's name. Only someone whose name appeared in the register of the State Chamber of Literature could publish in Nazi Germany. As a Jew, Edith Stein was denied access to the State Chamber of Literature.

According to testimony by my wife, Anna Maria Renate, née Borgmeyer, her father traveled to Holland after Edith Stein had fled to Holland following *Kristallnacht* in 1938. He hoped to pursue publication there. This enterprise failed, because the Nazis occupied Holland in 1940 and controlled everything; besides, this long philosophical work would have had to be translated into Dutch.... The publisher Otto Borgmeyer, who was also personally involved in the rescue of Jews in Nazi Germany, was cruelly abused when troops entered Germany in 1945. He lost an eye and escaped death by the skin of his teeth.

This brave publisher and upright Christian ought not to be forgotten. He committed himself to Edith Stein's work to the very end of the war. He died in Karlsruhe on November 8, 1951.

Ludwig Martin *is chief federal prosecutor in Karlsruhe, Germany, and the son-in-law of Otto Borgmeyer.*

Richard Erb

Bad Bergzabern, 1987

...Mrs. Pikl, then ten years old, lived in Bergzabern "on the hill," opposite the Bergkirche. I, then six years old, lived four houses over.

The town of Bergzabern belonged at one time to the duchy of Zweibrücken. When the dukes accepted the reformed faith of Calvin, the main church, the *Marktkirche*, turned Calvinist. The *Bergkirche* was built for the Lutherans, close to the castle. Thus there existed two parishes until the so-called "union of 1818." The two parishes continued to exist in the now unified parish to the present day. On the lectern of the *Bergkirche* lay the Bible with its dedication by the Lutheran grand duchess of the province of Hesse, who was a widow and lived in a nearby castle. Unfortunately, after the last war this Bible was taken along as a souvenir by a Jewish clergyman.

During the summer vacation of 1920, Edith Stein stayed with the Protestant Conrad-Martius family in Bergzabern. She attended the *Bergkirche* very often and asked the child Maria Hümmer (Mrs. Pikl) to get the key from Father Born in the nearby Protestant vicarage.... She then entered the church and stayed there about an hour, solemnly reading and praying.

The children were, of course, curious about the church, which was very rarely used (especially in winter), and explored it when it happened to be unlocked. When I knew how to read, I too read in this big book [i.e., the Bible], but of course not like Edith Stein. I was just six and could not understand what this woman absorbed and what brought her closer to her decision.

Dr. Conrad did not own a large orchard, but a big fruit garden. Because he was often found near the many yellow plum trees, he was called simply the "plum doctor." People thought he lived off them. He was a skilled man who later repaired radios for people.

Richard Erb is a minister in Bergzabern, Germany.

...On weekdays Edith Stein went into the church and sat in the last row on the "men's side," but I think that on Sundays I saw her further toward the front, accompanied by a woman....

Publisher Otto Borgmeyer, Breslau

Susanne Wannemacher

Kaiserlauten, 1987

...For six years we lived under the same roof with Dr. Stein at the teachers' college in Speyer, Convent of St. Magdalen. She taught us German composition and literature. She took six of us on our senior trip to Munich in 1929. Father Przywara, SJ, was our guide, and we had audiences with Archbishop Faulhaber and the mayor.

For me she was an eminent and outstanding personality, strict in our working relations, but kind, lovable, and helpful in her relationship with us. It was admirable how straight she went her way, and yet she was so mysterious in her general bearing....

Susanne Wannemacher *is a teacher in Kaiserlauten, Germany.*

Dorothy Scheid, OSF

Aliwal North, South Africa, 1987
...My memories of Edith Stein are very few, and I shall probably disappoint you. Edith Stein gave a lecture about "Women of the German Council of Catholic Women" in my hometown of Sinzig/Rhine; I believe it was about 1927 or 1928. I was a young girl then. A family acquaintance took me along to the lecture. She told me that the lady who was going to lecture was very intelligent. That impressed me. I cannot remember anything Edith Stein said at the time; I was probably too young, but her personality impressed me deeply. She was very simply dressed and spoke quietly, without haste; she was simplicity itself and so modest in her demeanor, really, not at all conceited (so unassuming). She made a deep impression on me, and I have never forgotten her and can still picture her clearly....

Sr. Dorothy Scheid, OSF *is a missionary in Aliwal North, South Africa.*

M. Ruth Cronauer, OP

...Allow me to tell you the following impressions of Edith Stein, as far as I can remember from my school days.

—a definite love of truth and honesty
—relentless openness, deep faith and piety
—magnificent simplicity and simple modesty
—gentility and discretion
—extreme control over her emotions and expressions
—goodwill and helpfulness
—concise, focused and clear answers to questions and problems of her students, both personally and professionally
—something holy emanated from her; in her presence one felt as if in an atmosphere of something noble, pure, exalted....

Sr. M. Ruth Cronauer, OP, *has served as a missionary and high school teacher in England and South Africa.*

Maria Hroswitha, ISSM

Remembering Dr. Edith Stein

Rockport, Texas, 1986

I was a student at the University of Münster and lived in the Marianum on Frauenstrasse. The house was inhabited by student nuns and was administered by Marian Sisters. A dining hall facing the street was also available to other university students; they ate their main meal there at midday.

In the spring of 1932 a lady moved into the house; it was Dr. Edith Stein. Her room was distant from those inhabited by the Sisters, so she had little contact with them. But every morning she came to the house chapel for Holy Mass. The organ was all the way in the back, and the Sisters in the choir, of whom I was one, sat in the pews in front of it. Dr. Stein always knelt on the left side behind the rest of the Sisters or with them in the last occupied pew. That meant she was always a few pews in front of us, so we could observe her.

This was the time of the Liturgical Movement, and most people used the "Schott"[1] as a prayer book during Holy Mass. The aim was to celebrate Holy Mass exactly along with the priest so as to exclude private devotion. Dr. Stein was exceptional. I can't remember ever having noticed that she followed Holy Mass in the book. Perhaps she could hear the priest pray, and since she knew Latin perfectly, she could have been following the prayers of the Mass without a book. Every morning we had two Holy Masses. Dr. Stein stayed for both. She knelt, unmoving, profoundly composed. It was evident from her appearance that she had an intense prayer life of mystical depth. I became convinced: She is the most devout woman in the entire house! None of the many Sisters were as profoundly composed. True, there are saints who don't necessarily look the part, but Dr. Stein was one of the few who literally radiated saintliness. Otherwise she appeared plain and was inconspicuous. She went

Maria Hroswitha, ISSM, *a Schoenstatt sister, has been a high school teacher and a missionary in Africa. She now lives in Rockport, Texas.*

her way quietly and modestly; her dress was simple, a reflection of the attitude of her soul. Fashion did not matter to her.

Twice I got into a conversation with her. One day I met her in the hallway outside the chapel. She waited for me. She brought me regards from former fellow-students at the academy, who were now attending her lectures.... She was very reserved, and we had little contact with her. She was already living like a Carmelite in the Marianum. Nor did I ever see her in the garden behind the house where Sisters usually gathered for a recreational walk after supper.

My second talk with Dr. Stein happened like this: I was the first Marian Sister [of the Schoenstatt Secular Institute][2] to go to Münster to study. In the spring of 1932 there were three of us. In Münster there were several groups of women and girls, among them student teachers and students, who belonged to the Schoenstatt Movement. I received invitations now and then to go there and tell them more about Schoenstatt. In the long run this took too much of my time, and I asked them to come to me all together as a group, to the Marianum, on Sunday afternoon. I asked the Mother Superior for permission to use the lecture hall in the house. She agreed. Next Sunday not only the people I knew arrived but they had also invited friends and acquaintances, and so a whole crowd came and marched up the stairs. On the floor between the stairs and the lecture hall was Dr. Stein's room. So she heard that something was going on outside. I myself was a bit embarrassed, when I saw the many beginners and decided to give them an introduction to the Schoenstatt Movement. From then on they came every Sunday afternoon. One day, as they were leaving, Dr. Stein appeared in the hall and asked me what I planned to discuss with them. I gave her a short explanation about Schoenstatt as a renewal movement in the spirit of the Church. She listened attentively. I cannot recall, however, whether she had any reaction to my report. The Schoenstatt Movement was in its infancy at the time and not so well known. Our founder, Fr. Kentenich, didn't know the philosopher Dr. Stein personally, only by reputation.

In spring 1933 I returned to Schönstatt for my tertianship. It was then that the decision was made that I be sent to the Africa Mission with the first group of our Sisters. We left in December of that year. Before my departure I heard that Dr. Stein had joined the Carmel in Cologne. I was not surprised. It was undoubtedly the best place for her, for she had already lived the life of a Carmelite in the world.

I am happy to have known her and to have lived in the atmosphere of her sanctity. People give their environment something of themselves, even without a lot of words. What we are speaks louder than words. When I read in the newspapers that her beatification process had been started, I made my small contribution to the Holy Father with great joy, with the request for her beatification. I congratulate you and all your fellow-sisters.

Margarete Otto

Conversation on the Occasion of
Edith Stein's Beatification

Hildesheim, 1987

Editor: Mrs. Otto, we read in the Catholic press about the impending beatification of Edith Stein. Edith Stein—Jewish philosopher from Breslau, convert to Catholicism, later, as a religious, gassed in Auschwitz. A shattering life journey; a multi-layered personality. To get to know her is presumably worthwhile for Protestant Christianity as well.

Mrs. Otto: Yes, Mrs. Ceglarski, I really believe that Edith Stein should not only belong to the Catholics.

Editor: You have the souvenir photo from Edith Stein's clothing ceremony with her personal signature. So you knew Edith Stein personally?

M. O.: Yes, I am grateful for this stroke of fate. "Knew" in the true sense would be presumptuous, for I did not know at the time what a great person I was meeting. When during my first semester, in the summer of 1933, I came to Münster, I found a room in the Collegium Marianum, where Edith Stein also lived.

Editor: Do you recall what she looked like then?

M. O.: I see her before me very clearly, a delicate figure, with a pale face, very dark hair parted in the middle. Edith Stein was dressed very simply and often wore a white blouse. Upon her face there was always a hint of sadness, and therefore she probably seemed to us unapproachable. Actually we saw her only in the dining hall and rarely had contact with her.

Editor: Did the people in the house know anything about her origins?

M. O.: We learned that Edith Stein was a Jew and had studied philosophy in Göttingen and Freiburg, that she had assumed

---

Margarete Otto *is a teacher in Hildesheim, Germany.*

the Catholic faith, had worked as a teacher for a while and was now a lecturer at the Educational Institute in Münster.

Editor: You mentioned a sorrowful look in her eyes. Could that have had anything to do with her origins?

M. O.: Certainly. The attacks against the Jews increased. The trend was clear. We felt how Edith Stein suffered with her people. Never would we have dared to speak to her about it, but on a walk my girlfriend and I got the idea to bring her a bunch of climbing roses. She accepted it and was much moved.

Editor: How did you feel when the esteemed scholar, the educator known far and wide for her lectures, entered the convent?

M.O.: Actually we were not surprised. Edith Stein was very devout, and this path was consistent with her inner life. It is known that she had been harboring this desire for eleven years. April 15, 1934, was the day of her clothing ceremony; now she was a member of the Carmelite order in Cologne and received the name "Teresia Benedicta a Cruce." The name "Teresa" points to her veneration of St. Teresa of Avila, through whose autobiography her interest in Christianity was aroused. "Benedicta a Cruce" means "the one blessed by the Cross."

Editor: That name, isn't it almost a prophesy?

M. O.: Let me point out to you how comprehensive Edith Stein's personality was. However reticent she may appear, she was radical, in the true sense of the word ("down to the root"): Thus she decided to become a Christian, even though she knew that by doing so she would inflict great pain on her family, especially her beloved mother. Likewise, at one time she wanted to make philosophy her life's work and remained as assistant to Husserl. She was also radical when she wanted to be independent and turned to teaching, perhaps also out of a certain pride to accomplish something on her own as a woman.

Editor: How is this radicalism consistent with the obedience required for life in the Order?

M. O.: Here, too, she sought the utmost. After the study of mysticism of St. Teresa, she sought the deepest internalization and self-surrender in Carmel.

Editor: Don't they also call Edith Stein a great "advocate of women" (not only "the great woman of prayer")?

M. O.: That she definitely is. On her lecture tours it was especially important to her to encourage women to dare to enter the professional world. She believed that women were also needed in leadership positions. As for her, a professorship was denied her.

Editor: As a member of such a strict order, did she have to renounce all scholarly work?

M. O.: She wanted to give it up, but the order urged her to continue her scholarly work. She continued to maintain contact with scholars and kept abreast of current politics.

Editor: What was the relationship between the convert and her original belief?

M. O.: She continued to feel Jewish. In 1933, for example, she asked for a private audience with the pope—which, however, did not come to pass—in order to do something for the Jews in Germany. She remained connected to Judaism; after all, she encountered in the church liturgy (which she loved so much) texts from the Old Testament, e.g., the psalms. But especially because of her love for her family.

Editor: Do you know what was Edith Stein's relationship to the Protestant Church?

M. O.: Her friends were predominantly Protestants. Thus a lively exchange of ideas ensued. Edith Stein suffered because of the division of the faiths, but she did not emphasize it. Instead she focused on what unified them. Even her godmother, also a former Jew, was a Protestant.[1]

Editor: What further happened to Edith in the Carmel?

M. O.: In the meantime, anti-Jewish measures in Germany intensified. There were difficulties for Edith Stein and for the Cologne Carmel. First she was sent to a monastery in Holland. When even there safety from the Gestapo no longer existed, efforts were made to get her to Switzerland. But it was too late. On August 7, 1942, she was deported to Auschwitz. There she was gassed—it was the end of her way of the cross.

Editor: Mrs. Otto, in conclusion let me ask: What message does the nun Edith Stein have for our time? And what does her beatification mean?

M. O.: Edith Stein was not divorced from reality. She participated in public life before entering the convent and she felt responsible for others. She was not a "yes-person," she asked to be convinced and then would convince others. She connected active life with inner life, because she wanted to give meaning to life. She was ready for renunciation.

Edith Stein was surely an exceptional phenomenon. She should also be valued for her sacrificial death. But the church wants, above all, to recognize her faith and her unshakable confidence and to place Edith Stein before us as a role model in this respect—that is the meaning of the beatification.

Editor: Mrs. Otto, I thank you very much for this conversation.

Edith Milz

My Encounter with Edith Stein

Grönenbach-Thal, 1988

I met Edith Stein in the Home for Women Students, the "Marianum," in Münster. She lived there during the year of her work as a lecturer (1932–1933) at the German Institute of Scientific Pedagogy. Since I was studying at the university and working on my doctoral dissertation, I was not Edith Stein's student. I only remember hearing that things were being made difficult for the lecturer Stein.

A few times I met her at lunch in the Marianum. She arrived, like myself, only shortly before the end of the meal; by then only one or two tables were still occupied.

I can still see her coming down the wooden staircase that led to the lunch room. She appeared very serene and composed. Her dress underlined the impression of beautiful simplicity. I believe she always wore the same thing: a light blouse and a dark skirt.

She quietly yet firmly rejected any deference from the others at the table. She was never the first to serve herself from the bowls of food. Sometimes I was alone with her at the table; sometimes we were three. Since we were all tired from the long, hard work of the morning, little was said.

However, once I experienced an event of a totally different sort with Edith Stein. It was in early 1933. Decisive elections lay ahead. The great political excitement of the time had seized the Catholic students and their sororities as well. The leaders met to call a pre-election students' meeting, to caution them about the negative effects of a victory by the National Socialist party. I was present as a member of the New Hochland Students' Sorority. We were profoundly impressed by the Liturgical Movement, by Guardini, Pinsk, and the Renouveau Catholique, Claudel, Péguy and Bloy. We had discovered within us a deep love for the church

Edith Milz, Ph.D., *is a high school teacher in Grönenbach-Thal, Germany..*

as the body of Christ encompassing all people. Edith Stein, too, was part of this spiritual renewal. It was this movement that led us to reject the Nazi system.

I cannot forget the words a fraternity brother spoke to me the first time I saw an SA cohort. "There's a new day marching in, and we'll never be able to march along." We knew that National Socialism was incompatible with a connection to Christ and his church. It distressed us at that time, as it did Edith Stein. The question about the fate of the Jews hit me a year later for the first time, when I celebrated Easter with a Jewish Christian, a member of the Hochland Sorority, in the Benedictine Abbey Gerleve. She said to me, "Your Easter joy is unbearable to me." Of course we had no inkling of the dreadful future of the Jews. We found out about it from her after 1945.

But let's get back to the pre-election meeting and to our experience with Edith Stein: As our election speaker, we invited the most famous Christian woman politician of our time, Helene Weber, a Member of Parliament. I was instructed to pick her up at the train station in Münster upon her arrival from Berlin. The seriousness of the moment led the politician to avoid any personal remarks. "How large is the hall? How many chairs do you have?" She didn't say much else after handing me her suitcase as a matter of course.

One of us visited Edith Stein and asked her to help us in the debate that was to follow. We saw her as a respected philosopher like Hedwig Conrad-Martius. Her Jewish origins were irrelevant. We had no aversion to Jews per se, even if we were angry at the current cultural scene: immoral and un-Christian tendencies in the theatre, movies, and magazines, many of which were in the hands of rich Jews. Edith Stein agreed with us in this matter as a devout Christian. Our meeting was to bear this out in an unpleasant way.

The auditorium in the Marianum was jammed. It quickly became obvious that the women students sitting in the first row were National Socialists. I myself sat in the second row and noticed Edith Stein diagonally behind me in the third row. After Helene Weber's speech, in which Jews were not a subject, the Nazi girls offered their reply. They had the charisma of conviction. None of us dared to say anything. We were hoping that Edith Stein would come to the rescue. I looked back in disquiet, in her direction. Finally she rose, but her remarks disappointed all of us. She spoke softly, unaggressively, factually. It disappointed us terribly, when she conceded a modicum of guilt on the part of the Jews, although it was completely unnecessary in that setting. It seemed to us grist for the Nazis' mill. In this tense and disturbing political situation there remained no opportunity for her to add anything positive about the Jews. A discussion of the political problems of the times, especially unemployment and the poor career prospects for young university students, everything that was for us a burning issue, simply did not suit her quiet, introverted personality. Had we ourselves not been basically unpolitical—unfortunately—we probably would not have thought of pushing Edith Stein into a situation that was so foreign to her.

Many years later my cousin Hedwig Eilert, a student in Münster who would become a nun, reminded me of this meeting, saying "Do you remember how Edith Stein disappointed us that time?" Simultaneously she recalled an unforgettable evening of conversation at which Edith Stein had spoken stirringly about "Women and Careers." Edith Stein meant a lot to my cousin (who died in 1967) and me. She was one of the women of that time who inspired us with hope.

Paula Bittner

My Reminiscences of Edith Stein

Oschatz, 1986

A s an active member of the youth group of our parish of St. Michael in Breslau, I was in the parish house frequently then (about 1932 and 1933), and occasionally helped our chaplain with small projects which involved the youth group. He also expected us older girls to attend Mass before school, and many of us did so. During early Mass we noticed a lady, simply but well dressed, with a plain but attractive hairdo. We girls wondered who she might be. After all, she was not always present.

Some time later when I visited the parish house, our chaplain was just saying good-bye to this lady. He said to her: "Here comes one of my young helpers." Dr. Stein smiled pleasantly, shook hands with me and asked what school I attended. When I replied, "public school," she only said, "a pity."

I did something that is not good manners. I asked our chaplain, "Who is this lady?" He only said, "Don't be so nosy."

Before I went home, he said to me: "This lady is Dr. Stein. She lives at Friesenplatz.[1] The large lumber yard belongs to the Stein family also."

A few weeks later I saw Dr. Stein again during early Mass at 6 o'clock. That afternoon the chaplain told me that she was working at a teachers' college and educating young women teachers there.

He asked me and another girl to go to her apartment and take a letter there. We were taken to a large hallway with strange furniture.

A few weeks later our chaplain told me: "Let us pray for Dr. Stein, and sacrifice, for hard times are coming for her; she is a Jew."

Unfortunately he had to leave St. Michael's and was given a post as parish priest. Shortly before his departure he said to me, "Dr. Stein is in Carmel now." I didn't know what to make of this statement, and he said that she was in a monastery on the Rhine.

Paula Bittner *is a pastoral assistant in Oschatz, Germany.*

His successor, who had the same name as he, told me that Dr. Stein was now a nun. I was upset and said, "then I shall never see her again." He said, "Oh yes, later, with our Father in heaven." Meanwhile I was already involved in youth work and in the first few years of professional work or studies. Our meetings were, of course, forbidden, and so we disguised our meeting nights as birthdays, etc. News about the nun grew ever scarcer. During a short meeting with Father Görlich I learned her name in the Order and that she had already made her perpetual profession. Since the second chaplain Görlich was also transferred, I did not hear about her for quite some time.

In the spring of 1944 Vicar Görlich telephoned me and said he wanted to talk to me, but I should not go to see him, nor could he come to my house. After work he stood in front of the office and said briefly, "Sr. Benedicta was killed in a KZ (concentration camp)." He forbade me to talk to anyone about it.

Unfortunately both these clergymen were murdered in the summer of 1945....

Anni Lohner

Reminiscences of Edith Stein from July 25, 1932

Munich, 1987

First let me say that I heard the lecture by Dr. Edith Stein in Augsburg 54 years ago, when I was a simple young girl from St. Martin in the parish of Nuremberg.... The personality of Dr. Edith Stein strongly impressed me, or rather, influenced me. She stood behind every word and both her content and her delivery made her fascinating, stirring. This lecturer was totally unknown to us; at the time she had not yet entered Carmel. I can still see her in her simple, blue-grey dress, with dark, smooth hair, parted in the middle.

In 1932, the beginnings of the problem of "woman in public life" were already in evidence; hence the subject of her lecture was especially timely: "Woman's Task as Leader of Youth: Woman's Incorporation Into the Mystical Body of Christ in the Place Appropriate for her According to God's Will."

The fact that in this lecture three possible types of vocation were discussed led me to treat them in detail in group discussions. Under the guidance of Dr. Edith Stein, good material was easy to find: For example, in Ida Friederike Coudenhove (Görres)'s trilogy "Of the Two Towers," in Gertrud von Le Fort's book "The Eternal Woman," in Pater Manuwald, in [Romano] Guardini the various types of vocations could be well presented. The idea of acknowledging each of them as a particular vocation in accord with God's will and of recognizing the opportunity to be fulfilled as a person in any of the three vocations, was received with special openness....

On the basis of my experience in Augsburg, I was really genuinely convinced, and enthusiastic about the idea that in every vocation one can be pleasing to God. I continued to profit from the remarks of Dr. Edith Stein; she really had an enormous radiant power. I carried away not only ideas for my youth work, but much

---

Anni Lohner *is a secretary in Munich, Germany.*

more. Something emanated from [her] that carried an existential obligation, that hit home, with implications for one's own life as well.

Since the thirties until today I am at home in a circle in which all three vocations are represented....

In any case it was Edith Stein who kindled the fire within me. On reading that lecture today, a sadness creeps over me....

Eric E. Hirshler

Granville, Ohio, 1989

...My mother, physician Dr. Helene Hirschler, née Riess, was a friend of Edith Stein. Both came from Breslau....

My father was a surgeon (Dr. Max Hirschler) and a school friend of Ernst Bloch. My parents were close friends of Bloch. Bloch's parents lived in Ludwigshafen (my hometown). He often came to visit my parents. Sometimes he stayed for longer periods.... According to testimony by Frau Lochner he met Edith Stein at our house one evening and had a long and serious conversation with her. According to a statement by Dr. Lochner, Edith Stein had given a lecture in Ludwigshafen on the subject: "What message does the Christ Child have for us today?" After the lecture, she came to see us. Frau Lochner and my mother had heard the lecture. Bloch had preferred to talk to my father. As far as I know this was either in 1930 or 1931.

I remember that my mother visited Edith Stein several times in the Speyer convent and once in Cologne.

In 1937, Edith Stein wrote in her letter to my mother:

Dear Lene!
...I can well imagine that you don't have any inclination for Palestine. I wouldn't want to go anywhere else, if the need should arise some day for me to leave Germany. It has always been a pleasant thought for me that there are several monasteries of our Order there. Is Peter already professionally active or is he still studying? According to my estimation, he must be about nineteen years old now. And did Ernst Erich not lose his joyous nature due to the many difficulties which he very likely has experienced already? Margot once visited me here. I had a very sad impression [of her] at that time, too.

Eric E. Hirshler *is a professor of art history at Denison University. His parents were freinds of Ernst Bloch and Edith Stein.*

I don't know whether you have any news from Breslau. Did you hear that my dear mother died last September after many months of suffering? I had not seen her again since my entry into the Order (October, 1933). That was the hardest thing about my life in the Order. And yet it has not shaken my conviction that I am where I belong. What you have been told about me is something rather insignificant. It is true that I have written a big book during the last two years. The manuscript of the first volume has been with the publishing house of Anton Pustet in Salzburg, but external obstacles have delayed the start of publication. However, the fact that a Carmelite philosophizes is something unusual and by far not the main thing in her life. And if her fortune depended on it, it would stand on rather weak legs. I may say that mine does not depend on it. I have been nursing a sick fellow-sister for seven weeks, and of course, little time is left for scholarly work, but I am happy at each such interruption that I can make myself a bit useful to my cloistered family.

The Bibersteins are still in Breslau.[1] Hans kept his position as senior physician and lecturer surprisingly long. Finally, however, it is at an end. Now he has a fair private practice (Kaiser Wilhelmstrasse 80) and works at the Jewish Hospital part-time. Erna's practice, or Lili Berg's respectively, which she was asked to take over in 1933, has melted down to a minimum. The children, now sixteen and fifteen years old, still attend Victoria School and Friedrichsgymnasium—despite all difficulties. But in a few years, their parents will probably have to part with them. Sometimes they think about emigrating, but they haven't taken any serious steps toward that end.

Margarete Helferich

My Reminiscences of Edith Stein

Schweinfurt, 1984

To this day I remember her great patience—also her great simplicity and profound quiet piety before the tabernacle.

I never spoke to Edith Stein privately and did not know at the time that she was Jewish and had converted to Catholicism.

I am still vividly aware that the head of our seminary spoke with enthusiasm about Edith Stein's work, [a translation of] St. Thomas Aquinas's *Disputed Questions on Truth*. Only after Edith Stein had left Speyer and was forbidden to teach in 1933 did Sr. Stephana report everything in detail. The news of August 7, 1942, from Schifferstadt, which I was told about soon after, shook me up and thus made me aware of the situation of the times much more clearly.

The path of Edith Stein influenced me strongly to think about Judaism, Israel, the Old Testament, and so on.

"It has always been far from my thoughts to assume that God's mercy is tied to the limits of the visible church. God is truth. Those who seek truth seek God, whether they are aware of it or not." These words [which Edith] addressed to Sr. Adelgundis gave me hope and peace in my relationship to a colleague and later friend....

Margarete Helferich *is a teacher at the School for Vocational and Domestic Sciences in Schweinfurt, Germany.*

Dietrich von Hildebrand

New Rochelle, 1976

Dear Sr. Johanna!

...Unfortunately, I must disappoint you, since I met Edith Stein only twice in my life. The first time was at the funeral of my greatly respected and beloved teacher Adolf Reinach, who played a decisive role in Edith Stein's life, too. At that occasion I did not speak to Edith Stein. We only saw each other, or rather, we met, and she heard me, since I was giving the eulogy at the funeral.

The next occasion was in the summer of 1930 at a convention of the Catholic Academics' Society in Salzburg.

I gave the first lecture about Catholic Professional Ethos and she gave the second lecture, about the Vocation of Woman. Unfortunately we hardly spoke on this occasion. Of course, I have heard a lot about her—especially from Adolf Reinach's widow, Anna Reinach, and from my friends Balduin and Leni Schwarz, who occasionally met Edith Stein in Münster in 1932.

I find it very interesting to hear from you that Edith Stein mentioned me now and then in her writings and letters. The most I heard about Edith Stein was from Mrs. Hedwig Spiegel, in whose conversion Edith Stein played a significant part. However, I assume that you have been in touch with Dr. Spiegel for a long time. I met her in America in 1942. She spoke about Edith Stein with special admiration and enthusiasm, more than any of the others who spoke to me about her.

Dietrich von Hildebrand was a noted philosopher and disciple of Edmund Husserl. He taught for many years at Fordham University in New York City.

Andrea Loske

My Longing for Truth
Was One Continuous Prayer (Edith Stein)

Munich, 1967

At the "University Study Weeks in Salzburg" in 1930, I sat in one of the first rows when a famous professor spoke. As happens often with young students, I felt an urge to make fun of the speaker's little idiosyncracies. And so I found it amusing when the professor, with each sentence he wished to emphasize, banged his fist on the table. This caused a glass of water to jump around on the tray in more or less large leaps. The expectation that the glass might finally jump from the edge to the floor was fascinating. I was disappointed that the expected catastrophe did not happen after all. The professor had not even noticed his unintentional capers, yet someone else had.

A slender lady of medium height, with dark, large eyes and smooth hair parted in the middle, quietly advanced to the front, took glass, tray and water jug from the lectern and placed them all on the floor in the rear. When she turned around, our eyes met. With a restrained, merry smile she looked into my mocking face. It was Edith Stein. She was the second speaker that day, with the subject: "The Ethos of Women's Vocation." At the time I could hardly imagine anything more boring. It was a fashionable subject; by the Twenties it had already been pretty much talked to death. I had planned to play hooky during this second lecture, but the incident with the glass of water had awakened my sympathy for the speaker. Her matter-of-factness, her humor—without the tendency to mock, as in my case—and her charm held me spellbound. And so I stayed.

Edith Stein spoke for almost two hours. For two whole hours, over midday in August, about a thousand people listened to her without making a sound. No scraping of feet, no clearing of throats, no cough could be heard. Captivated, we all listened to that delicate

---

Andrea Loske *is a high school teacher in Munich, Germany.*

woman who spoke with charming simplicity, her refined face now and then animated by an indefinable smile, in a soft, clear voice, audible to the farthest corners. Not even the tiniest piece of paper did she have before her. Her hands remained quietly folded on the lectern, and yet a restrained dynamic was contained in every sentence. I cannot remember having felt tired for even one minute. For here one sensed a great power of mind, a rich, yet disciplined inner life, born of utmost self-assurance.

The thunderous applause after this lecture, however, scarcely reflected what had occurred in those who attended. Professor Vierneisel from Heidelberg expressed it thus in a review of the lecture series:

> At the Salzburg convention, one woman made an unforgettable impression. By chance, her significant lecture was delivered at the beginning of the session....
>
> Edith Stein's lecture was most convincing because it was free of the pathos of the *feminist movement* and because the speaker herself markedly and visibly personified her own thoughts. Her bearing when she descended from the podium recalled those paintings in which ancient masters depicted Mary's visit to the temple. (*Heidelberg Bote,* October 1, 1930; see *Essays on Woman,* pp. 20–23)

From "In Search of God—Edith Stein," Bavarian Radio Munich, church broadcast (September 17, 1967): 127-128.

Bernhard Rosenmöller, Jr.

Edith Stein and the Family of the Religious Philosopher Bernhard Rosenmöller

Münster, 1990

I have been asked repeatedly to talk about the connection between the philosopher and later Carmelite Edith Stein and my father, Bernhard Rosenmöller, professor of religious philosophy, as well as his family. I hesitated to comply with this request, because at the time I was a boy of 12–13, and therefore can only repeat the reports of my parents, who have died in the meantime.... Perhaps my modest contribution can serve for the understanding and veneration of this saintly woman and may also serve to honor her biological sister Rosa Stein whom I was privileged to meet in Breslau. Looking back over my life I can only confess, in great gratitude toward God, that I was granted the grace to meet several saintly people, people who quite clearly were martyrs, blood witnesses of their God. Out of this gratitude I dare, after all, to write these lines.

My father had worked for his doctorate in the Twenties, under the philosopher Ettlinger, and was lecturer or assistant professor at the University of Münster until 1934. In his home on Heerdestrasse an extremely lively intellectual life was going on. University students held discussions with my father, sitting on the carpet in our small living room. The conversations that the young Protestant theologian Karl Barth held in our home with leading Catholic theologians...are common knowledge. My father's position on the board of the Union of Catholic Academicians, his close friendship with the highly important Franz X. Münch (not yet rediscovered by church historians), and father's activity as Chapter Secretary in Münster, brought many significant people to our house.... Very illustrious names are to be found in our guest book; what riches could I have experienced there if I had been a little

---

Bernhard Rosenmöller, Jr. *is a high school principal in Münster, Germany, and the son of Edith Stein's friend, Bernhard Rosenmöller.*

older then! In this way, quite by chance, I recall Peter Wust, who, with his pince-nez, inspired respect in us, and above all, of course, those who paid attention to us children, guests who could be witty, like Karl Adam and "Uncle" Münch. Those were especially likable and unforgettable.... We kids, of course, did not realize at all that we were witnesses of a highly important radical change: the beginning liturgical movement and the youth movement, as with Guardini, or the ecumenical beginnings, especially through Father's friend Paul Simon, or the emergence of German Catholicism from the cultural ghetto, substantially promoted by Prelate F.X. Münch. This time of emergence and its importance for the later Council has not yet been explored. During the Nazi period, this era of change was increasingly pushed underground, of course....

Toward the end of the time when my father was active in Münster, Edith Stein, too, visited our house. My parents had met her at meetings of the Union of Catholic Academics or the Salzburg University Lecture Weeks that followed them. Now Dr. Stein had come to Münster, and she worked at the German Institute for Scientific Pedagogy together with my father, who was one of the editors of its quarterly journal. Philosophically their views diverged quite a bit. Both were greatly influenced by phenomenology, Father more by Max Scheler's philosophy, and Edith Stein much more directly by Husserl. Within Christian philosophy Edith Stein turned strongly toward the philosophy of Thomas Aquinas, while the philosophy of my father was much more imprinted by St. Augustine and Bonaventure. Certainly, Edith Stein participated actively in the discussions in our house, but her friendship toward our family was also personal in nature.... Surely Edith Stein must have noticed at once that my parents detested anti-Semitism, precisely because they considered it deeply un-Christian. For them Jews were human beings, and in the deepest sense, those members of the Chosen People who had not found the faith in the Jew Jesus of Nazareth, or better, had not found it yet.

At any rate, during that time, when anti-Semitism was spreading like the plague, Edith Stein was a frequent guest in our house, particularly Sunday afternoons. She especially enjoyed my youngest brother Anselm who was an infant at the time. Later when my brother decided upon the priesthood, he put special trust in this friendship. For his ordination as a priest in 1957, he chose among other things, a photo of Edith Stein as a souvenir holy card, thus at a time when her beatification lay far in the future. We as a family also put our trust firmly in Edith Stein when my brother Anselm was taken from us quite suddenly as a young priest by an accident in the mountains. Again the photo of Edith Stein served as one of the funeral pictures. Let the love that Edith Stein felt for my little brother serve as an example that her connection to our family was of a very personal nature. The threat of the then triumphant National Socialism, for both a horrible experience, must have created a special tie between my father and Edith Stein. My father had no illusions concerning the danger everywhere, a danger that especially threatened Jewish fellow-citizens.

Of course, I only learned some details through my parents. A remark by Edith Stein to my father, that she considered the story "Der versiegelte Engel" ("The sealed angel") by Leskow [1] the most important work of fiction became meaningful for me; thus I myself became a great lover of this author and his work.

My mother told me that, during the short time of Edith Stein's stay in Münster, she spent a weekend with her in the nearby Benedictine Abbey of Gerleve. They stayed in the retreat house, Ludgeri's Rest. Decades later my mother, ordinarily quite down-to-earth, was still deeply impressed by her companion's intensity of prayer. She said she could feel the power of her prayer through the wall of the adjoining room.

I myself could scarcely remember Edith Stein—a twelve-to-thirteen-year-old boy has other things on his mind than "aunties" who come for a visit on Sundays and who take special interest in the baby—if our last encounter had not left an unforgettable imprint on me.

For me it seems more than coincidence that upon our return from a walk along the promenade in Münster—I still remember the spot today—we met Edith Stein. My mother whispered to me: "Tomorrow she will enter Carmel. That is a convent that you can never leave." This remark made a deep impression on me, and full of awe I looked up to this woman who gazed at me long with her dark eyes. She did not speak a word to me, but I remember those eyes to this day.

Edith Stein did not forget us children later. Even in Breslau, hence after 1937, each of us received poems by her and small paper cutouts she had made in her cell. But, ungrateful as we were, we did not know how to appreciate these signs of friendship properly. What would we give today if we still had these treasures in our possession. They all remained in Breslau.

After Edith Stein's departure from Münster, my father, together with his friend Peter Wust, was invited to the Cologne Carmel for the clothing ceremony, about which he reported after his return. He was very touched. Shortly thereafter our family left Münster, too, and spent three years in Braunsberg in East Prussia. From the summer semester 1937 on, my father taught at the University of Breslau. Our move to Breslau meant a strengthened bond with the Carmelites in Cologne, in two respects. For one, Edith Stein established for us very good relations to the newly founded Carmel of Breslau. The nuns, by the way, were driven out of their Wendelborn monastery and found refuge with the Ursulines in town. I remember that as a boy I visited the Carmelite Sisters in Wendelborn as well as the Ursulines on behalf of my father. Our friendship with Sr. Marianne de Deo remained after the war, when she resettled the Carmel of Breslau anew "on the cliff" high above Witten in the Ruhr valley, not without having first sought advice from my father. Sr. Marianne de Deo, like Edith Stein, came from the Cologne Carmel.

The bond with Edith Stein was intensified above all by the fact that she, who could do so little from inside the monastery for her greatly threatened family, had presumably asked my father to look after her siblings, especially her sister Rosa, who, in the meantime, had converted to Christianity. Because my father rightly feared that his mail was being watched, I was sent as a messenger to the house of the Stein family several times. In this plain, middle class home, however, I always encountered only Rosa Stein. I learned to venerate this extremely modest woman very much at that time. To my parents she never uttered a word of complaint, although the situation had become quite threatening for her. Mrs. Tworoger, too, another sister of Edith Stein who visited us in our house in Breslau, refrained from any reproach, although she feared the worst for the future. My parents were greatly impressed by this. Sadly, she, too, became a victim of persecution.

In the short period between 1937 and her departure from Breslau, Rosa Stein was our guest occasionally. In our home she always experienced a Christian Christmas on Christmas Day. She always came after dark in order to cause us no problems. She was very considerate, almost shy. Thus in the kitchen of her house she told me once that she always attended Mass at 5 a.m. in a small chapel near the Breslau cathedral. She did not want to endanger the officiating priest, because she was obliged to wear the Jewish star.[2] Thus Rosa Stein appeared rather reticent. Compared to Rosa, her sister Edith was thoroughly self-assured and goal-oriented. For my brother Johannes, Rosa was the image of humility: Like her sister she was kind and deeply religious. And then, of course, she went to her death for the Jewish people like her sister. I myself always turn with my concerns to both sisters at once, they belong together, not only in their dying, but probably also for all eternity....

The fact that my brother and I were allowed to experience the beatification in Cologne-Müngersdorf next to the Jewish relatives and that I was the first one to introduce the niece of Edith Stein, Mrs. Susanne Batzdorff and her family, to the pope and to Cardinal Höffner, we felt as a high honor for our parents who were as devout as they were fearless.

Mathilde Herriger

Solingen, 1986

Dear Mr. Sanders![1]

...Sadly, an unpleasant feeling comes over me and my family when there is talk about the philosopher and Carmelite Edith Stein. When Sr. Benedicta was taken to Echt in Holland on the evening of December 31 of the dreadful year 1938, it was Paul Strerath, M.D., the brother of my father, who carried out this courageous trip by night. He practiced in Schlebusch, where he also looked after the orphanage named Nazareth House. The connection he had to Cologne and the Jesuits is based on the fact that two of his brothers were also active in the Jesuit Order (partly in missionary work). I still remember a few names: Fathers Zaun, Schütz, Sudbrack, who were often his and our guests on the estate near Schlebusch. Now you will surely think, what is this all about? We are just upset by the fact that this deed is simply being passed over. At least, a human being is worthy of having his courage at that time acknowledged by mentioning his name. I would be happy if you could respond to this, and my sisters would be even happier if I received a positive answer....

Mathilde Herriger *of Solingen, Germany, is a niece of Dr. Paul Strerath, who drove Edith Stein to Holland on New Year's Eve, 1938.*

Paul Strerath

Strerath Delivered Edith Stein in 1938 By Taking Her Across the German Border

Cologne-Schlebusch, 1987

The SS attack during the night from November 9 to 10, 1938, opened many people's eyes. A smell of death lay upon the streets of Germany on the morning of November 10. Jewish citizens had been driven from their homes at night with rubber truncheons, their businesses were demolished and expropriated. With one blow the livelihood of the Jews had been swept away. The synagogues were on fire. No one dared to level accusations out loud.... In the darkness of New Year's Eve a friend of the (Cologne) Carmel, Dr. Paul Strerath, drove Edith Stein across the Dutch border by car.

Waltraud Herbstrith, The Real Face of Edith Stein, *pp. 152–153*

Only a very reliable person could be entrusted with such a mission during the Nazi period. After the pogroms against the Jews in November 1938, it had become clear to Edith Stein that she ought no longer to endanger her monastery. The Carmel Echt in Holland had offered to take Edith Stein in. She had obtained all documents required for legal departure. Despite all precautions it was known that the guards at the Dutch border were especially strict. But Dr. Strerath had the pleasure of escorting Edith Stein safely to the Sisters in Echt at 8 o'clock at night. Strerath, his two Jesuit brothers, and his friends opposed National Socialism. The country doctor from Cologne-Schlebusch was known as a selfless, kind man who sacrificed himself completely to his profession. He

---

Paul Strerath, *a noted physician in Schlebusch near Cologne, cared especially for the children in Nazareth House.*

was especially popular in the children's home, Nazareth House. There are still acquaintances alive who testify, with the patients of the country doctor from Schlebusch, that you could go to him unannounced, at any hour, without insurance and without money. Dr. Strerath died on March 5, 1945.

Fr. E. Läufer, "Ein Leben an der Hand des Herrn"
(A life at the hand of the Lord)
Church Bulletin Cologne, *Nr. 8, February 20, 1987.*

Leo Sudbrack

Companion on Trip from Cologne to Echt

Perl, 17 August 1967
Apacherstraße

I consider it urgent for me to inform you that, as his traveling companion, I helped Dr. Paul Strerath, MD, bring your Sister, Dr. Edith Stein, across the border into Holland. I still recall she brought along a manuscript codex that she showed me. On each page of the book a large heart was drawn, accompanied by antiquated writing. This heart greatly impressed me and influenced considerably my work of preparing young children for their first Holy Communion. I am still happy today to have met this great woman and to have been able to share with her one of the stops along her Way of the Cross.

May her heavenly intercession bless my priestly ministry.

Most devotedly yours in the love of Christ,
Dr. Leo Sudbrack, Pastor of Perl

Rev. Dr. Leo Sudbrack *was known to the nuns of the Cologne Carmel because his brother, Jesuit Karl Sudbrack, used to give them conferences. This letter reveals his little-known role in accompanying Edith Stein and Dr. Paul Strerath from Cologne to Echt on New Year's Eve, 1938. As a friend of the driver, Dr. Leo Sudbrack was a natural choice to provide companionship on the journey. With the permission of the Cologne Carmel's archivist, Sr. Amata Neyer, OCD, this previously unpublished letter has been translated by John Sullivan, OCD, and added to the English language edition of* Never Forget.

Herman Leo van Breda, OFM

Commemorative Address
Honoring Edith Stein

Echt, 1967

Dear Chairman, Attentive Listeners!

First, I want to describe the impression of my personal encounter with Edith Stein in April 1942. It was a weekday during the second half of April 1942, April 28 or 29 in that unholy, fear-ridden war year, that I announced myself in the Carmel of Echt. There I met for the first and last time Sr. Benedicta a Cruce, Edith Stein. Was it really a personal meeting in that small, poorly furnished speakroom on the first floor in Bovenste Straat? Behind the familiar iron grille a heavily veiled woman sat opposite me in the dark.

The long, anxious hours I spent there—I stayed about three days in Echt and talked with Edith Stein for hours in that small room—are etched into my memory as one of the most impressive encounters of my life. Encounter? Only God knows how often in life the grace of an encounter was granted to me. Here I found it in the richest and deepest sense of the word, despite the grille and veil and despite the salutation prior to each dialogue, in my view a bit pietistic. You surely know the custom of the Carmelites. This conversation was not explained or underscored by facial expressions or a radiant or smiling look. In spite of that, I could not for a moment dismiss the feeling of a strong spiritual presence during those hours. This 51-year-old Edith Stein impressed me as quiet and controlled, yet attentive and altogether present. Edith Stein wore the dark habit of the professed nun. Like hundreds who had experienced it before, I must admit that during this conversation I was irresistibly impressed by this small, somewhat shy and not exactly charming woman.

Herman Leo van Breda, OFM, *was the first director of the Husserl Archives in Louvain, Belgium. He rescued Husserl's manuscripts from Nazi Germany, and tried to rescue Edith Stein in 1942.*

This impression was not absolutely connected to her outward appearance. Many who had been granted a longer conversation with her had experienced this. Surely, Edith Stein had a good character; she showed genuine, spontaneous interest in the concerns of other people, in their work, their problems, and their troubles. This characteristic alone cannot account for the wonderful magnetism emanated from her and with which she influenced the mind and heart of all she met. Even though her interest in the other person was very great, she almost always remained reserved and somewhat closed off, sometimes even cool. Her natural kindness was somewhat limited by the care that she evidently had to expend in order to understand other people in their lack of decisiveness or their weakness. The concept "relentless" was applied repeatedly to everything she did, to herself and others. The love of neighbor that Edith Stein demonstrated abundantly, at times heroic love of neighbor, must not be confused with what is called natural charm, even though she certainly had her own charm.

Edith Stein, in my view, had the extraordinary talent to be tuned in to those people who encountered her, with an alert, empathic attention. The root of her irresistible attraction lay elsewhere. Already as a child and adolescent, more strongly as a student and young woman, she immediately inspired confidence. She often attracted, unaware, the friendship of others, and became a support and refuge for many. Throughout her whole eventful life, so brutally cut off, Edith Stein testified through word and deed that God, the giver of all that is good, had granted her this charismatic gift so that she would understand her fellow-humans and help them to a better insight. Sometimes she did so almost prophetically, in that she showed people the direction toward a goal for which God had destined them. She received this charism, from birth and throughout her whole life, in accordance with the word of the Gospel, "Give, and it will be given unto you: full measure, pressed down, shaken together, and overflowing, will be poured into your lap" (Luke 6:38). I experienced and observed this charism when I met with this blessed woman in April 1942 for two or three days and exchanged ideas with her for hours.

In this memorial lecture I would like to bear witness publicly to this special talent that Edith Stein possessed in such great measure.

It is my intention to interpret, in the light of this charismatic gift, the rich personality and the life of this exceptional woman whose tragic death twenty-five years ago has brought us together today in this memorial celebration to honor her. My attentive listeners, for this celebration I have thought it appropriate to wear the decoration that the State of Israel kindly bestowed upon me in 1965, at Yad Vashem—the solemn place that bears witness to the tragic destruction of a large part of the Jewish people—for the help that I was privileged to give to Jews during the war.

Whoever wants to become totally convinced of Edith Stein's charism should read the detailed autobiographical account of her youth. She wrote these reminiscences mostly in Carmel. The title of her book is *Life in a Jewish Family*. In the large, hospitable house in Breslau where Auguste Stein, née Courant, Edith Stein's mother, kept the family together, her youngest daughter became the confidante of all early on. Apparently everything was entrusted to her, life's profoundest emotions and intimate secrets. In her, one found understanding but also the courage for action. This was true for her siblings, for her many relatives, and for the ever-growing number of friends and acquaintances who were guests in the Stein home. Edith Stein's mother, the strong woman who, like Deborah in Israel, ruled the town with all her worldly goods, also found in Edith, even though she was the youngest, the faithful Ruth who comprehended swiftly and completely, who was always ready to help and who, over the course of years, offered counsel and leadership.

In this impressive account of her memoirs her personal and human contacts are most surprising of all. The number of persons and personalities of both sexes with whom Edith was in contact is amazing: Men and women, young people, children, professors, fellow-students, artists and politicians, nonbelievers and devout believers, not to mention the many nurses and patients in the military hospital in Mährisch-Weisskirchen. This life story surprises above all by the immediate confidence that this young, vivacious, somehow manly, reserved and sometimes severe woman inspired in everyone who came near her; by the great influence that she had by word and example upon many, e.g., Richard Hönigswald in Breslau, the phenomenologists in Göttingen, e.g., Adolf Reinach among others, Edmund Husserl in Freiburg. In the exhibit here, we only see pictures of Edith Stein's professors at the university. For these very learned people she was not only a talented philosopher and a diligently working student and researcher, but also someone to whom one eagerly listened in conversation, a wise woman whose advice was sought and listened to with rapt attention. Edith Stein was the heart and center of the large circle of enthusiastic Husserl pupils, Hedwig Martius (later Mrs. Conrad-Martius), Jean Hering (the famous exegete who taught in Strassburg), Hans Lipps, Fritz Kaufmann, Roman Ingarden (professor at the University of Cracow and best known Husserl student), to name only the most famous here. She accepted everything and linked all of them with one another. This also characterized her life as a high school teacher in Speyer, lecturer in Münster, and Carmelite in Cologne and Echt. Meanwhile, through her conversion, she became conscious of the theological deepening of her charism: the unity of all beings, of all people in Christ.

St. Paul writes: "He destined us for adoption to himself through Jesus Christ." God has decided, "as a plan for the fullness of times, to sum up all things in Christ, in heaven and on earth" (Eph 1:5, 10). And of his cares about the people he writes: "in everything we commend ourselves as ministers of God, through much endurance, in afflictions, hardships, constraints, beatings, imprisonments, riots, labors, vigils, fasts; by purity, knowledge, patience, kindness, in a holy spirit, in unfeigned love" (2 Cor 6:4-6). Edith Stein felt the burning urge to help and serve all she encountered, during the twenty years from her entrance into the church in 1922 until her death.

Everywhere and in the most difficult situations this highly sensitive and learned woman acted simply and almost spontaneously as *an ancilla servorum ac servarum Domini,* as the servant of the servants of the Lord. I say, almost spontaneously.... In not a few cases it was rumored that the readiness to help and the service of this charismatic woman was not child's play. For her it was often a difficult duty, a virtue acquired in a tough school. She stood by her beloved mother[1] in her last years with limitless devotion and respectful sorrow, although her mother had not been able to cope with her entry into the Catholic Church. For her siblings and their children, she remained ever the zealous one who wanted to be everything for everyone. This is demonstrated particularly by her support for her sister Rosa. Her teaching in Speyer, the devotion with which she carried out her tasks as an educator, were in her eyes a service. This is confirmed by her first biographer, Sr. Teresia Renata Posselt OCD. The many relationships that Edith Stein maintained with her friends and acquaintances, the lectures she gave, the visits she paid, the letters she wrote, in short, everything she did and accomplished in those years, can be expressed succinctly with the old Dutch motto "Ich diene ("I serve").

Edith Stein's fellow-sisters, too, appreciated and stressed her sensitivity to the troubles and suffering of others and her ready helpfulness.

As I thought about all this I recalled the marvelous prayer by the poet Rainer Maria Rilke [from *Das Buch von der Pilgerschaft* (The Book of Pilgrimage)]. Thus Edith Stein, too, might have spoken at the end of the day:

> And my soul is a wife before you,
> Like Naomi's daughter-in-law.
> By day she walks around your sheaves
> Like a maidservant doing servant's chores.
> But at eventide, she enters the waters
> To bathe and dress in beauteous garments.
> She comes to you, when all is still around you,
> And comes and at your feet removes the covers.
>
> And if at midnight you ask, she will reply
> With deep simplicity: I am Ruth, the maid,
> Spread your wings over your maid.
> You are the heir....
> And then my soul sleeps till it's day,
> At your feet, warmed by your blood,
> And is a wife before you. And is like Ruth.

During her painful journey to Auschwitz, Edith Stein was a charismatic helper for those who were being led to death.

A few weeks after my visit to Echt, on Sunday, August 2, 1942, twenty-five years ago, Edith Stein, together with her sister Rosa, was taken from the Echt Carmel at dusk. Her last journey began, her way of the Cross. She started on the long, final road to her death in Auschwitz.

To honor Edith Stein's memory, I went on a pilgrimage to Auschwitz in the autumn of 1957. About my hours-long visit to this unholy place I want to say just this:

No human eye has ever seen,
no ear has ever heard,
and it has never penetrated a human mind
what was perpetrated there, in Auschwitz, by human hands.

After I had turned my back to this place of misfortune again, I needed many hours before I could bear to hear again the sound of a human voice or simply talk to anyone. In one of those ovens, which I had seen, Edith Stein was gassed and murdered in the summer of 1942. In one of those pits her earthly remains were burned to coal and her ashes scattered to the winds.

To this woman the word of Paul applied in full measure: *Mihi vivere Christus est et mori lucrum* (For to me life is Christ, and death is gain) (Phil 1:21).[2] *Mori lucrum,* this shining word gives Edith Stein the courage, to embark, strong and unbroken, on her last Exodus from Echt to Westerbork, from Westerbork to Hooghalen, and, in the words of Paul "when we are flogged, or sent to prison..." (cf. 2 Cor 6:4-6) in sleepless nights, from Hooghalen into that hell, her own valley of death.

Mori lucrum, "for me death is gain." But next to that it says, *Mihi vivere Christus est,* "life to me is Christ." This gave Edith Stein the strength to be, for the last time, charismatic during her humiliating road of pain: Support and refuge for her sister Rosa Stein, for her friend Ruth Kantorowicz, and for those many who, together with her, were facing certain death.

For this "small remnant of God," who traveled through the wilderness with her—the wilderness of the Germany of that time—Edith Stein was Blessed....

From Als een brandende toorts *(Echt, 1967): 103ff.*

Stephanie a Magna Domina, OCD

Reminiscences of Sr. Benedicta — Edith Stein

Echt Carmel, 1967

My memories of Sr. Benedicta are of a rather personal nature. That is because we novices were separated from the older Sisters during regular recreation hours. True, I saw them in the choir, chapter, refectory, etc. However, we novices had quite a lot of contact with Sr. Benedicta during our daily Latin lesson.... I had already formed my first impression of her before entering, during one of my visits to the Carmel in Echt, when I was officially introduced to the Sisters.

After the questions back and forth had been answered, Sr. Benedicta leaned over a bit, out of the row of the Sisters, and asked me when I was coming. Her voice was a little masculine, but very agreeable and low. So much friendliness and charm lay in her question that it resembled, as it were, an invitation. That gave me much courage and confidence. At that time I knew nothing about her, but her personality made a deep impression on me, so that I could never forget that moment. I met Sr. Benedicta the second time when, upon entering Carmel, I greeted the Sisters one by one. Sr. Benedicta embraced me cordially and whispered mischievously: "Rózsika, nem szabad!" That is a Hungarian expression that means, "Not allowed!"[1] That was something she had remembered from the First World War, when she nursed Hungarian soldiers in the Austrian military hospitals as a Red Cross nurse. I replied, "Oh, I suppose I shall hear this quite often from now on." Sr. Benedicta smiled teasingly.

During the lessons she gave us, Sr. Benedicta proved to be an excellent teacher. Nothing was too much for her, and she gave of herself with great devotion and patience when that was necessary. She immediately recognized whether our ignorance stemmed from the fact that the lesson in question had not been learned or

---

Stephanie a Magna Domina, OCD, *was a sister with Edith Stein in the Carmel of Echt, Holland.*

whether it was a matter of lacking diligence; in the latter case she was pitiless. Without mothering us (that was not her way) she had something warm and maternal about her, and she had a keen eye for situations in which one of us was overly fatigued or feverish. Then she sent us immediately to the Directress of Novices.

In our lessons we dealt not only with grammar; Sr. Benedicta also provided interesting details. During the lesson about hymns, the dates when they were written and their authors' names came under discussion. Once she was quite disappointed when she noticed that some of us did not know the meaning of the *Tantum ergo*. How can it be that one sings something for years without knowing what it means!

One time she was criticized for going into more detail than was necessary in order for us to understand the Liturgy of the Hours. She accepted this criticism quietly, without protest, but simply continued in her own way—she remained herself wherever that was required. Sr. Benedicta had been in the Carmel in Echt for three years, and she spoke Dutch quite well by then. And yet she sometimes asked us for the correct Dutch word for something. Each of us would then contribute her share, glad to be able to help her. But finally, to our amusement, Sr. Benedicta herself always found an even better Dutch word than we.

She observed silence very faithfully; and yet Sr. Benedicta would not have suppressed a necessary remark. She also asked me, outside of recreation, for a prayer for a friend of hers who had emigrated to England and who was celebrating her birthday just then.

Once during our lesson, we talked about the antiphon *Euge, serve bone*.[2] Our convent had always used the wrong pronunciation for the first word. Sr. Benedicta told us a bit wistfully that she had mentioned it before, but that it had done no good. We should know the correct pronunciation, but should adapt to the convent and continue mispronouncing it. Never would she have told us: Let them hear how it ought to be!

At that time we had no heat yet, and during the last year we had a harsh winter. Sr. Benedicta coped as best she could, but when we came for a lesson she took us to a room that had a heater, so that we should not be so cold. In the refectory she always finished her meal quickly. There, too, she paid special attention to others. She saw to it that they got what they were supposed to receive, and then she would relieve either the reader or the one who served at table.

During recreation on feast days, which we were allowed to spend with the professed Sisters, she was very nice, especially when student pranks were involved. She always contributed her share to the good humor. Although she did not laugh uproariously, she would sometimes laugh pleasantly, in a delicate manner, and even giggle.

Her conversations, even when they were carried on more or less in jest, always had worthwhile content. She would never have talked nonsense. It was easy to see that she couldn't stand that. Sr. Benedicta could also direct dramatic performances well. And yet I never saw her as an actor; that wasn't her forte. At work, laundry, etc., she was always first, and yet she was not at all adept.

Although her personality, as I mentioned before, was conspicuous for a certain attraction and charm, I could never have guessed what she actually was. Her reticence and ascetic lifestyle only let you assume that she was an excellent nun. She never showed that she was such a learned woman. True, at the prioress's request she gave a lecture on our Father St. John of the Cross. She gave this lecture standing up, and one could tell that such activity was nothing unusual for her. But I only realized what she really was after she was taken from us and after some facts about her were made public.

In the choir she was respectful and reserved. When we knelt thus for hours before the Blessed Sacrament, she occasionally would doze off and sleep, resting on her heels. That also happened because at night we sometimes had air raids and bombardments, as in the last Whitsun night. Then Sr. Benedicta sat motionless in front of the tabernacle with outspread arms, while we moved around anxiously. The situation grew ever more unsettled and threatening. Three weeks before her departure, when we had our last lesson with her (from then on Mother Prioress wanted her to devote every moment to her *Science of the Cross* and no longer to give lessons) she showed me a photo of the Carmel in Switzerland where she wanted to go. Her eyes filled with tears (she wasn't so unmoved and stiff, after all) and she asked me to pray for her, for it wasn't so easy to move to another Carmel so often!

On the eve of the feast of St. Alphonsus [i.e., on August 1] we novices sat outside in the garden. Sr. Benedicta came to us with another sister, an emissary from the "Big Sisters," in order to congratulate Sr. Alphonsa with a rose on her name day. That was the next to last image of her that I remember.

On the feast of St. Alphonsus [i.e., on August 2], Sr. Benedicta read something aloud as usual during meditation. She had to interrupt the reading, because Mother Prioress, who had been called into the speakroom before, came to get her.

Shortly thereafter, Sr. Benedicta returned. She knelt before the Blessed Sacrament, then she turned to us and, red-faced but quietly and self-controlled, she ran back from the choir, saying in a sad voice: "Please, Sisters, pray!"

I can still hear her saying that. A few Sisters were also called out of the choir (they were supposed to get something ready for her), but no one called us out of the choir to say good-bye. In their consternation, those involved did not think of it in the rush. And thus she left us…without a farewell. We did not know she was leaving. Sr. Benedicta, *auf wiedersehen* in Heaven!

Another personal memory is the following: Sr. Benedicta was acquainted with the history of Hungary. She knew that King Stephen, the Saint, had dedicated his country to the *Magna Domina* ["Great Woman," i.e., the Virgin Mary] Patroness of Hungary. Before my clothing ceremony Mother Prioress asked the Sisters in the recreation room: "What name should we give her (me)?" Sr. Benedicta answered spontaneously: "Let the child be given the name Sr. Stephanie a Magna Domina!" And that is the name I received. Sr. Benedicta told me that during a feastday recreation one time.[3]

Written from the Carmel of Beek, Holland

Daniel Feuling, OSB

Short Biographical Sketch of Edith Stein

Beuron, 1956

Regarding her *human* qualities, Sr. Teresia Benedicta's uniqueness, I find, lies in her far-ranging vision and in the striving and feeling of her heart that result from it. In her inner self there dwelled the urge to a deeper sense of human existence and life; because of this urge, she looked continuously—in her life and in her research—for the great existential interconnections of humanity, the world, and being. This she shaped in her own thought and feeling and in the overall goal of her work among people—as a high school teacher and as a lecturer on human, women's, and religious problems for Catholic audiences. She united penetrating intellect and vivid feeling in an exceptional manner. Above all, by combining concept and feeling, she influenced the more mature girls as well as educated, thoughtful women. And this connection opened the way for her to the greater religious truths. She carried her knowledge and love from the shadow of the Old Testament to the light of the Gospel of Jesus and to the security of the church of Christ.

A pull toward *philosophy* was deeply rooted in Stein's personality. Philosophy is, after all, the search for truth, for being and life in those profound relationships that reveal themselves to us in a clarified and enlarged concept, if we seek to grasp all that we encounter persistently and logically in accordance with its being and its working. This philosophical endeavor had become second nature to young Edith Stein. She carried it to the study of philosophy itself, which she pursued successfully with the founder of phenomenology, Edmund Husserl. Like Martin Heidegger and Koyré she was among the assistants of Husserl. Up to her entry into Carmel and until his death, Husserl continued to be favorably inclined toward his former student and remained connected to her in

Daniel Feuling, OSB, *is a professor of philosophy and theology, and a monk of the Benedictine Abbey of Beuron, Germany.*

thought. Edith Stein remained faithful to the study of philosophy all her life. A chief fruit of her work relating to this was the German translation of one of the most important works of St. Thomas Aquinas, *Quaestiones disputatae de veritate* (Disputed Questions about Truth). It was her concern, with this difficult, brilliantly successful work, to immerse herself more deeply into the thought world of Aquinas and thereby to attain a philosophical analysis of the great teacher and to broaden her own philosophical insight. The reputation that Edith Stein enjoyed, beyond the borders of the German language area, as well as her familiarity with the teachings of Husserl and other representatives of the phenomenological school of research and thought, are what prompted the leadership of the Société Thomiste to invite her to participate in the discussion among selected researchers and scholars in philosophy that took place in Juvisy near Paris in September 1932. In the discussion following the two lectures of this conference (Journée d'études), Dr. Edith Stein participated in exemplary fashion; in contrast to other German participants, she spoke in fluent French, and without notes, since her remarks had to be in response to what had been presented and to what had been asked and stated in the discussion. Her various remarks received great applause in the assembly, composed mostly of important men. After Edith Stein had entered the Cologne Carmel, she was pleased that her superiors had the vision to allow her gladly to continue her involvement with philosophical research in the framework of the cloistered life. Even as a Carmelite she remained a philosophical human being.

Sr. Benedicta as a *Carmelite* I saw only once, or should I say, heard only once, since according to the rules of the Carmel she was veiled in black. Had I had an inkling then that one day I would be asked for reminiscences about Sr. Benedicta, I would have asked for a dispensation from this rule, in order to get a better impression of her appearance, her face, and especially her eyes, and to be able to describe her better now. This way I am confined to two things: her words and the revealing sound of her voice. Both together entitle me to say the following: Sr. Benedicta appeared to me to have matured beyond her earlier self in three ways—as a woman, as a spiritually-religiously secure human being, and as a personality dedicated to God and belonging to God, in the true sense of the word. As a woman, Sr. Benedicta appeared to me more womanly, ennobled. By that I mean two things. One is that in Carmel, Sr. Benedicta attained an even higher relationship between heart and mind, beyond that connection of both sides that had been noticeable in her even before. The other, however, is that the particularly feminine (the sense of being supported and guided in life, and also a deeper discernment) had broken through much more strongly in her by means of the spiritually illuminated feeling than before, when I first met her. In her *spiritual-religious security*, I sensed a greater maturity in Sr. Benedicta. Formerly she had been engaged in a struggle of the mind, as a participant in the great intellectual battle of our time, striving for clarity of knowledge and a firm basis for cognition. But now she had entered into a new way of living the truth: a way of fortifying, with the help of her experience, the decisive philosophical and religious certainties. She had reached the other shore, so to speak, saw the realities and truths more in the divine light of faith than predominantly with philosophical and theological reason; she had that *cognitio affectiva experimentalis* in a higher degree, that understanding of truth that draws upon experience and intuition that St. Thomas connects with the gifts of the Holy Spirit.

That, again, leads to the third thing that I felt during my visit to the Cologne Carmel, the deepened *religious character* of the inner life of our Sister Benedicta as a bride of God, totally surrendered, totally dedicated to the Lord. If one of the main goals of the great St. Teresa of Avila for her Carmelites was the contemplative, in the final analysis mystical life in dedication to love—Sr. Benedicta, I felt, was surely on the road to it. I sensed her as definitely at the right place in the hidden life of Carmel. I felt that she spoke the truth when she assured me how happy and joyful she was to be allowed to be a Carmelite now. And when I parted from her, I did so in the joyful certainty that she had chosen great things when she went into the seclusion of Carmel and bound herself closer to God in holy vows. Later, when she had to exchange her beloved Cologne Carmel for another house of her Order, when she was finally torn from her hallowed silence by elements hostile to humans and hostile to God and had to embark on a difficult, dark path of suffering, I can have no doubt that, according to God's loving decision, Sr. Benedicta thus became even more that which she wanted to be, with mind, heart and will: The one dedicated to God, the one totally connected to God, the true Carmelite.

From Edith Stein, Frauenbildung und Frauenberufe *(Women's Education and Women's Professions) (Schnell & Steiner, 1956).*

Valentin Fouquet

Edith Stein: Her Greeting on August 7, 1942
At the Schifferstadt Train Station

Schifferstadt, 1953

On August 7, 1942 around noon, I was waiting for the express train from Saarbrücken to Ludwigshafen. The train arrived, and a prison car, which had been attached to it, halted in front of me. From this car, a lady in dark clothes spoke to me, asking whether I was from Schifferstadt and whether I might know the family of Father Schwind. I answered in the affirmative, that the family of Dean Konrad Schwind, my classmate, was well known to me. She then asked me to give them regards from Sr. Teresia Benedicta, that she was Edith Stein and was traveling east. The lady appeared calm, friendly. Only a short time later, I was able to pass this message on to Miss Schwind, the sister of the Dean and niece of Edith Stein's spiritual mentor, Vicar General Joseph Schwind....

Valentin Fouquet *was the stationmaster in Schifferstadt, Germany.*

Hedwig Conrad-Martius

Arnstorf, 1948

Dear Father! [1]

...I want to write a few things down that came to mind concerning Edith Stein....

1) On a walk to work together in the upper part of our fruit farm I asked her whether it might be possible to lead a life of total obedience without having a spiritual mentor, whereupon she answered in her decisive manner, and rapidly: "No." That was still before her baptism.

2) In the same time period we once went to the Protestant church in Bergzabern, where the United Reformed service, I must admit, was more than sober and "liberal" besides. Afterwards she said: "In Protestantism, heaven is closed; in Catholicism it is open."

3) At a time when she was entertaining the idea of entering Carmel—I can no longer say when that was—she said to me, in answer to a question on that topic: "For this you have to have a vocation." I would like to add that I never tried to dissuade her, already because of my own deep sympathy for this....

4) Now I want to write something to you about which I have never spoken before, but which suddenly (only just after my return home) showed me a new and essential aspect of the story of her conversion, but which I ask you to treat with the most intimate delicacy possible. She loved Hans Lipps, the phenomenologist who was part of our group and who later became a full professor in Frankfurt and died as a [military] doctor before Petersburg. I am

---

Hedwig Conrad-Martius *was a professor of philosophy. After the war she held a professorship honoris causa at the University of Munich. She was Edith Stein's closest friend.*

also certain that she would have married him if he had wanted it. But he did not want to. When that was absolutely clear, I had a talk with her—concerning the photograph that, all by itself, still stood on her small desk in our Bergzabern home. I said to her that it didn't seem right to surrender totally to God and to want to dedicate oneself to him and yet to keep on the table the picture of a man who didn't want to marry you (perhaps I said to hold it in your heart, I'm not sure). She was deeply affected and shortly thereafter, perhaps even immediately, the picture disappeared from her desk. After all this came back to me, I believe for certain that this profound disappointment of her life contributed not a little to her conversion and baptism, yes, even to the choice of cloistered life. And yet I am far from thinking that such a disappointment could be the entire valid reason for a conversion, as the world cynically might. But divine mercy uses such incidents in order to draw near persons who are called. As for this entire sequence—if you wish to make use of it—I ask that you mention it without giving its source, i.e. my name.

5) A small detail: Once when we were washing dishes together (I had a very energetic and quick style, while hers was very slow and calm, though inwardly it was perhaps almost the other way around), I said something to her that burdened my mind immediately afterward and now that I remember it, it bothers me a bit once again: "You are working too slowly; this way we'll never get anywhere" or something like that. She was silent, without any contradiction, but I felt how much she had to struggle against that.

From my report to the Cologne Carmel I select in addition the following single traits about which I think I haven't written you before.

1. When, around the year 1932, she visited me on the way back from Breslau, where she had visited her relatives, I was in the hospital for an operation. She was extremely wretched and thin. She had suffered a bad flu in Breslau, and the doctor had imposed a very strict diet because of lingering intestinal trouble (not just no meat, but also no sweets, etc.). I had the definite impression that, for her, these restrictions were very welcome—with respect to her

hidden Carmelite lifestyle, which she already observed insofar as possible....

2. Toward the end of her novitiate, when I was allowed to speak to her for an extended time behind the double grille and she told me...how difficult the novitiate had been for her, especially learning the rule with all its details, she also told me that, during the winter, despite cold and unheated rooms, she had not suffered nearly so much from cold in hands and feet as before. I myself remember that in the winter she always had very swollen and bluish hands. Then she merrily pulled out her large, dark brown handkerchief, as if it were her most beautiful possession. She said that she had resumed scholarly work and writing, only upon orders, i.e., in obedience, but that it was outwardly very difficult, because each time she had to ask for "our" pen. A heavy, constant sorrow evidently burdened her, because of the fate of her large family. She constantly spoke about that....

Hedwig Conrad-Martius with her husband

Hélène Vérène Borsinger

Attempt to Bring Edith Stein to Safety
In Switzerland in 1942

Basel, 1945

In a letter of December 31, 1941, ...Sr. Teresia Benedicta asked me to let her know whether an entry permit and visa for Switzerland could be obtained on the condition that she and Rosa were accepted by a monastery there. As her reason for her decision to go abroad, Sr. Teresia Benedicta stated that, because of a German decree, all non-Aryan Germans in the Netherlands had been declared stateless and that they were required to register for emigration before December 15.

Sr. Teresia Benedicta and her sister had followed this order because it had been imposed under threat of severe punishment. Nevertheless, at the same time they made a request to the occupation forces to grant them an extended stay in the Carmel of Echt and to strike their names from the list of emigrants. If this request were denied, they would have to look for other possibilities. Her superiors, Edith Stein continued, would prefer to see them go to a Swiss Carmel.

> If we cannot get out this way, we will certainly be deported by the authorities.... You will understand that our superiors would like to spare us this fate. Besides, I am obligated by my vows to use all available means to continue to live according to our holy rule. (December 31, 1941)

I inquired at once from a (Catholic) official with the Swiss Immigration Service about ways and means in this matter. He advised me to get in touch first of all with a Swiss Carmel and to

---

Doctor of Law Hélène Vérène Borsinger *did research on women's status according to the canon law of the Catholic Church. She was Edith Stein's friend, and attempted to rescue her.*

obtain a declaration of acceptance and guarantee from them. Only in this way would there be any prospect for an entry permit and visa, which would have to be issued for both sisters by the Immigration Service. With the help of the diocesan chancery in Fribourg, I got in touch with the prioress of the Carmel Le Pâquier, the only Carmel for Discalced Carmelites in Switzerland. The prioress of the Carmel in Le Pâquier, Sr. Marie Agnes de l'Immaculée Conception, informed me that she and her monastery were willing to take Sr. Teresia Benedicta, but that, for lack of space, they could not accept her sister Rosa in Le Pâquier. Msgr. Besson, Bishop of Geneva, Fribourg, and Lausanne, advised me, just as Mother Prioress of Le Pâquier had done, to send a request for Rosa's admission to the Seedorf convent, and I did so immediately. After I had received an affirmative answer to my request for Rosa's acceptance, on February 12, 1942, I sent a formal request to the Swiss Immigration Service, in which I explained the mortal danger threatening the two sisters. In the course of the following months, all sorts of *difficulties* arose, which I shall briefly describe here:

1) ...On April 9, 1942, Edith Stein informed me by postcard that the Occupation Authority had informed her in January and March 1942 that, "an emigration was out of the question prior to the end of the war." I did not let this information keep me from continuing my rescue efforts in Switzerland, telling myself that the Occupation Forces might perhaps change their position.

2) ...After the superiors at Le Pâquier and Seedorf had readily given their approval to acceptance the two fugitives, they afterward created difficulties about accepting the two sisters. Based on my knowledge of Dr. Edith Stein's character, I succeeded in defusing this objection.

3) Meanwhile, the Swiss Immigration Service demanded two additional lay sponsors, besides the declaration of guarantee by the two monasteries. Miss Maria Stadlin and I myself gladly served as sponsors.

4) A new delay with severe consequences resulted when Sr. Teresia Benedicta wrote to me on June 22, 1942, that the Congregation for Religious in Rome made the following stipulations, based on canon law:

a) Both monasteries had to submit chapter decisions stating their willingness to accept the two sisters.

b) The Ordinary of the Diocese of Fribourg had to give official certification accepting the two sisters in his diocese.

c) "Une assertion de Rome." Because I sent the postcard in question from Sr. Teresa Benedicta to the Carmel, I no longer recall what this "assertion de Rome" was all about. While we obtained the first two stipulated documents relatively quickly, the "assertion de Rome" was delayed so long that I, in utter despair, wrote to the Mother Superior of Le Pâquier, that she should inform the authorities in Rome that both sisters were in mortal danger, and that they should hurry, for heaven's sake. Mother Prioress did so....

d) Then the Swiss Immigration Service came up with new difficulties. A senior official telephoned me at the end of July and said that they were basically willing to give Dr. Edith Stein an entry permit, but not her sister. I answered most forcefully that Dr. Edith Stein had stated to me repeatedly in writing that she would not leave without her sister Rosa; that she felt responsible for her. I pleaded with the government official to make no further difficulties, since two convents and two lay guarantors had vouched for the two sisters. I said it was Switzerland's duty to intervene to help them, since the two sisters were in mortal danger.

In order to influence the Immigration Service positively, I wrote quickly to a very influential acquaintance who was a friend of Dr. Rothmund, head of the Immigration Service, asking her to intercede in behalf of the two sisters. She answered immediately and sent me a copy of her letter to Dr. Rothmund. Despite all these efforts, on August 2, 1942, the very day on which Sr. Teresia Benedicta a Cruce and her sister were deported, I received the reply from the Swiss Immigration Office that the application for an entry permit from the two sisters had been denied....

Thus my country renounced the distinction of having helped an eminent woman like Edith Stein and her sister to asylum, and of saving their lives. This attitude can only be explained, up to a point, by the threatened position in which Switzerland found itself at that time and the thousands of applications for entry besieging the authorities. Probably the occupation authorities in the Netherlands would not have allowed the two sisters to leave anyhow, as Edith Stein indicated on a postcard dated April 9, 1942....

From Als een brandende toorts *(Echt, 1967): 57ff.*

P. O. van Kempen

Eyewitness in Westerbork

Maastricht, 1942

Three days after the Gestapo arrested Sr. Benedicta a Cruce and Rosa Stein, the Carmelite Sisters in Echt received a telegram—it was Wednesday, August 5, 1942—from the concentration camp Westerbork. They were to send a messenger with warm clothes, blankets, and travel necessities for the sisters Stein. The Ursuline Sisters in Venlo received a similar telegram that day for Ruth Kantorowicz, a friend of Sr. Benedicta. The prioress, Mother Antonia, quickly found her messengers: Messrs. Pierre Cuypers and Piet van Kempen of Echt. They were the last ones to have a conversation in Westerbork with Sr. Benedicta, several days before her death in the gas chambers of Auschwitz. Both gentlemen were witnesses for Edith Stein's beatification process in Cologne in 1963.

After their return from Camp Westerbork they gave the following account of their meeting with Sr. Benedicta and Rosa Stein:

With the luggage that the Carmelites had prepared, we left early in the morning on August 6, on the first train going from Echt to Drenthe. Camp Westerbork was located near Hooghalen. We had never heard of Hooghalen nor of a camp Westerbork before. After we changed trains several times, we arrived at the Hooghalen station at about five o'clock in the afternoon. There we met two gentlemen from Venlo whom we had seen several times while changing trains. They, too, had to go to the "Jew camp" in Westerbork. They had been sent as messengers by the Ursulines of Venlo in order to take luggage to a certain Dr. Ruth Kantorowicz—just like us.

At the station we were told that the camp was about five kilometers outside of Hooghalen. The only connection with the camp

---

P. O. van Kempen was editor-in-chief of the Episcopal Newsletter Roermond, in Maastricht, Holland. He and Pierre Cuypers were the last to see Edith and Rosa Stein in the transition camp of Westerbork, Holland.

was a pair of trucks taking loads of dirt there. One of the drivers took our luggage along. About ten meters before the high barbed wire fence surrounding the entire camp, the truck stopped. We reported to the Dutch police sitting in a wooden pavilion outside the camp. They read the telegram the prioress had given us to take along, several times. We offered them cigars and cigarettes, discussed the situation, and got into a friendly conversation. At first the policemen objected. We did not know whether we were dealing with Nazis or whether they were doing their job here under duress. After our discussion, one of the policemen left. I assumed he wanted to telephone the camp commander from the small pavilion. A little Jewish boy was called who worked as a sort of orderly. The little chap was sent to the camp with the telegram. We got the impression that the Dutch police were afraid of the SS people. They were amazed—or pretended to be—when they learned from us that we wanted to visit nuns in the camp. "Surely there are no nuns in the camp," they said. Only after they had inquired and been assured that it was true did they believe us. We remained in suspense. Things were quiet in the camp. On the high barbed wire fence, machine guns were placed on scaffolding. Together with the policemen, we waited with a small group of people outside the small wooden building. The little Jewish boy had disappeared into one of the camp barracks. The luggage stood near us on the ground. A letter from Mother Antonia for Sr. Benedicta was in our pocket. We were to give this letter to Sr. Benedicta secretly.

We smoked another cigarette. Then the little Jewish boy returned with two Sisters. I did not know Sr. Benedicta or Rosa Stein. Both sisters wore the yellow Jewish star. The black veil had been turned back over the cap. The two sisters came through the camp gate to the wooden pavilion of the Dutch police. We introduced ourselves and shook hands. It was an encounter that was sad and joyful at the same time. We told of the telegram and the luggage we had brought. "Did Mother send a habit also?" was one of the first questions put by Sr. Benedicta. Both were grateful for the greetings and prayer of their fellow-Sisters from the Carmel in Echt. With the knowledge of the police we could give Sr. Benedicta the letter from the Mother Superior. She tucked the letter right into her habit. Sr. Benedicta listened to the news from the monastery very attentively, and also to the reaction that their brutal deportation from the monastery had evoked from the inhabitants of Echt. We could speak freely with her, and the conversation was quite normal and unconstrained. Rosa Stein was very quiet. She did not say much. Of course we were interested—just like Mother Antonia—to learn what had happened to her since her arrest that Sunday afternoon in Echt. Sr. Benedicta told us the following:

After the rushed departure from the monastery that Sunday afternoon, the two officers—their names have remained unknown—took Sr. Benedicta and Rosa to a police van that stood waiting near the monastery. Several persons were already seated in it. From Echt the trip took them to the local headquarters in Roermond. That same evening two police vans left Roermond, destination unknown. Thirteen persons sat in one van, and fourteen in the other. Since the driver lost his way somewhere…the prisoners did not arrive in Amersfoort until 3 a.m. The guarding by the German soldiers had been friendly until now. In the camp of Amersfoort, treatment by the guards became brutal and hardhearted. The prisoners were hit in the back with rifle butts and driven to the dormitories. The non-Catholic Jews got something to eat, and after a "night rest" of several hours on bunk beds, the transport of the Jews continued very early the next morning by freight train to Hooghalen. From the train station [they traveled] on foot to Camp Westerbork. In the camp, Sr. Benedicta met several acquaintances and even relatives. With the help of the *Jüdischer Rat* (Jewish council) it was possible to telephone. "The *Jüdischer Rat* was very good to us, especially to the Catholic Jews," said Sr. Benedicta.

By order of the German authorities, the Catholic Jews were separated from the others in the camp. They sat, together with Sr. Benedicta and Rosa Stein, in separate barracks, left of the main entrance of the camp. Beyond that the *Jüdischer Rat* couldn't do anything for them.

While she told their experiences, we both smoked cigarettes. To lighten the tension a little, we jokingly presented Sr. Benedicta with a cigarette as well. She, too, laughed about that and told us that, formerly, in her student days, she had certainly smoked cigarettes and also danced. Sr. Benedicta was completely calm and self-controlled. One could not detect any trace of fear in her about the uncertain future. Calmly and in complete surrender she had placed her life into the sure hand of God. In her clear eyes shone the glow of a holy Carmelite, who related events in a gentle voice but said nothing about her personal experiences. Rosa Stein also said that she was all right. She found much support in the example of her sister Edith. We were to tell the Carmel in Echt specifically that she was still wearing the habit of the Order, and all the other nuns as well—there were ten of them. If possible she would like to keep wearing her holy habit. Sr. Benedicta also told us that the camp prisoners were glad that there were also Catholic nuns and priests in the camp.

From the spot where we stood we saw two Trappist nuns—as Sr. Benedicta told us—and several priests, all with the star of David, walking to and fro in front of the barrack. In the camp, the religious were a great support for all prisoners who were deprived of everything, literally everything. Sr. Benedicta helped wherever she could help. Mothers who had been deported with their children were helpless. She was happy to be able to help through comforting words and her prayer. She told us repeatedly that Reverend Mother need not worry about her and her sister Rosa. They were able to pray all day, interrupted only three times by meals. She did not complain, neither about the food nor about the treatment by the camp guards or the soldiers. Her deep faith and unconditional surrender encircled Sr. Benedicta with an atmosphere of heavenly life. In her cheerful calm there was a certain happy joy. She did not know how long she would remain in Camp Westerbork. It was rumored in the camp that they were waiting for a transport of Jews from Amsterdam. Also, it was said in the camp that the prisoners would be transported that very night or the following day—that was August 7—to Silesia, her home. In the camp, Sr. Benedicta had heard that those deported were to work in the Silesian mines. She said she was familiar with work in the mines. If she were to leave, her prayer—regardless of what job would be given to her—would always occupy first place. She wanted to sacrifice her suffering for her Jewish people, for the blind persecutors, and for all who had lost God from their hearts.

Upon a sign by the SS camp guard we broke off the conversation, which had lasted quite some time. We shook hands with Sr. Benedicta and Rosa Stein. Together they walked toward the high fence that offered entry to the camp. No complaint had passed their lips during our talk.

Upright, strong and full of trust she went her way, where the cross awaited her, as if she were going to her cloister cell to pray. Once more Sr. Benedicta looked back and bowed in greeting. The broad, high fence of pine poles, woven through with much barbed wire, opened. Behind the two sisters, the barbed wire was closed immediately. Together, Sr. Benedicta a Cruce and Rosa Stein stepped through the door of the low barracks.

From Als een brandende toorts *(Echt, 1967): 149ff.*

Pierre Cuypers

Eyewitness in Westerbork

Echt, 1942

At 5 o'clock we had arrived in Hooghalen. There we met two gentlemen from Venlo, who had been sent by the Ursulines to Dr. Ruth Kantorowicz, an acquaintance of Sr. Benedicta. The camp is about five kilometers distant from Hooghalen. We were lucky; we got a ride on a truck carrying dirt to the camp.

In front of the camp, consisting of barracks, stood a small building where we were instructed to report to the Dutch police. We turned the telegram over to them; we offered cigars and cigarettes, and very soon a friendly dialogue developed. It seemed that these military policemen performed their duties reluctantly. Upon our request, they sent a little Jewish boy with the telegram to the barracks where Sr. Benedicta and Miss Rosa were staying. After a few tense moments, the high barbed-wire fence opened, and from the distance we could see the brown habit and black veil of Sr. Benedicta, who was accompanied by her sister. Our meeting was sad and joyful at the same time. We shook hands, and, due to the joy of seeing people from Echt, the first words were a bit halting. The ice, however, was quickly broken, and we turned over everything that the Carmel had given us. Sr. Benedicta especially was very grateful for the greetings and prayers of her fellow-sisters. All written greetings as well as the note from Mother Prioress were put in Sr. Benedicta's hands, sealed, with the help of the Dutch police. She told us straight away that she had met very many acquaintances and even relatives in the camp. The trip had proceeded as follows: from Echt, with the squad car to the local headquarters in Roermond. In the evening the trip continued with two squad cars from there; one car with thirteen persons, the other with fourteen. The route went via Amersfoort, but because the driver lost his way, they did not arrive until 3 o'clock in the morning. From Echt to

---

Together with P. O. van Kempen, Pierre Cuypers *was the last to see Edith and Rosa Stein in the transition camp of Westerbork, Holland.*

Amersfoort the German soldiers (SS) were very friendly toward the prisoners. In Camp Amersfoort the treatment turned hard-hearted and brutal. They were hit in the back with rifle butts, and with curses were driven to the dormitories without food. Thanks to other non-Catholic Jews, they got something anyway to relieve their hunger, and after a short night's rest in bunk beds, the transport continued very early Tuesday morning to Hooghalen and from there to the camp. Through the intervention of the *Jüdischer Rat,* sending a telegram was possible.

The *Jüdischer Rat* is very kind, especially toward the Catholic Jews. At the behest of the German authorities, the Catholic Jews are kept separate from the others. The Council can't do anything for them. They are together in a separate barrack.

Sr. Benedicta related all this calmly and with self-control. In her eyes shone the glow of a holy Carmelite. With soft words and quiet resignation she told all these experiences, but she said nothing about her personal experiences. We were asked especially to report to the Carmel that she was still wearing the habit of the Order, and that all nuns, ten in all, wanted to retain their holy habit if at all possible. Further, she told us that the people in the camp were glad that there were also Catholic Sisters and Fathers in the camp. They were the only support in camp for all these people who were deprived of literally everything.

Sr. Benedicta was happy to be able to help with comforting words and prayer. Her deep faith surrounded her with an atmosphere of heavenly life. She stated repeatedly that Reverend Mother need not worry about her and her sister. They could pray all day long, interrupted only three times by meals. She had no complaint about food or the treatment by the soldiers. She did not know how long they were to remain at this camp. Rumor had it that that day (on August 7, a Friday) they might leave for Silesia, her homeland, but she did not yet know for sure. Miss Rosa, too, was well. She had a lot of courage for the future. The two girls from Koningsbosch are also very devout and trusting. They, too, find in the example of Sr. Benedicta a powerful support. If she were to leave, her prayer would certainly be in first place, no matter what work she might be assigned. Sr. Benedicta had written a letter to Mother Superior. She did not know whether it had arrived.

From Als een brandende toorts *(Echt, 1967) pp.153ff.*

Notes

PART I: EDITH STEIN — A FIGURE FOR OUR TIME

INTRODUCTION
By Waltraud Herbstrith, OCD

1. "Edith Stein und Geistliche des Bistums Speyer: Erinnerungen von Altbischof Isidor Markus Emanuel," *Der Pilger: Kirchenblatt für das Bistum Speyer* (1987), nos. 32–35.

2. Prior Gaudentius Sauermann, "Feierstunde zur Einweihung der Kapelle im Haus St. Ansgar," May 1, 1987.

3. Pope John Paul II in Hannes Burger, *Der Papst in Deutschland: Stationen der Reise 1987* (Munich: Südwest Verlag, 1987), p. 72.

THE PATH TO BEATIFICATION
By John Sullivan, OCD

1. Cf. Kenneth Woodward, *Making Saints: How the Catholic Church Determines Who Becomes a Saint, Who Doesn't, and Why* (New York: Simon and Schuster, Touchstone Book, 1996).

2. Cf. Michael Freze, *The Making of Saints* (Huntington, IN: Our Sunday Visitor, 1991).

3. Eszer, Ambrosius, "Edith Stein: Jewish Catholic Martyr," *Carmelite Studies* 4 (1988): 310-27.

4. Of interest for English-speaking countries, in 1986 the Discalced Carmelites' Institute of Carmelite Studies began publication of the series "The Collected Works of Edith Stein." Its first volume, the moving *Life in a Jewish Family,* captured the Catholic Press Association of North America's prize for the best "Spiritual Book" of the Year.

5. At present, interest in Edith Stein continues to flourish in a medium to which she frequently contributed, i.e., publications. Since the appearance of *Life in a Jewish Family,* ICS Publications has

distributed just under 50,000 copies of the five volumes currently in its series of "The Collected Works of Edith Stein." All her original works will one day be added to the series. Other supplementary titles are being readied to take their place alongside the exegetical content of Carmelite Studies 4, with its set of papers from a symposium about Stein held in 1984 in Washington, DC, as well as all the papal pronouncements made about Stein in Germany at the time of her beatification.

Most recently two scholarly works designed to delve into this holy woman's importance for philosophy have taken their place alongside ICS's publication output, viz., Mary Catherine Baseheart's *Person in the World: Introduction to the Philosophy of Edith Stein,* and Marianne Sawicki's *Body, Text, and Science: The Literacy of Investigative Practices and the Phenomenology of Edith Stein* (both published in 1997 and available from Kluwer Academic Publishers). May the work grow in breadth and depth to the praise of God, whose glory shines forth in the saints.

Edith Stein's Beatification: Annoyance or Sign of Reconciliation?
By Anna Maria Strehle, OCD

1. All quotations from *Der Pilger: Kirchenzeitung für das Bistum Speyer* 19 (May 10, 1987): 711.

2. Cf. *Die Welt,* April 27, 1987; *Deutsche Tagespost,* May 12, 1987.

3. Edith Stein, *Life in a Jewish Family: Her Unfinished Autobiographical Account,* ed. Dr. L. Gelber and Romaeus Leuven, trans. Josephine Koeppel (Washington, DC: ICS Publications, 1986), p. 77. Hereafter referred to as *Life in a Jewish Family.*

4. See Edith Stein, *On the Problem of Empathy,* trans. by Waltraut Stein, 3d rev. ed. (Washington, DC: ICS Publications, 1989), p. 119. [The wording here has been slightly modified.—Trans.]

5. Stein, *Life in a Jewish Family,* p. 24.

6. Ibid., p. 89.

7. Stein, *On the Problem of Empathy,* p. 31.

8. "Declaration on the Relation of the Church to Non-Christian Religions, Promulgated October 28, 1965" in *Vatican Council II: The Conciliar and Post-Conciliar Documents,* ed. Austin Flannery, new rev. ed. (Northport, NY: Costello, 1984), p. 741.

9. "Beiträge zur christlich-jüdischen Begegnung, Sonder-Vorabdruck zum 89. Deutschen Katholikentag Aachen, 1986," *Freiburger Rundbrief* 37/38 (1985/86), nos. 141–148, p. 3.

10. *L'Osservatore Romano,* weekly edition in German, 17 (May 8, 1987): 11.

11. Ibid., p. 12.

12. *Kölner Stadt-Anzeiger* 102 (May 2–3, 1987): 5.

13. *Jüdische Allgemeine Zeitung* 41 (July 25, 1986): 30.

14. *Kölnische Rundschau,* May 2, 1987.

15. *Kölnische Rundschau,* April 4, 1987, Supplement: "Der Papst in Köln," p. 3.

16. *Deutsches Allgemeines Sonntagsblatt,* March 5, 1987.

WHAT SIGNIFICANCE DOES EDITH STEIN'S BEATIFICATION HAVE FOR HER FAMILY?
By Susanne Batzdorff

1. [We should thankfully note recent progress in Jewish-Catholic relations, including the signing of an agreement establishing diplomatic relations between the Vatican and Israel on December 31, 1993.—TRANS.]

2. [The Carmelite convent has since been moved from its first site adjacent to the Auschwitz death camp to an area further away.—TRANS.]

LIFE IN A JEWISH FAMILY—AUNT EDITH'S LEGACY TO HER DESCENDANTS
By Susanne Batzdorff

1. Stein, *Life in a Jewish Family,* p. 234.

2. Ibid., p. 66.

3. Ibid.

4. Ibid., p. 78.

5. Ibid., p. 66.

6. Ibid., p. 202.

7. Ibid.

8. Ibid., p. 203. [The translator, Sr. Josephine Koeppel OCD, has charitably rendered the German word *Herde* as "flock" and not as the less flattering term "herd."—TRANS.]

9. Teresa Renata Posselt, *Edith Stein,* trans. Cecily Hastings and Donald Nicholl (New York: Sheed & Ward, 1952), p. 60. See

also Letter #14 to Roman Ingarden, in Edith Stein, *Self-Portrait in Letters,* ed. L. Gelber & Romaeus Leuven, trans. Josephine Koeppel (Washington, DC: ICS Publications, 1993), p. 17.

10. Stein, *Life in a Jewish Family,* p. 215.

11. Reply to my questionnaire.

12. Stein, *Life in a Jewish Family,* pp. 326–327.

13. Ibid., p. 142.

14. Page 22 of his unpublished remarks addressed to his children.

15. Letter to Sr. Theresia Margareta, OCD.

16. Stein, *Life in a Jewish Family,* p. 239.

17. Ibid., p. 34.

18. [My translation here is closer to the original text than that of Sr. Josephine Koeppel; cf. *Life in a Jewish Family,* p. 69.—TRANS.]

19. Ibid., pp. 212–213.

20. Ibid., p. 81.

21. Ibid., p. 391. [The translation here has been slightly modified.—TRANS.]

22. Ibid., p. 394.

23. Ibid., p. 343.

24. Ibid., p. 127.

25. Ibid., pp. 342–343.

26. Ibid., p. 123.

27. Ibid., p. 206.

28. Ibid., p. 204.

29. Ibid., p. 240.

30. Ibid., p. 291.

31. Ibid., p. 304.

32. Ibid., p. 35.

33. Ibid., p. 191.

34. Ibid., p. 294.

35. Ibid., pp. 297, 299.

THE FAMILY AWAKENS TO EDITH STEIN'S DESTINY
By Waltraut Stein

1. [The quote here attributed to Susanne Batzdorff was "Maybe she did the right thing after all." The translator has added a qualifier, as she thus recalls her own statement to Waltraut Stein on May 1, 1987.—TRANS.]

My Experiences With My Aunt Edith
By Gerhard Stein

1. [It is debatable whether the two situations are indeed comparable. As for the extent of Auguste Stein's pain, the translator (who lived under the same roof with her during that time) remembers her anguish and daily weeping. Gerhard Stein lived in another city and was thus removed from the scene.—Trans.]

2. [Note that the the concerns usually raised about the church's role during the "Shoah" have to do not with what measures it might have taken to save Edith Stein in particular during her final days, but whether a more courageous attitude on the part of the church leadership at a much earlier stage could have prevented or lessened these persecutions.—Trans.]

3. [The role of Pope Pius XII during the Nazi regime and the Second World War continues to generate widespread discussion among both his critics and his defenders.—Trans.]

4. [In 1942, the Ninth of Av, a Jewish day of mourning for the destruction of the Holy Temple in Jerusalem and for other disasters in Jewish history, fell on July 23. The lunar calendar, by which Jews reckon their festivals, varies from the Gregorian calendar. Hence the observance of Jewish feast and fast days varies from year to year, according to the secular calendar. Thus, while the Ninth of Av always occurs during July or August, it did not coincide with the death date of Edith Stein.—Trans.]

A Great, Exceptional Human Being
By Ilse Gordon

1. [The picture referred to appears here on p. 58.—Trans.]

2. [In fact, this omission occurred because the first edition of *Aus dem Leben einer jüdischen Familie* in 1965 was abridged. At the request of family members, a number of passages were deleted because of their detailed revelations about family problems. The later German edition that appeared in 1985, as well as the English translation, *Life in a Jewish Family* (Washington, DC: ICS Publications, 1986), offer the complete text. The passages Ilse Gordon refers to appear on pages 88–102 of the English-language text.—Trans.]

284 Notes to Pages 64–86

EDITH STEIN: A JEW'S PATH TO CATHOLICISM
By Daniel Krochmalnik

1. Her secular name was Posselt.

2. [Edith Stein, *Selected Writings* (Springfield, IL: Templegate, 1990), p.16.—TRANS.]

3. Ibid., p. 17.

4. [A detailed description of the draft for this encyclical has been omitted, since this document was never finalized nor promulgated. For a more recent analysis of the draft, see Georges Passelecq and Bernard Suchecky, *The Hidden Encyclical of Pius XI* (New York: Harcourt Brace, 1997).—TRANS.]

5. ["Ahasuer" here refers to a legendary cobbler of Jerusalem who is said to have taunted Jesus on his way to the crucifixion and was cursed to live and wander for ever until the return of Jesus. He is also referred to as the Wandering Jew. See R. J. Z. Werblowsky, ed., *Encyclopedia of Jewish Religion* (Holt, 1965), p. 100.—TRANS.]

6. [*Purim* is a minor Jewish festival that commemorates the end of Jewish persecution by the Persian King Ahasuerus and the execution of his anti-Semitic prime-minister Haman.—TRANS.]

EDITH STEIN AND CHRISTIAN-JEWISH DIALOGUE
By Waltraud Herbstrith, OCD

1. Erich Przywara, "Die Frage Edith Stein," in Waltraud Herbstrith, ed., *Edith Stein: ein Lebensbild in Zeugnissen und Selbstzeugnissen* (Mainz: M. Grünewald, 1992), p. 161.

2. Edith Stein in Felix M. Schandl, *Ich sah aus meinem Volk die Kirche wachsen: Jüdische Bezüge und Strukturen in Leben und Werk Edith Steins (1891–1942)* (Sinzig: Sankt Meinrad Verlag, 1990), pp. 117 and 118.

3. Stein, *Life in a Jewish Family*, p. 23.

4. Ibid., p. 24.

5. Edith Stein, "The Prayer of the Church," in *The Hidden Life*, ed. L. Gelber & Michael Linssen, trans. Waltraut Stein (Washington, DC: ICS Publications, 1992), pp. 7–8.

6. Ibid., p. 8.

7. Ibid., p. 9.

8. Edith Stein, *Selected Writings*, pp. 100–101.

9. Teresa Renata (Posselt), *Edith Stein*, p. 188.

10. Bishop Franziscus von Streng, in *Ernst Ludwig Ehrlich und der christlich-jüdische Dialog*, ed. Rolf Vogel (Frankfurt/M.: Knecht, 1984) p. 125.

11. Herman van Breda rescued the unpublished philosophical works of the "non-Aryan" Edmund Husserl from Nazi Germany.

12. Herman von Breda, in *Als een brandende toorts*, ed. Friends of Dr. Edith Stein (Echt, 1967), p. 108.

13. Chaim Herzog, "Und mein Schmerz ist immer bei mir," Speech by the President of Israel in Bergen-Belsen, *Deutsche Tagespost* 41 (April 7, 1987): 2.

EDITH STEIN'S TIMELY MESSAGE
By Irmgard Rech

1. Edith Stein, *Essays on Woman*, ed. Dr. L. Gelber & Romaeus Leuven, trans. Freda Mary Oben, 2d ed. rev. (Washington, DC: ICS Publications, 1996), p. 81.

2. Ibid., p. 83.

3. Ibid.

4. Ibid., p. 84. [Note that the author, like Edith Stein herself, wrote prior to the Vatican's most recent declarations on the question of the ordination of women.—TRANS.]

5. Ibid., p. 76.

6. Ibid., pp. 60–61.

7. Ibid., pp. 79–80.

8. Ibid. p. 80.

9. Ibid.

10. Ibid.

11. Ibid., p. 61.

12. Ibid., p. 62.

13. Genesis 2:24

14. Edith Stein, *Essays on Woman*, p. 65.

15. [Male chauvinism, as we might call it today.—TRANS.]

16. [My translation. Compare Edith Stein, *Essays on Woman*, p. 72.—TRANS.]

17. Ibid., p. 72.

18. Ibid. p. 73.

19. Ibid., p. 84.

20. Ibid.

EDITH STEIN: REMEMBERING A COLLEAGUE
By Nikolaus Lauer
  1. [The Palatinate is a part of the State of Bavaria.—TRANS.]

SERMON FOR THE TWENTY-SECOND GERMAN PROTESTANT
CHURCH CONGRESS
By Leonore Siegele-Wenschkewitz
  1. Gotthard Fuchs, ed., *Glaube als Widerstandskraft: Edith Stein, Alfred Delp, Dietrich Bonhoeffer* (Frankfurt/M.: Knecht, 1986), p. 73.
  2. Edith Stein, *Selected Writings*, p. 16.
  3. Edith Stein, *Self-Portrait in Letters*, p. 295 (Letter #287).
  4. Ibid., p. 341 (Letter #330 to M. Ambrosia Antonia Engelmann, Echt).
  5. Edith Stein, *In der Kraft des Kreuzes: Textauswahl* (Freiburg: Herder, 1987) p. 74.
  6. Edith Stein, *Self-Portrait in Letters*, p. 54 (Letter #45 to Sr. Callista Kopf).

NOT LIKE THAT! — ON THE BEATIFICATION OF EDITH STEIN
By Friedrich Georg Friedmann
  1. *Erbe und Auftrag*, 1962, p. 28. [As Friedmann later suggests, the authenticity of the remark attributed to Edith Stein regarding the "mark of Cain" is questionable.—TRANS.]
  2. Waltraud Herbstrith, *Edith Stein auf der Suche nach Gott* (Butzon and Bercker, 1963), p. 221.
  3. [See Teresia Renata Posselt, *Edith Stein*, p. 184.—TRANS.]
  4. *Pope John Paul II on Jews and Judaism, 1979–1986,* with introduction and commentary by Eugene J. Fisher and Leon Klenicki, eds. (Washington, DC: United States Catholic Conference, 1987), p. 82.
  5. Ibid.
  6. Holy See, Commission on Religious Relations with the Jews, *Notes on the Correct Way to Present the Jews and Judaism in Preaching and Catechesis in the Roman Catholic Church* (Washington, DC: United States Catholic Conference, 1985), para. 10.
  7. [A note with the text "unterwegs ad orientem" ("on the way to the East,"signed "Sr. Teresa Benedicta a Cruce") dropped from the window of her railway compartment, was delivered into the hands of Sr. Placida Laubhardt of St. Lioba, just two days before she

herself was arrested and deported to Ravensbrueck, because of her own part-Jewish origins. Sr. Placida burned the letters from Edith Stein, including this last one, just before her arrest.—TRANS.]

8. [Friedmann, in quoting Batzdorff's article, neglects to mention that she and her brother were then 12 and 11 years old respectively, and that the viewpoint here described is that of youngsters of that age. It would thus not be fair to equate their perspective with the outlook of the Stein family.—TRANS.]

9. [As noted above, this Carmelite convent has since been moved from within the parameters of Auschwitz to an area outside the death camp in April 1993, and an agreement was signed establishing diplomatic relations between the Vatican and Israel on December 31, 1993.—TRANS.]

OF SAINTS AND MARTYRS
By Menahem Benhayim

1. [i.e., Edith Stein, *Life in a Jewish Family* (Washington, DC: ICS Publications, 1986).—TRANS.]

2. [He is probably referring to the testimony of P. O. van Kempen and Pierre Cuypers, the two messengers who were sent to Westerbork by the Carmel of Echt, to take travel necessities to Edith and Rosa. They were Dutch civilians, not German soldiers.—TRANS.]

EDITH STEIN AND FREIBURG
By Hugo Ott

1. [A measure designed to exclude Jews from civil service employment.—TRANS.]

COMPANION IN HUMAN FATE
By Joachim Köhler

1. Joseph Cardinal Höffner, "Dem Herrn im Zeichen des Kreuzes vermählt," Lenten Pastoral Letter 1987 on the Occasion of the Beatification of the Cologne Carmelite Edith Stein, in *Zeitfragen: Eine Schriftenreihe,* ed. Public Relations Office of the Cologne Archbishopric, no. 39 (Cologne, 1987), p. 5.

2. Ibid.
3. Ibid.
4. Ibid., p. 6.
5. Ibid.

6. Ibid., pp. 6ff.

7. Ibid., p. 7.

8. Teresia Renata (Posselt), *Edith Stein,* p. 64.

9. Sr. Teresia a Matre Dei (Waltraud Herbstrith) in a conversation observed how Sr. Teresia Renata [Posselt] had transposed some facts from the sober letter of P. Johannes Hirschmann, SJ, this way. Such sentences, she said, could only fascinate in the language of Sr. Teresia Renata.

10. Teresia Renata (Posselt), *Edith Stein,* p. 59.

11. These sentences are quoted in *Kölner Selig- und Heiligsprechungsprozess der Dienerin Gottes Sr. Teresia Benedicta a Cruce (Edith Stein), Professe und Chorschwester des Ordens der Allerseligsten Jungfrau Maria vom Berge Karmel* (Köln, 1962), p. 94.

12. Höffner, op. cit., p. 6.

13. Quoted according to *Edith Stein: Wege zur inneren Stille,* ed. Waltraud Herbstrith, (Aschaffenburg: Kaffke, 1987), p. 60.

14. Höffner, op. cit., p. 10.

15. Edith Stein, *Self-Portrait in Letters,* p. 178 (Letter # 174, to Fritz Kaufmann, May 14, 1934).

16. Höffner, op. cit., p. 11.

17. Ibid.

18. Ibid.

19. Stein, *Self-Portrait in Letters,* p. 295 (Letter # 287 to Mater Petra Brüning OSU, Dorsten, December 9, 1938).

20. Cf. Höffner, op. cit., p. 5.

21. Ibid., p. 13.

22. Ibid., p. 15.

23. Quoted in note 29 of Höffner's Lenten pastoral letter, p. 23.

24. Ludwig Volk, "Die Fuldaer Bischofskonferenz von der Enzyklika 'Mit brennender Sorge' bis zum Ende der NS-Herrschaft," *Stimmen der Zeit* 178 (1966): 241–267; 256.

25. Ibid.

26. Waltraud Herbstrith, "Eine deutsche Patriotin. Über Edith Steins Haltung zum Staat und zum Nationalsozialismus," *Christ in der Gegenwart* 37 (1985): 277ff.

27. Ibid.

28. Ibid.

29. Cf. Wilhelm Josef Doetsch, *Württembergs Katholiken unterm Hakenkreuz* (Stuttgart, 1969), p. 27. More recent biographical research

on Raphael Walzer pays scant attention to the political structure in the personality of the archabbot. Cf. Elisabeth Endres, *Erzabt Walzer, Versöhnen ohne zu verschweigen* (Baindt bei Ravensburg, 1988); Heinrich Kirchner, "Wege der Versöhnung. Vergessen und wiederentdeckt. Zum 100. Geburtstag von Erzabt Raphael Walzer," *Katholisches Sonntagsblatt* (Diözese Rottenburg-Stuttgart) 136 (June 5, 1988): 5ff.

30. Teresia Renata (Posselt), *Edith Stein*, pp. 150–155.

31. Edith Stein, *Self-Portrait in Letters*, p. 284 (Letter # 274 to Maria Mayer, Beuron, August 12, 1938).

32. Ibid., p. 340 (Letter # 328 to M. Johanna van Weersth OCD, Beek, November 18, 1941).

33. Ibid., p. 291 (Letter # 281 to M. Petra Brüning OSU, Dorsten, October 31, 1938).

34. Ibid., p. 295 (Letter # 287 to M. Petra Brüning OSU, Dorsten, December 9, 1938).

35. Ibid., p. 305 (Letter # 296 to M. Ottilia Thannisch OCD, Echt, Passion Sunday, March 26, 1939).

36. Edith Stein, *Selected Writings*, p. 16.

37. Ibid.

38. Ibid., p. 17.

39. Ibid.

40. Cardinal Adolf Bertram to the German Bishops, quoted from *Akten Deutscher Bischöfe über die Lage der Kirche 1933–1945*, vol. 1: *1933–1934*, ed. Bernhard Stasiewski, Veröffentlichungen der Kommission für Zeitgeschichte, Series A: Quellen, vol. 5 (Mainz, 1968), p. 42.

41. *Akten Kardinal Michael von Faulhabers, 1917–1945*, vol. 1: *1917–1934*, ed. Ludwig Volk, Veröffentlichungen der Kommission für Zeitgeschichte, Series A: Quellen, vol. 17, (Mainz, 1975), pp. 716ff.

42. Ibid., p. 717.

43. Ibid., pp. 682ff.

44. Ibid., pp. 709–711.

45. [As noted above, "Ahasuer" here refers to a legendary cobbler of Jerusalem who is said to have taunted Jesus on his way to the crucifixion and was cursed to live and wander for ever until the return of Jesus. He is also referred to as the Wandering Jew. See R. J. Z. Werblowsky, ed., *Encyclopedia of Jewish Religion* (Holt, 1965), p. 100.—TRANS.]

46. Michael Kardinal Faulhaber, *Judentum, Christentum, Germanentum: Adventspredigten* (Freiburg, 1933) p. 10.
47. Ernst Ludwig Ehrlich, "Katholische Kirche und Judentum zur Zeit des Nationalsozialismus. Eine geschichtliche Erfahrung und eine Herausforderung an uns," *Judaica* 40 (1984): 155.
48. Edith Stein, *Selected Writings,* p. 17.
49. [A detailed discussion of the drafts for the proposed encyclical has been omitted, since this document was never finalized nor published. For a more recent analysis of the draft, see Georges Passelecq and Bernard Suchecky, *The Hidden Encyclical of Pius XI* (New York: Harcourt Brace, 1997).—Trans.]
50. Quoted in from *Ecclesiastica* (1934): 59–62.
51. Quoted from Visser t'Hooft, *Holländische Kirchendokumente* (Zürich, 1946): 58–62.
52. Ehrlich, "Katholische Kirche und Judentum," p. 155, note 46.
53. Teresia Renata (Posselt), *Edith Stein,* 7th ed. (Nuremberg: Glock & Lutz, 1954), p. 288. [This edition not available in English translation.—Trans.]
54. Ibid.
55. Ibid., p. 289.
56. Edith Stein, *Self-Portrait in Letters,* p. 310 (Letter # 302 to Peter Wust, Münster, August 28, 1939).
57. Christian Feldmann, "Gottsuche mit Herz und Verstand. Edith Stein, Frauenrechtlerin, Philosophin, Karmeliin. Die facettenreiche Biographie der getauften Jüdin, die am 1. Mai seliggesprochen wird," *Rheinischer Merkur/Christ und Welt* 16 (April 17, 1987): 25.

Edith Stein and Catholic-Jewish Relations
By Eugene J. Fisher
1. These concerns are well articulated by the Jewish contributions to this volume. I would also point to the essays included in a collection edited by Harry James Cargas for the Studies in the Shoah series: *The Unnecessary Problem of Edith Stein* (Lanham: University Press of America, 1994). Particularly helpful are the essays by Daniel Polish (which won a Catholic Press Association Award when it first appeared in the October, 1987 issue of *Ecumenical Trends*), Judith H. Banki, Nechama Tec, Zev Garber and Susanne Batzdorff, "On Witnessing My Aunt's Beatification."

2. It seems to have been the NBC-TV miniseries, entitled "Holocaust," that precipitated the move of the term from the purview of the few to a word known and widely used. I vividly recall an argument between the French and English-speaking representatives (with the disputants split not according to religion but language group) at the 1980 meeting of the International Catholic-Jewish Liaison Committee held that year in London over whether to use the term "Holocaust" in a statement condemning Holocaust deniers. The French speakers, Jews and Catholics alike, were adamant that it could not be used in our joint communiqué (the official record of the meeting) because "there is no such word in French; we have only the word 'genocide'." We ended up using the latter term, even though the communiqué was issued in English. The term *Holocaust* is now commonly accepted in France. A side irony is that the term "genocide" was itself a post-World War II invention because no language had a term that could approximate the intent and scope of the Nazi attempt to exterminate all the Jews of Europe.

3. Both the Pope's address and that of Chief Rabbi Elio Toaff are contained the volume of papal addresses I co-edited with Rabbi Leon Klenicki, *Pope John Paul II, Spiritual Pilgrimage: Texts on Jews and Judaism 1979–1995* (New York: Crossroad, 1995): 60–73. Survivors were again present in numbers for the moving Holocaust Memorial Concert held at the Vatican itself on April 7, 1994, in conjunction with Yom HaShoah (see ibid., pp. 188–191). The concert was attended by virtually the entire Roman Curia and by Catholic leaders from throughout Europe.

4. For the prayers and remarks of Rabbi Elio Toaff and the Pope at the Assisi World Day of Prayer, see ibid. pp. 75–79. During a meeting with Jewish leaders in Australia on November 26, 1986, the Pope declared the 20th Century to be "the century of the *Shoah*" and stated that "For the Jewish People, Catholics should have not only respect but also great fraternal love for it is the teaching of both the Hebrew and Christian Scriptures that the Jews are beloved of God, who has called them with an irrevocable calling. No valid theological justification could ever be found for acts of discrimination or persecution against Jews. In fact, such acts must be held to be sinful."

5. Ibid., p. 87.

6. I go into the significance of the entanglement of Jewish and Catholic religious symbolism in these controversies in greater detail in "*Mysterium Tremendum:* Catholic Grapplings with the Shoah and Its Theological Implications," in Steven L. Jacobs, editor, *Contemporary Christian Religious Responses to the Shoah,* Studies in the Shoah, vol. VI (Lanham, MD: University Press of America, 1993): 59–84.

7. Texts of the documents and discussion of their implications and implementation in church teaching can by found in my *Faith Without Prejudice: Rebuilding Christian Attitudes Toward Jews and Judaism* (New York: Crossroad, 1993); E. Fisher and L. Klenicki, *In Our Time: The Flowering of Jewish-Catholic Dialogue* (Mahwah, NJ: Paulist Press, Stimulus Books, 1990); J. Bemporad and M. Shevack, *Our Age: The Historic New Era of Christian-Jewish Understanding* (Hyde Park, NY: New City Press, 1996); and Philip Cunningham, *Education for Shalom* (Collegeville, MN: Liturgical Press, 1993). The Cunningham volume updates my own 1976 analysis of the treatment of Jews and Judaism in Catholic religious education materials on the primary and secondary levels. It shows continuing progress but still much to do.

8. I do not mean by the use of "so-called" here to disparage the personal integrity of the members of these congregations, but the title by which they call themselves is at the heart of the issue. The Jewish community, one may say, clearly has "title" to the use of the term "Judaism," which means "faith of the Jewish people" (derived from "Judea," land of the Jews in the ancient world). Just as clearly, the Jewish community rejects any and all Christian attempts to apply to itself the term "Judaism," whether by Gentile Christians or Christians who were born Jewish but who have, through conversion to Christianity, opted out of what they understandably consider to be the "faith of the Jewish people." So it cannot simply be presumed here that the title, "Messianic Judaism," is one to be accepted without question, as those who use it seemingly argue.

9. The Edith Stein Guild, which has been active in pushing her cause for sainthood over the years, has been very careful to avoid any theological triumphalism in describing her conversion, has explicitly eschewed any conversionary intent, and, indeed, has promoted the dialogue of mutual esteem between Catholics and Jews in any way that it could.

The Canonization of Edith Stein
By Daniel F. Polish
1. At the very least, the church, as I have noted elsewhere, is fully capable of appropriating the *sancta* of various peoples or other religious communities for the purpose, or with the consequence, of incorporating those groups into itself.
2. Certainly the death of Edith Stein must cause the Catholic Church to examine what its own role has been over the centuries in perpetrating the denigration of Jewish religion and hatred for Jews.

Part II: A Great, Exceptional Personality — Edith Stein Remembered

Heinrich Spaemann
1. [In a fall down a flight of stairs, Edith Stein had suffered a broken wrist and ankle and was in the infirmary. Thus she was able to attend the baptism of her sister.—Trans.]

Bruno Thiebes
1. [A note with the text "unterwegs ad orientem" (on the way to the East), signed "Sr. Teresa Benedicta a Cruce" dropped from the window of her railway compartment, was delivered into the hands of Sr. Placida Laubhardt of St. Lioba, just two days before she herself was arrested and deported to Ravensbrueck, because of her own part-Jewish origins. Sr. Placida burned the letters from Edith Stein, including this last one, just before her arrest.—Trans.]

Sr. Maria Hroswitha, ISSM
1. [Schott was the editor of this German missal. Hence, this missal was frequently referred to as simply "The Schott." —Trans.]
2. [The Secular Institute of the Schoenstatt Sisters of Mary was founded by Father Joseph Kentenich (1885–1968). During the Nazi regime, Father Kentenich was a prisoner in Dachau for some time. In the United States this Institute is located in Waukesha, Wisconsin.—Trans.]

Margarete Otto

1. [Though she had a Jewish grandmother, Hedwig Conrad-Martius was in fact Protestant from birth. —Trans.]

Paula Bittner

1. [Edith Stein lived at Michaelis Strasse 38, not on Friesenplatz.—Trans.]

Eric E. Hirshler

1. [This refers to Edith Stein's sister Erna, Erna's husband Hans Biberstein, and their children Susanne and Ernst Ludwig.—Trans.]

Bernhard Rosenmöller, Jr.

1. [Nikolai Semianovitch Leskov (1831–1895).—Trans.]
2. [In fact, wearing the Jewish star did not become obligatory until September, 1941. By then Rosa had left Breslau.—Trans.]

Mathilde Herriger

1. [Mr. Sanders (or Sander) a journalist who contributed to the Church newspaper in Cologne.—Trans.]

Herman Leo van Breda, OFM

1. [Actually, during the last years of her mother's life, Edith Stein was unable to "stand by her beloved mother." Upon entering Carmel in October 1933, she was not to see her any more. Her mother died in September 1936. This separation caused grief to both mother and daughter.—Trans.]
2. [Closer to the Latin text quoted here would be the more familiar version: "For me to live is Christ and to die is gain."—Trans.]

Stephanie a Magna Domina, OCD

1. [This phrase is mentioned by Edith Stein in her account of her volunteer nursing work during World War I in Mährisch-Weisskirchen. See Edith Stein, *Life in a Jewish Family*, p. 334.—Trans.]

2. [The proper pronunciation of the word "euge" is to sound out each of the two vowels, E and U separately and distinctly, instead of pronouncing them "oy" (as in "oyge," as was customary among German-speaking people).—TRANS.]

3. [While on ordinary days, silence was kept as strictly as possible, feastdays afforded a rare opportunity for the Sisters to converse with each other during the day and even engage in one-on-one talks, while during regular recreation the conversation was almost exclusively general, i.e. addressed to the whole community. Sr. Stephanie obviously cherishes this remembrance of a private moment shared with Edith Stein.—TRANS.]

Hedwig Conrad-Martius

1. The priest thus addressed was Msgr. John M. Oesterreicher in New York. See *Christliche Innerlichkeit* 26 (1991): 189.—TRANS.]

Select Bibliography

I. Volumes to Date in the *Collected Works of Edith Stein* from ICS Publications (1986–)

Vol. 1: *Life in a Jewish Family*. Edited by L. Gelber and Romaeus Leuven. Translated by Josephine Koeppel. Washington, DC: ICS Publications, 1986.

Vol. 2: *Essays on Woman*.Edited by L. Gelber and Romaeus Leuven. Translated by Freda Mary Oben. 2d edition, revised. Washington, DC: ICS Publications, 1996.

Vol. 3: *On the Problem of Empathy*. Translated by Waltraut Stein. 3d revised edition. Washington, DC: ICS Publications, 1989.

Vol. 4: *The Hidden Life*. Edited by L. Gelber and Michael Linssen. Translated by Waltraut Stein. Washington, DC: ICS Publications, 1992.

Vol. 5: *Self-Portrait in Letters*. Edited by L. Gelber and Romaeus Leuven. Translated by Josephine Koeppel. Washington, DC: ICS Publications, 1993.

Vol. 6: *Science of the Cross*. Edited by L. Gelber and Romaeus Leuven. Translated by Josephine Koeppel. Washington, DC: ICS Publications, 1998.

II. Other Writings of Edith Stein in English Translation

Daily Readings With Edith Stein: To Live at the Hand of the Lord. Edited by Amata Neyer. Translated by Susanne M. Batzdorff. Springfield, IL: Templegate Publishers, 1994.

Science of the Cross; A Study of St. John of the Cross. Edited by L. Gelber and Romaeus Leuven. Translated by Hilda Graef. Chicago, IL: Regnery, 1960.

Selected Writings, With Comments, Reminiscences and Translations of Her Prayers and Poems by her niece, Susanne Batzdorff. Springfield, IL: Templegate Publishers, 1990.

The Writings of Edith Stein. Selected, translated and introduced by Hilda Graef. Westminster, MD: Newman Press, 1956.

Ways to Know God. Translated by Rudolf Allers. Ed. Josephine Koeppel. (New York: Edith Stein Guild, 1981). Reprinted from *Thomist* 9 (July 1946): 379–420.

III. Books About Edith Stein in English

Baseheart, Mary Catharine. *Person in the World: Introduction to the Philosophy of Edith Stein.* Dordrecht, Netherlands: Kluwer, 1997.

Bordeaux, Henry. *Edith Stein: Thoughts on Her and Her Times.* Translated by Donald and Idella Gallagher. Milwaukee, WI: Bruce Publishing Co., 1959.

Cargas, Harry James, ed. *The Unnecessary Problem of Edith Stein.* Lanham, MD: University Press of America, 1994.

Fabrégues, Jean de. *Edith Stein: Philosopher, Carmelite Nun, Holocaust Martyr.* Translated by Donald M. Antoine. Staten Island, NY: Alba House, 1965.

Graef, Hilda C. *The Scholar and the Cross: The Life and Works of Edith Stein.* New York, NY: Longmans, Green, 1955; Westminster, MD, Newman Press, 1955.

Herbstrith, Waltraud. *Edith Stein: A Biography.* 2d English ed. Translated by Bernard Bonowitz. San Francisco, CA: Ignatius Press, 1992.

———. *In Search of God, with Teresa of Avila, John of the Cross, Thérèse of Lisieux, Edith Stein.* Translated by Edward Flood and Gary Brandl. New York: New City Press, 1989.

Koeppel, Josephine. *Edith Stein: A Biographical Essay and "Ways to Know God," by Edith Stein.* New York: Edith Stein Guild, 1981.

———. *Edith Stein: Philosopher and Mystic.* Collegeville, MN: Liturgical Press, 1990.

Marinelli, Donald, ed. *Arthur Giron's "Edith Stein": A Dramaturgical Sourcebook.* Pittsburgh, PA: Carnegie Mellon University Press, 1994.

Muller, Gerald [Brother Roberto]. *The Broken Lamp: a Story of Edith Stein.* Notre Dame, IN: Dujarie Press, 1957. [A biography for children]

Neyer, Maria Amata. *Edith Stein: Her Life in Photos and Documents.* Translated by Waltraut Stein. Washington, DC: ICS Publications, 1998.

Oben, Freda Mary. *Edith Stein: Scholar, Feminist, Saint.* Staten Island, NY: Alba House, 1988.

Oesterreicher, John M. *Walls Are Crumbling: Seven Jewish Philosophers Discover Christ.* New York: Devin-Adair, 1952. (Chapter on Edith Stein: pp. 325–372.)

Posselt, Teresia de Spiritu Sancto. *Edith Stein.* Translated by Cecily Hastings & Donald Nicholl. New York, NY: Sheed and Ward, 1952.

Sawicki, Marianne. *Body, Text, and Science: The Literacy of Investigative Practices and the Phenomenology of Edith Stein.* Dordrecht, Netherlands: Kluwer, 1997.

Schlafke, Jakob. *Edith Stein: Documents Concerning Her Life and Death.* Translated by Susanne M. Batzdorff. New York: Edith Stein Guild, 1984.

Sullivan, John, ed. *Carmelite Studies IV: Edith Stein, Teresian Culture.* Washington, DC: ICS Publications, 1987. [Contains papers by Freda Mary Oben, Mary Catherine Baseheart, Jan H. Nota, and Ralph McInerny from a 1984 Syposium on Edith Stein at the Catholic University of America, as well as texts for the beatification of Edith Stein from Ambrosius Eszer and Pope John Paul II.]

Index

The Institute of Carmelite Studies promotes research and publication in the field of Carmelite spirituality. Its members are Discalced Carmelites, part of a Roman Catholic community—friars, nuns, and laity—who are heirs to the teaching and way of life of Teresa of Jesus and John of the Cross, men and women dedicated to contemplation and to ministry in the church and the world. Information concerning their way of life is available through local diocesan Vocation Offices, or from the Vocation Director's Office, 1525 Carmel Road, Hubertus, WI, 53033.